Hospitality and Catering GNVQ: Intermediate Textbook

Hospitality and Catering GNVQ: Intermediate Textbook

Series editor: Yvonne Johns

Butterworth-Heinemann Ltd
Linacre House, Jordan Hill, Oxford OX2 8DP

 A member of the Reed Elsevier plc group

OXFORD LONDON BOSTON
MUNICH NEW DELHI SINGAPORE SYDNEY
TOKYO TORONTO WELLINGTON

First published 1995

British Library Cataloguing in Publication Data
A catalogue record for this book is available from the British Library

ISBN 0 7506 1944 9

Composition by Genesis Typesetting, Laser Quay, Rochester, Kent

CONTENTS

LIST OF CONTRIBUTORS

Series Editor

Yvonne Johns, Head of Faculty, Business, Care & Hospitality, Leicester Southfields College; BTEC External Verifier; BTEC External Education Adviser

Series Consultant

Michael Rimmington, BTEC Chief Examiner; Principal Lecturer, Sheffield Hallam University

Contributors

Peter Trigg, Head of Department, Hotel Management and Leisure Studies, Wirral Metropolitan College; BTEC External Verifier

Christine Parry, Lecturer, Wirral Metropolitan College

Stephen Moore, GNVQ Coordinator, Blackpool & Fylde College; BTEC External Verifier

Margaret Weaver, FCCA, Lecturer, Stockport College of Further and Higher Education

Patricia Morrell, Lecturer, Macclesfield College

Hilary Firth, Deputy Head of Faculty, Business, Care & Hospitality, Leicester Southfields College; Chief Examiner, City and Guilds; BTEC External Education Adviser

Carol Johnson, Lecturer, Sheffield College

Irene Norman, Lecturer, Llandrillo College

INTRODUCTION

This book offers a new approach to study. It is designed to closely mirror the four Intermediate Mandatory Units of the GNVQ in Hospitality and Catering. Its aim is to encourage you to take a journey through each unit of the book which relates to the elements and performance criteria to be found in the Mandatory units. You are invited to attempt the many tasks and test your knowledge by answering the questions to reinforce the underpinning skills. Throughout the book you will find assignments which incorporate core skills. The evidence from these assignments will be useful in creating your portfolio of evidence.

We have taken account of the National Council Vocational Qualifications (NCVQ) Mandatory Units and Test Specifications, together with comments from lecturers who piloted the units and the many recommendations of industry. This book is therefore concerned with:

- Investigating the diverse nature of the hotel and catering industry
- Customer requirements, their needs and methods of assessing them
- Customer service practice and procedures
- Health and safety
- Front Office operations such as bookings and cashiering
- Accommodation operations including cleaning and servicing of rooms
- Key factors in the provision, production and service of food and drink.

In addition there is a tutor resource pack to provide additional support for both teacher and student.

The authors have tried to keep as closely as possible to the four units of the Intermediate GNVQ, encouraging you to travel the journey from the unknown to the known as simply as possible, gathering evidence for your portfolio on your way.

Throughout the book we have endeavoured to avoid sexist terms. People have been referred to as customers, clients, guests, patients, managers, supervisors and staff. In all sections of the book these terms, in line with current trends, refer to both male and female personnel.

We hope that you will enjoy your journey of discovery using this book, both for its text and as a reference, and in some part encouraging you to invest your future in the hospitality and catering industry.

The industry is known to have job opportunities for both sexes, regardless of sexual orientation. A wide range of abilities from all ethnic groups and cultures find worthwhile and enjoyable employment within our industry. It is hoped that this book will help you to achieve the success that you hope for, either to progress into employment or for further study of the hotel and catering industry.

Y. Johns

INVESTIGATE THE HOSPITALITY AND CATERING INDUSTRY

This unit introduces you to the hospitality and catering industry. The industry consists of many different parts, dependent on each other and on other industries for their success. When we think of the hospitality and catering industry we often think only of hotels and restaurants, but in fact the industry spreads a great deal further than these two types of outlet, and we will learn about its scale and scope in this unit. We will also look at sources of information about the industry, and use them to discover what the industry does, and how it is changing to meet the needs of those who use it. We will consider the contribution that the industry makes to the economy of the country, and examine the factors that influence its growth or the goods and services it provides. Finally, we will look at the wide range of job opportunities offered in the industry, the kinds of qualifications and experience needed in these jobs, and we will explore the ways in which individuals can plan their own career progressions.

This unit is one which requires us to investigate for ourselves, rather than simply read and listen. We can find a wealth of information on the industry in our local area, as well as looking further afield to the rest of the country. Even in our own schools and colleges there is a need for hospitality and catering. In other words, you should be looking for examples of the industry in your everyday life and collecting evidence and information as you go through the course. There is no external test in this unit, therefore your portfolio of evidence is especially important.

Many of the tasks in these units need you to look at different kinds of outlets in the industry and to compare them. You are unlikely to be able to investigate the industry properly from within your own school or college. If you live in a very rural area with poor transport facilities, you will find it much more difficult to investigate different areas of the industry in person. Take every opportunity you can to visit places while you are on holiday or visiting relatives. Your tutor should be able to arrange group visits to some outlets, and you may like to join with other members of your class in writing to a wide range of different establishments. You should aim to visit as many different kinds of outlets as possible, to interview those who work there or use the facilities, and to question any speakers from the industry, who visit your school or college. To help you in collecting evidence for the tasks, those tasks which might need you to look at other outlets are marked with **** in the top right-hand corner. You would be advised to read through this unit and note those which are marked in this way, so that whenever you visit an outlet, or have a speaker, you can have your questions ready.

▪ EXPLORING THE HOSPITALITY AND CATERING INDUSTRY ▪

In this section we will look at the various parts which make up the industry. Some of these are well known to us, and we can find examples in our everyday lives; others are less obvious and we will discover more about them here. We will explore ways of finding out more about the industry, and consider how it affects people – those who use its facilities, those who work in it, and those who are connected with other industries. We will also consider the contribution that the industry makes to the economy of the country, and discover just how large and complex it is, and how important it can be to us.

What is hospitality and catering?

Let us first consider what we mean by *Hospitality* and *Catering*.

Definition

- ***Catering** is quite straightforward – it means the provision of food and drink. The food might be cooked or uncooked, but it is usually prepared in some way. For example, the industry does not include grocers' shops as these usually sell unprepared food.*
- ***Hospitality** can have quite a wide meaning. To be hospitable means to provide shelter, warmth, kindness etc. to visitors.*

The hospitality and catering industry is extremely old. The Bible mentions places where people stayed, including the fact that there was no room at the inn for Joseph and Mary. Monasteries and other religious houses were used by pilgrims in the Middle Ages. Ale houses existed from an early date, where people used to gather to discuss trading deals and plot crimes. When people began to travel by horse or horse-drawn coaches, inns began to appear at the side of the road to offer shelter and refreshment to the traveller. When railways were developed, hotels were built near to stations to cater for the needs of passengers.

Nowadays, the industry is a large and complex one. It covers many different types of outlets, from the simple hot-dog stand to the large hotel with 1000-plus bedrooms. The industry changes constantly to meet the needs of its customers, which makes it an industry requiring staff who are well trained and adaptable. It provides the basic necessities of life, such as food and shelter, and therefore is likely to remain an important industry in the future.

The sectors of the industry

The industry consists of two sectors:

- The *commercial* sector
- The *catering services* sector

The commercial sector

This is the sector which we all think first about when we are asked what the industry comprises. It contains those parts of the industry where hospitality and catering are the principal activities. It includes outlets such as:

- Hotels
- Guest houses
- Public houses
- Clubs
- Wine bars
- Restaurants (including cafés, fast-food outlets, take-aways, etc.)
- Contract catering (caterers who supply prepared meals to other organizations)

In all these outlets hospitality and catering is the main activity. There may be other activities taking place in the same area, such as leisure facilities in a hotel, but the main purpose is to provide hospitality and catering. These outlets normally exist to make a profit, therefore their goods and services are sold to the customers in exchange for money.

The catering services sector

This sector may provide the same goods and services as the commercial sector, but the difference is that the provision of hospitality and catering is not the main activity or purpose of the organization. It exists for some other purpose, and the provision of food, drink, shelter, etc. is a *secondary* or *indirect service*.

Definition

- *A **secondary** or **indirect** service is one which is not the main activity of the organization.*

This sector includes:

- Hospitals
- Prisons
- Residential homes
- Schools, colleges, universities
- Armed forces (army, air force, navy)
- Leisure and tourism outlets
- In-house staff feeding

People in all of these areas need the goods and services of hospitality and catering, but that is not their prime reason for being there. A patient in hospital is there to undergo treatment, but needs a bed, food and drink during the period of stay.

Although very few outlets like to make a loss on their hospitality and catering activities, some of those in this sector do make a loss, or very little profit. Often, profit making is not a priority. The school meals service, for example, may be subsidized through the local authority; similarly, a works canteen might be subsidized as a 'perk' to the people who work there. Some of the hospitality and catering services included in this sector are provided 'free of charge' to the customers (e.g. patients in National Health hospitals or inmates in prison). In these cases, the money to provide the service comes from the health authority or direct from the government.

Task 1.1

Make a list of establishments which exist in your own local area or in the surrounding areas which provide hospitality and catering services. Which ones are part of the commercial sector *and which are part of the* catering services sector?

Outlets in the hospitality and catering industry

Within each sector of the industry, there are several different *outlets* for goods and services provided.

Definition

- *An **outlet** is a part of an organization which provides hospitality and catering services.*

An organization, such as a chain of hotels, might have several outlets. Each outlet might provide several *facilities*.

Definition

- *A **facility** is a type of hospitality or catering service (e.g. a room, a restaurant, a bar) which earns* revenue.
- ***Revenue** is money earned by selling goods and services.*

There is another, more general, meaning of the word 'facilities' which can describe supporting services such as toilets, automatic doors, trouser presses and hair dryers in rooms, swimming pool, etc. We usually call these *amenities*.

Definition

- ***Amenities** are the physical goods provided for the convenience of customers.*

Each facility, or outlet if there is only one facility in the outlet, might contain several *operations* or activities.

Definition

- *An **operation** is an activity or group of activities, which may provide facilities (i.e. they may bring in revenue) or which may provide supporting services (e.g. housekeeping, reception).*

For example, a hotel restaurant will have a Food Preparation operation and a Food Service operation. Hotel bedrooms will be supported by the Housekeeping operation, and perhaps a separate Laundry operation. Operations such as Reception, Porterage, Administration, Maintenance, etc. will support the entire outlet. Operations are sometimes referred to as *departments*.

Figure 1.1 might help to clarify the structure of an organization.

Task 1.2

Using the list you made for Task 1.1, think carefully about the types of outlets on the list, and the facilities offered by them. Make a list of them as follows:

Establishment	Sector	Type of outlet	Facilities offered
e.g. Ritz Hotel	*Commercial*	*Hotel*	*Two restaurants* *Bar* *Coffee shop*

Task 1.3

Join with other members of your class to produce a wall chart showing the information you have gathered. You can produce textual information, supported by leaflets and advertisements. You can also present your results in the form of a bar chart, using a computer.

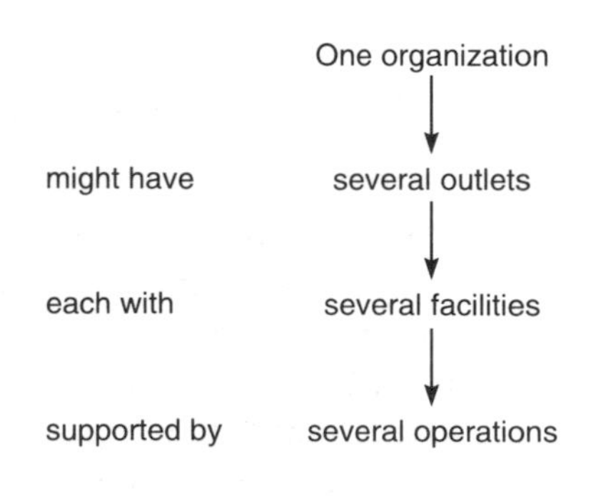

Figure 1.1 The structure of an organization in the hospitality and catering industry

Types of outlets

There are many different types of outlets in the hospitality and catering industry. Some have already been mentioned and examined. Depending on where you live or attend school or college, you will have covered some of them in two tasks you have already done. It is useful to know what other types of outlet exist in other parts of the country or in different kinds of towns.

In a large town or city you might find lots of *commercial sector* outlets, such as:

- Fast-food outlets and sandwich bars
- Ethnic take-aways
- Large restaurants
- Foreign and speciality restaurants (e.g. Greek, Turkish)
- Large hotels (e.g. with over 200 beds)
- Wine bars

In addition there might also be outlets in the *catering services sector,* such as

- A college or university
- A large hospital
- Employers offering in-house staff feeding

The large hotels found here might belong to national or international groups of hotels, such as International Hilton and Forte Hotels. This is especially true if there is an airport nearby.

In an area near the coast there may be *commercial sector* outlets, such as:

- Guest houses and boarding houses with only a few beds
- Small hotels (e.g. between 25 and 30 beds)
- Holiday camps
- Fish restaurants
- Beach kiosks (e.g. ice-cream, hot-dogs)
- Larger resort hotels catering for families
- Caravan parks

and there might be *catering services sector* outlets such as:

- Homes for the elderly or sick
- Private hospitals
- Leisure outlets such as fun-fairs, swimming pools, etc.

The hotels in this area might be privately owned, perhaps with two or three owned by the same small family company. Some may be members of a local 'consortium', which means they join together to discuss local situations and to make decisions about the future of the industry in their area. They also help each other by buying in goods in bulk, and referring business to another hotel in the consortium if their own hotel is full.

In a country area you might find the following *commercial sector* outlets:

- Country pubs
- Country hotels
- Small restaurants and cafés

Catering services sector outlets might include:

- A prison
- A base for one of the armed forces, such as the Army or Royal Air Force.
- Leisure attractions such as theme parks

The majority of hotels here will be privately owned but there may be one or two who are members of a national chain, especially in areas which attract tourists or which are near to larger towns and cities.

Hotels and the facilities they provide

All hotels provide facilities for eating and sleeping. You might think that makes them all the same. But in fact there are many different types of hotels to suit different types of customer. They are often classed in the following way:

1 *International hotels* These are called international because they are owned by companies with hotels in many countries of the world. Some of them are built, furnished and decorated in exactly the same style, and offer exactly the same facilities and service throughout the world. Customers who travel abroad can be confident of finding the same

standard wherever they stay. Room charges are often high and do not include meals. Meals might be taken in the hotel restaurant or elsewhere. The guest is usually able to ask for any kind of service and the hotel will be able to provide it.

2 *Commercial hotels* These are found in towns and cities where there is business activity. They are used by these businesses to provide overnight accommodation for their guests, to entertain clients or to provide conferences. The hotels have a wide range of services, including mini-bars in rooms, trouser press, hair dryer, room service, etc.
3 *Resort hotels* These are found in seaside areas and cater for people who are on holiday. Services are more restricted than in commercial hotels. *Guest houses* and *bed and breakfast* accommodation is similar but often smaller. Most hotels have a restaurant, offering a choice of meals, and one or more bars. Guest houses might have fixed meal times and limited choice, and perhaps no bar.
4 *Transient hotels and motels* These are often found near motorways or on major routes, and are used by motorists, often without a prior booking. They are often adjacent to a restaurant which is open to other travellers as well as residents.
5 *Residential hotels* These offer long-stay accommodation, often for the elderly or homeless. Some might be permanent residents. They often have shared bathrooms, fixed meal times and limited choice. Those for the homeless might have no provision for meals, but there may be cooking facilities in a shared kitchen.

Task 1.4

Look at the list or chart you have compiled for Task 1.2, showing the outlets and facilities in your area. Make a list of outlets which do not exist in your area, and find out where the nearest ones are. You might need to look in Yellow Pages *or* Thomson's *to find this information. Motoring organizations, such as the AA or RAC publish data on some establishments. Your local tourist information office might also help. Label each outlet on your list as being part of the* commercial sector *or part of the* catering services sector.

Pubs, clubs and wine bars

These three outlets have a major similarity – they all provide alcoholic drink as one of their main revenue-earning activities. Pubs have been long established, starting out as ale-houses for men only, but now provide pleasant surroundings for all kinds of people to meet and chat over a drink. Relaxation in the licensing laws has meant that pubs stay open for longer than they used to, and are starting to provide day-long facilities such as breakfasts throughout the morning. Many pubs serve bar meals and some have a restaurant attached. Families are made much more welcome, sometimes in separate rooms which have play facilities for little children. Menus contain a wide variety of traditional dishes, including Sunday roast dinners and more modern foods such as burgers and pizzas. Many pubs attract regular customers, and loyalty to a particular pub is very common. Originally only serving beers, pubs now offer a wide range of drinks, including medium-priced wines, spirits and soft drinks. Entrance is free, but the surroundings may not be plush in all pubs. Most villages have a pub – some boast a pub on every corner.

Clubs tend to attract younger age groups, 18–24-year-olds mainly. They offer music and dancing as well as drinks and some provide light refreshments. Entrance fees can be quite high, but entertainment is included and the surroundings are often very modern and well decorated. Many insist on guests being smartly dressed, and they employ 'bouncers' to turn away unlikely guests at the door. Clubs tend to exist in areas of high population because they need large numbers of guests to pay for the high cost of running the club. There are some smaller clubs in towns and villages, such as 'working men's' clubs, political clubs, etc. These attract older age groups.

Wine bars also attract younger age groups. These exist in medium-sized and larger towns. They primarily serve alcoholic drinks, though some also provide bar food. Background music is often played, and entrance is usually free. Many impose restrictions on the style of dress which can be worn, and few allow children in.

Restaurants

This category includes cafés, fast-food outlets, take-away outlets, sandwich bars, etc. whose prime function is the provision of food. Drinks will also be served. Many restaurants have a full wine list, while cafés and fast-food outlets are more likely to serve soft drinks. Take-aways and sandwich bars might serve only bottled or canned drinks.

Restaurants are open during the main meal times, perhaps until quite late at night. They tend to be well furnished and comfortable, with waitress service, cloakroom facilities, etc. There are many different types of restaurant. In rural areas there will probably be only traditional restaurants, but foreign restaurants are found in towns and cities.

Cafés might only open until early evening, and often have poor toilet and cloakroom facilities; decor can vary widely from one outlet to another. Some cafés cater particularly for those who want a quick, filling and inexpensive meal and do not want luxurious surroundings – transport cafés are a good example of this. Motorway cafés serve fast food and traditional meals, usually on a self-serve basis, with a good standard of decor.

Fast-food outlets are also self-service, with a pleasant decor. Some are open until very late in the evening. Take-aways also stay open until quite late. Sandwich bars, baked-potato stalls, etc. tend to open during working hours.

Hospitals

Hospitals provide for three types of customer – patients, visitors and staff. Improvements in the attitude towards patient-feeding means that patients now have some choice of meals, including 'healthy' options; most are served on trays to patients with plain crockery and cutlery. Provision for visitors might be in a small café-style facility or self-service restaurant. Staff might be fed in the same restaurant or in a separate 'canteen'. Senior staff may have waitress service.

Because food and drink for visitors might be needed at unusual times, vending machines are used to supplement the normal facilities.

Private hospitals serve a wider choice of foods, both to patients and to visitors and staff, including alcoholic drinks. Many hospitals now use contract caterers as a means of economic provision of meals.

Prisons

These provide for the inmate, usually in a canteen or similar room. Food is self-serve or served to the 'guest', using plain crockery. Meals are basic and simple, but more variety has appeared in recent years as attitudes towards the treatment of prisoners has changed. Alcohol is not allowed.

Prisons also need to feed their staff, often in self-serve restaurants. Contract caterers are also used in this area.

Residential homes

These offer long-term accommodation to people, often the elderly. They tend to be fairly small establishments with 'home cooking' as one of their attractions. They usually try to offer a variety of meals to suit the tastes of their guests, but without undue expense. Service will probably be some form of table service in comfortable surroundings.

Schools, colleges and universities

Primary schools usually offer a cooked meal at lunch times only; some allow children to bring their own meals, and some are introducing sandwiches into the school meals service. Many school meals are cooked in central kitchens and distributed to nearby schools; an increasing number are using contract caterers.

Secondary schools offer a self-serve restaurant, with fast-food and 'healthy' options. Many pupils bring their own lunches, and often have nowhere to sit to eat it! Vending machines are used to provide drinks and snacks.

Universities and colleges often provide a more comprehensive range of foods and drinks. Many of the students will be living away from home and in situations where cooking a meal is not easy. Self-service restaurants provide a service at lunch times and evenings, with vending machines and snack bars to supplement the main service. Most colleges have a students' bar serving snacks and alcoholic drinks. Provision for staff is often in the same restaurant, with a separate eating area.

Armed forces

The forces are usually based in camps or barracks, with good kitchen facilities and trained staff. Although forces food has to be economical, it must also be highly nutritious. The standards of service are not luxurious, but are based on canteen-style self-service. Choice has greatly improved in recent years. Senior staff have separate dining rooms with waitress service.

Many camps have a bar, serving alcholic drinks and providing relaxation in a comfortable atmosphere.

Leisure and tourism

The range of facilities and type of service offered depends very much on the leisure and tourism outlet concerned. A theme park will contain snack bars, self-service restaurants, stands selling hot-dogs, burgers, baked potatoes, pizza slices, etc., and probably a bar. A golf club might have a formal restaurant. Some theatres have exclusive restaurant facilities and extensive wine lists.

In-house staff feeding

Many employers provide facilities for staff feeding. Some segregate manual workers' canteens from office staff restaurants, primarily to protect office staff from getting their clothes dirty, and to enable manual workers to eat in a relaxed atmosphere. Some are now combining different types of staff for feeding purposes. Most provide a self-serve system, with waitress service for senior staff. Menus are usually fairly restricted, with a small choice each day. Contract caterers are taking over a large share of this part of the market.

Contract catering

This area of business is expanding rapidly. It is now used widely in hospitals, prisons, schools and colleges and in-house staff feeding – in fact anywhere where large numbers are to be catered for. It is also used for separate, smaller areas. For example, many companies use contract caterers for special functions and promotions. The standard is dependent on the level required, from economical school meals to banquets.

Economic significance of the hospitality and catering industry

The industry contributes greatly to the UK economy; it earns money for the country and for those who work in the industry. It also provides income for other industries. As a result, the government obtains more in taxes from profits and earnings and saves money on state benefits.

Sources of information about the hospitality and catering industry

Information about the industry and its economic significance or importance can be obtained from a variety of sources. Some of these are described here.

Trade journals

These are magazines published by various bodies. There are many of them, and your tutor should be able to give you their addresses. Your college or school library may stock some of them, and you may be able to obtain them through your newsagent. Some of them are:

	Frequency of publication
Caterer & Hotelkeeper	Weekly
Catering Update	Monthly
Popular Foodservice	Monthly
Pub Caterer	Monthly
Chef	Quarterly

Professional bodies

These are organizations to which many hospitality and catering staff belong. They often offer qualifications for staff in the industry, and publish magazines and other data. Some are available only to members, so your tutor might be able to obtain these for you. The main professional body of the industry is:

HCIMA (Hotel, Catering and Institutional Management Association),
191 Trinity Road, London SW17 7HN

Published data

The government and other bodies collect data on the industry from various sources and publish it from time to time. Some of the places which might let you have such data are as follows:

Hotel and Catering Training Company, International House, High Street, Ealing, London W5 5DB
British Federation of Hotel, Guest House and Self-catering Associations, 5 Sandicroft Road, Blackpool, Fylde FY1 2RY
British Hospitality Association, 40 Duke Street, London W1M 6HR

The difficulty you might have with these sources is that they publish a great deal of data, and you really need to know exactly what you want before asking. Some textbooks are also a source of published data (like this one).

Scale and scope of the hospitality and catering industry

The industry grew rapidly during the 1970s and 1980s, even during the recessions which affected other industries. People generally have more spending power than they had in earlier years, and greater amounts of leisure time. Consequently, their expectations and lifestyles have changed. In the early part of the 1990s, the recession started to hit the hospitality and catering industry too, but to a lesser extent. The industry is still a very large one, as the following facts show:

- *Fact 1* – In 1991 there were 30.2 million meals served in state schools and 38.2 million meals served in health-care facilities. Meals served in businesses and industry were over 300 million (*Keynote, Contract Catering 1992*)
- *Fact 2* – In 1993, 2.5 million people were employed in hospitality and catering related industries – that is, about 10% of the total UK workforce (*Employment Gazette* April 1993/*Annual Abstract of Statistics 1993*)
- *Fact 3* – In 1991 there were nearly 600 million nights spent by visitors in the UK (Pannell Kerr Forster, *UK Trends 1993*)

- *Fact 4* – The average number of meals eaten outside the household in 1990 was 3.76 per person per week (*Keynote – The UK Catering Market 1992*).

The majority of all outlets are small and privately owned. Pubs are the largest commercial catering market, with fish and chip shops and small take-aways accounting for the next largest share. In contrast, there are a few very large hotel chains, some of them owned by breweries, which have a very high turnover (revenue).

Task 1.5

Contact a selection of sources of information and ask for the latest statistics on the number of outlets in different areas of the industry. You might prefer to do this in groups so that you are not all writing to the same organizations or using the same publications. Draw up a table of your results.

Employment patterns in the hospitality and catering industry

We have already seen that the industry provides employment for a large number of people. The total of 2.5 million in 1993 can be broken down into:

- 1,105,200 in the hotel and commercial sectors
- 1,350,000 in the catering services sector

The majority of employees in the hotel and commercial sectors in 1993 were female (over 60 per cent), and most of these (over 70 per cent) were part-time employees. Of the male employees, less than half were employed part-time. This is not surprising when you consider the types of jobs which are available in the industry. Many of them are low paid, thus men are reluctant to take them. Many are seasonal, so part-timers are best suited to them. Many involve unsocial hours, and therefore attract women with young children who cannot work during the day.

Over 50 per cent of all jobs in the industry are held by unskilled workers. About half of these employees stay in their jobs for less than five years and are replaced by other employees. Compare this with only 14 per cent of jobs in the industry being held by managers, and only 8 per cent of them leaving and being replaced. The low-paid jobs would seem to be the ones which cause most movement of staff.

On the bright side, there are over one million vacancies per year in the industry. So there are always jobs available in some areas.

Task 1.6

Make a list of the jobs you can think of in the hospitality and catering industry. At the side of each job state whether you would consider it to be a managerial/ supervisor's job, an unskilled job, or somewhere in between (craft and semi-skilled).

The large number of part-time jobs is due partly to the fact that customers require services at all hours of the day and night, and consequently certain areas of an outlet need to be staffed at unusual times. The reception area of a large hotel near an airport would need to be staffed 24 hours a day to deal with guests arriving or departing very late or very early. On the other hand, the majority of customers require breakfast between 7.00 a.m. and 9.30 a.m., so there is no point in putting a full staff in the restaurant at 11.00 a.m. Staff therefore work irregular hours to cope with the needs of the customers.

Many outlets and facilities operate a *shift system* of working. This means that employees work in blocks of about 8 hours, and at the end of the block or *shift* another group of employees takes over, and so on until 24 hours have been covered.

Task 1.7

Make a list of reasons why a hotel reception desk might need to be staffed 24 hours per day.

Some employees work *split shifts* which means that they work part of their hours at one time of day and the rest at another time. For example, a restaurant serving lunch and dinner might require staff from 11.00 a.m. until 3.00 p.m. and from 6.00 p.m. until 10.00 p.m.

The main advantage of working shifts is that you have free time when other people are working. You can do your shopping then, or visit the leisure centre at times when it is less busy. You might be able to enjoy the sunshine in the afternoon when most people are still at work.

Task 1.8

Make a list of different facilities in the industry which might require employees to work shifts in order to fulfil the needs of its customers. Describe briefly the types of job the employees would be needed to do.

The range of services and products provided by the hospitality and catering industry

The industry provides a wide range of services and products for the customer. The obvious ones are food, drink and accommodation, but there are many others.

In hotels, for example, leisure facilities are becoming popular, including swimming pools and gyms. A hotel might also provide beauty care, such as a hairdresser, manicurist, or make-up consultant. Personal laundry and valeting are also available in luxury hotels.

Wine bars provide food and fast-food cafés often supply alcoholic drinks. Pubs also have increased their emphasis on the provision of food, with bar-snacks and lunchtime menus for the businessperson. Pubs also provide entertainment, with music and games machines.

Hotel bedrooms are providing more and more facilities. It is now common to find tea- and coffee-making equipment, hair-dryers, irons, trouser presses, etc. Even caravan parks now provide modern showers and toilet facilities of a high standard.

Many hotels in business centres offer conference facilities, providing office equipment, stationery and even secretarial staff. Telephone facilities are available in rooms, or in public areas, using phonecards as well as coins. There are facilities for using facsimile machines (faxes), telex and computerized mailing.

Figure 1.2 A conference

Task 1.9

Imagine that you are a visitor to a large city for the first time, and you expect to stay in your chosen hotel for several days. You are meeting an important business client, and you find that you need urgent information from your office hundreds of miles away. After the meeting you will need to relax and unwind, before going on to another hotel, by train, for another important meeting.

List the services and products which you might need to use during your stay.

Industries associated with the hospitality and catering industry

There are several industries associated with the hospitality and catering industry, and which depend partly on the industry for their success. These include:

- The leisure and tourism industry
- The grocery trade
- The wine and spirits industries
- Breweries
- Fishing and agriculture
- Makers of catering equipment

In addition to the above there are many other industries which provide goods and services to the hospitality and catering industry as well as to other industries. These include:

- Manufacturers of furniture and furnishings
- Architects
- Builders
- Interior designers
- Accountancy and banking
- Staff recruitment agencies

Many large hotel chains employ their own teams of decorators, or have their own printing departments for the production of advertising leaflets, menus, tariff cards, customer questionnaires, registration documents, as well as all the internal stationery required to run any business. Some have their own marketing departments too.

Task 1.10

Look through your local newspaper and find the adverts from businesses and tradespeople. Make a list of those which could provide services or products to the hospitality and catering industry in your area, and identify the types of products or services that could be useful.

The benefit which the industry brings to the national economy

We have already seen how large the industry is in terms of numbers employed and the amount of business which is done. It is of considerable benefit to the economy. There are many ways in which the industry contributes to the economy and some of these are as follows:

1. Providing jobs in the industry. This enables people to maintain themselves and their families, and lessens the burden on the social security system. The employees are then able to pay taxes to the government to fund the country as a whole.
2. Providing jobs in associated industries. This then enables employees in those industries to look after themselves.
3. Making profits. These go partly to the owners of the business, partly in taxes to the government and some are left in the business and used to expand by building new premises or updating equipment. In those areas of the industry which are not profit making (e.g. schools, hospitals, prisons, etc.) the profits

help to reduce the overall cost of running those areas.

4 Encouraging overseas visitors to come to the UK. This brings in foreign currency which the government can then use to buy essential items from overseas.
5 Enabling business people to travel for their own firms and thereby allowing those firms to employ more staff and make more profits.
6 Providing services to state-run organizations, such as school meals, hospital and prison kitchens.

Connections with other industries

The hospitality and catering industry has many connections with other industries, in a variety of contexts. This means that each industry affects the other, and therefore the performance in one will have a bearing on the performance in the other. The main contexts or areas in which there are connections with the industry are:

- The entertainment industry
- Education
- Travel and tourism
- Sports and recreation
- Health and welfare establishments

We will look at each of these in turn, and examine the ways in which they are connected and the effects which they have on the hospitality and catering industry.

Entertainment

The entertainment industry is a growing one also, for many of the same reasons as the growth in hospitality and catering, namely increased spending power and leisure time, changing patterns of activity and expectations, plus the increased availability of entertainment throughout the country. The entertainment industry contains:

- Theatres and cinemas
- Theme parks
- Holiday parks and camps
- Watching sports

These outlets are expected to provide food, with a choice of styles – take-away or restaurant style. Some are also expected to provide alcoholic beverages. Even if the outlets themselves do not require it, nearby hospitality and catering establishments benefit from these areas. For example, people visiting the theatre in London to see a top musical will require a restaurant meal before the show and overnight accommodation afterwards. If the popularity of such entertainment decreases, then so will the popularity of the hospitality and catering industry.

Catering establishments need to be open at hours to suit the entertainment nearby. Restaurants near theatres may stay open late to encourage customers after the theatre has closed. The customers may consist not only of theatregoers but also of performers and theatre staff.

Task 1.11

Identify three entertainment providers in your area. Find out what times of day and year they are open. Then look for hospitality and catering outlets near each one, and the times of day and year which they are open. Can you see any outlets which could use the customers of the entertainment provider, but which have failed to take advantage of them?

In addition to the specialist entertainment providers, hotels and restaurants themselves often have entertainment. Many provide themed evenings or events, often connected with a local tradition, or a national celebration such as Valentine's day. Some pubs offer special food and drink on the day of important sporting events,

Figure 1.3 A Christmas party

together with large-screen viewing of the event. Events such as this may require extra staff to cope with the one-off demand.

Task 1.12

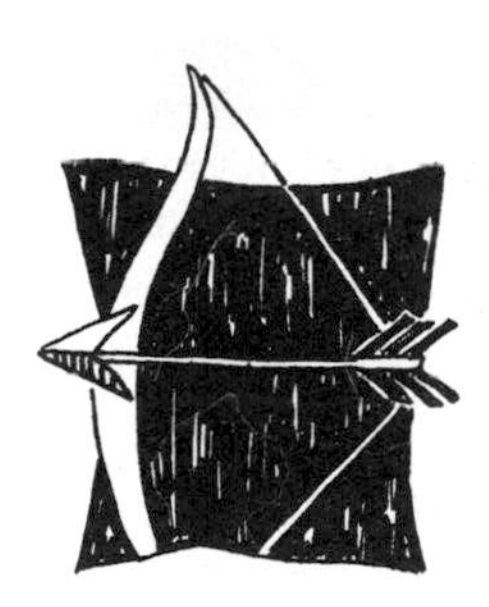

Look through your local paper for special events and offers at local hospitality and catering establishments in your area. Are there any special events coming up in the near future which establishments could use to boost their income?

Education

Education is also a user of the hospitality and catering industry. Again, all educational establishments require food of some kind. Some provide self-service food, others a table or tray service. Establishments for older students often have a take-away service.

Universities and colleges cater for older students who may enjoy pubs and clubs. These need to be fairly inexpensive, as students are often short of money.

Universities are often empty during the vacations, and therefore the industry needs to find other ways of attracting customers during those times. Many universities offer their facilities for conferences during vacations, so delegates may become customers of the empty pubs and clubs. In fact, this area is growing rapidly, with many colleges employing teams of hospitality and catering staff to provide services and standards similar to those found in hotels. Conference delegates use the rooms normally occupied by students, upgraded to contain tea- and coffee-making amenities, towels, etc. Many of the senior students at top universities also have en suite bathrooms, which are available to delegates during their stay. This also gives the university's catering staff an opportunity to extend their skills at times when they might not otherwise be employed. The lecture rooms and equipment are obviously already in place, and to a high standard. Some universities also offer their facilities for short breaks and family holidays.

Travel and tourism

This industry is a major provider of customers to the hospitality and catering industry. In 1991, tourism expenditure reached over £17,000 million!

People in business need to travel frequently, and use the facilities of hotels, restaurants, etc. Tourists need similar facilities, perhaps for longer periods. They may be happy to accept lower standards of luxury on holiday, because they are enjoying themselves and have more time, whereas business travellers often expect a little extra convenience, especially if it saves time.

Catering facilities are required throughout a person's journey as well as at the place of stay, and on trains, boats and planes it must be highly efficient. Motorway services are expected to provide quick meals in pleasant surroundings, with facilities for children and mothers with babies.

Figure 1.4 Off on holiday

Many UK residents take their holidays during the summer, thus hotels need to be fully staffed at those times. Christmas is also a busy time for hotels and restaurants. People celebrate with their firms, and with their families and friends. Longer Christmas breaks mean that the hospitality and catering establishment is busy for a longer period. On the other hand, many are partly empty at other times of the year and need to find ways of boosting their income.

Task 1.13

Design a short questionnaire for your family and friends. Find out what times of the year they prefer to travel in the UK, and what types of outlet they use both while they are travelling and when they reach their destinations. Ask also what method of transport they use during their journey and their opinion of the hospitality and catering services they use en route.

The travel and tourism industry is one of those being hit by the current recession. People are afraid to commit themselves in advance to long holidays, and are tending to take shorter, unbooked breaks. This in turn reduces the expenditure in the hospitality and catering industry.

On the other hand, the number of retired people in our society is increasing. Many of them retire early, with extra pensions from their employers. Women now have pensions, whereas in previous years they did not. People are living longer, and are more fit and active than previous elderly generations. This leads to increased demand for travel and tourism, as well as for entertainment. However, the industry needs to respond to this demand as recent trends have been to cater for the younger generations. Eventually, of course, the younger generations – who are now used to eating out and travelling – will also become older. Older people require more comfort, healthier foods and environments and demand value for money.

Sports and recreation

Increased leisure time and recent interest in health and fitness has led to an increase in the number of places providing sporting and recreational facilities, and in the number and frequency of people using them. They all require catering facilities, especially as physical activity increases the appetite, and some will need accommodation if people are travelling from home to compete in sports or other activities. Family and friends accompanying the sportsperson might also need accommodation.

Some sporting activities attract large numbers of people, such as football cup finals, snooker championships, motor racing, and of course Wimbledon tennis tournaments. The failed Olympic bid by Manchester to host the games in the year 2000 would have provided jobs and security, as well as a huge contribution to the local and national economy.

Sporting activities are often carried out after working hours and at weekends. This means that hospitality and catering facilities will also need to be provided at those times. Again, this probably involves shift working and part-time staff.

Sporting activities appear to have been less badly affected by the recession than other areas. Sports enthusiasts do not easily give up; many sporting activities are relatively inexpensive when compared to other activities, and so people are less inclined to abandon them to save money.

Task 1.14

Survey your local area for sporting and recreational facilities (this could be done in small groups). Include indoor and outdoor activities and both public and private ones. Find out what hospitality and catering provision there is nearby or within the recreational building. Identify any areas where the provision could be improved and state what those areas are.

Health and welfare organizations

These are places where several people reside at once. Some will be temporary residents and others permanent or long term. They include:

- Hospitals
- Hospices
- Prisons
- Residential homes for the elderly
- Centres for the disabled
- Mental homes

These all provide hospitality and catering services throughout the year. They are not normally affected by seasonal changes and do not react very quickly to changes in the economy, either local or national.

The services and products supplied need to be highly personal. Long-stay residents in homes for the elderly or disabled should be able to express preferences for food, decor and standard of service. Inmates in prisons are less likely to have their preferences considered. The food in hospitals may need to be geared to special diets, as well as to provide for the needs of visitors and staff.

Food which is served to very large numbers over a wide area, such as in hospitals, needs special systems to ensure that it is kept hot and does not lose texture or flavour while being transported hygienically. This can be costly to provide.

The income, and hence the profit, in welfare organizations is often low, and therefore does not always get the attention it deserves. The amount spent often depends on government and local authority grants, so if the national economy is weak then less money is available. However, the population in this part of the world is getting older, living longer, and is more likely to need hospital and long-term residential care in the future, so this area should not be ignored.

Staff, visitors and sometimes patients in hospitals need the services at all hours of the day and night, therefore shifts are worked and facilities are often open at all times, even if the services offered are reduced. The shift patterns worked also mean that staff have leisure time available during the day when other employees are at work, and hence might be able to travel, indulge in sport, etc. at unusual times of the day.

Task 1.15 

Visit a welfare establishment such as a hospital, near to your school or college. If there is none nearby, write to one as a group, and ask for information on the following:

- *The numbers of patients/inmates, etc. each day*
- *The numbers of visitors per day*
- *The types of facilities for the provision of food*
- *The hours of serving or providing such food*
- *Visiting times*

Classification systems in hospitality and catering

In an attempt to assist the customer in choosing the hospitality and catering provision which best suits his or her needs, several grading or classification systems have been developed over the years. Initially, these were introduced by the motoring organizations, such as the Automobile Association and the Royal Automobile Club. These grading schemes have been added to by the tourist boards and other bodies involved in hospitality, catering, leisure and tourism.

Accommodation grading schemes

Star grading

This scheme has been introduced by the motoring organizations, who award a number of stars to outlets which fulfil certain criteria. The criteria are based on the facilities (used in the general sense of the word, to mean the benefits offered by the establishment) and the amenities offered, compared to the number of customers. For example, an establishment which has en suite bathroom facilities for every room will gain more stars than one with only 50 per cent of rooms with en suite facilities. A dining room which offers a choice of meals and wines, with meal times spread over a longer period, will also gain more stars. All-night reception facilities, leisure facilities, direct-dial telephones, etc. all contribute to the grading. The grading is not based on the *standard* of goods and services offered, but rather than the quantity of them, though it follows that a good-quality establishment will attract profits which can be spent on adding extra amenities; poor-quality ones will be unable to afford them. Therefore it is normally assumed that a four-star hotel will provide good-quality food, drink and accommodation as well as a wide variety of amenities.

Despite the star rating, a hotel with four stars might be less suitable to a particular guest than one with two stars, depending on the needs of that guest. Hotels awarded four stars are among the larger hotels, and service could be less personal than with smaller hotels.

Rosette grading

This is a relatively new grading system, again used by the motoring organizations, to award to establishments which may have restricted facilities, giving them a lower 'star' rating, but which offer something special in other areas. For example, a hotel with a restaurant which serves dinner from 6 p.m. to 10 p.m. normally gets more 'stars' than one which has set dinner times. But the hotel with set dinner times may offer special dishes which appeal to particular guests, and hence will gain 'rosette' grading. Rosettes are often awarded to establishments with special atmospheres, e.g. country hotels, converted castles, in romantic settings, etc. even though their facilities may be restricted in some way.

Crown grading

The English Tourist Board awards a number of crowns to establishments of a certain standard. The scheme is currently being reviewed as it is felt that it is not fully understood by both hoteliers and guests. A recent survey of overseas visitors to England found that over half of them did not know anything about the crown system at all – they did not even know that it was connected with hotel accommodation.

There are other accommodation grading systems run by organizations such as the Caravan Club and other specialist groups, as well as several guidebooks published by travel organizations.

Food and drink grading schemes

These schemes are less common due to the fact that opinions vary so much on what constitutes 'good' food and drink. People's tastes and expectations depend on a variety of factors, and can cause much disagreement.

Michelin stars

These are awarded by the French organization, Michelin, to establishments on the Continent, but they also publish a *Michelin Guide to Great Britain and Northern Ireland*, listing restaurants who have been awarded this prestigious grading. It is very difficult to achieve a Michelin star grading, and hence chefs are very proud if their establishments are awarded one. Restaurants which serve less elaborate food, but which is well prepared, are awarded a red 'M' rather than a star. The *Guide* includes 1200 restaurants, but only 10 per cent of them have any kind of award. That should tell you that there are many good restaurants who do not achieve the award but nevertheless are popular and successful.

Other guides

Other guidebooks exist on food and drink standards. One is written by the famous chef, Egon Ronay, and includes not only restaurants but also pub food and smaller eating places.

Task 1.16

Obtain copies of the various guidebooks of organizations which award grades to hospitality and catering establishments and compare the criteria which each uses to determine the ratings. Prepare a chart showing your findings.

Conclusion

We have now looked at the hospitality and catering industry in outline. We have seen how it is made up of two sectors, with a variety of organizations, outlets and facilities. We have considered the importance of the industry to the economy, and have examined the connections which the industry has with industries in other contexts.

Test your knowledge

1 What are the two sectors of the hospitality and catering industry?
2 List six examples of outlets in each of the two sectors.
3 What is the difference between the terms 'outlet', 'facility', 'operation' and 'organization'?
4 What are the five main categories of hotel?
5 Can you remember any of the following facts about the hospitality and catering industry?

- How many meals were served in state schools in 1991?
- How many meals were served in businesses and industry in 1992?
- How many people were employed in hospitality- and catering-related industries in 1993?
- What proportion of employees in the industry were female?

6 Name six industries which depend heavily on the hospitality and catering industry for their success.
7 How does the hospitality and catering industry contribute to the national economy?

▪ THE HOSPITALITY AND CATERING INDUSTRY IN A LOCALITY ▪

Now that we have investigated the different sectors and the types of outlets and facilities within the sectors we can start to learn what products and services are offered and who uses them. Because the industry is so large, this section will look at the industry in your local area. Your investigations will help you to:

- Describe the range of outlets and facilities in your local area
- Describe the various sources of information on the outlets in your local area
- Identify the different types of customer, and their particular requirements
- Match the services and products to customer requirements

What is a 'locality'?

Definition

- *A **locality** is a geographical area which contains the facilities which people need for their daily lives.*

People have different needs, as we shall see later in this chapter, but generally most people need the following in their *locality*:

- Somewhere to live
- Somewhere to shop, for everyday things and for less frequent purchases
- Somewhere to work
- Somewhere to enjoy themselves
- Somewhere to learn
- Somewhere to cure them when they are ill

Every area has different characteristics. Several factors combine to make them different. These are:

1 *Size of population* Some areas are densely populated, others are sparsely populated.
2 *Ethnic background of population* Some areas have a high proportion of ethnic groups, with particular needs and customs; others have mainly white people, with traditional British likes and dislikes.
3 *Job opportunities* Some areas have plenty, including industry, commerce, tourism, etc.

Other areas are depressed or have few job opportunities. Some areas have seasonal job opportunities, such as holiday resorts.

4 *Social groupings* Some areas have a large proportion of well-off families, living in large houses with plenty of spare money; others have poorer families in crowded, rented accommodation, living on state benefits or low incomes.
5 *Nature of the area* Some areas are built-up with few open spaces. Some are country areas surrounded by steep hills and picturesque villages. Some are by the coast, others are inland.
6 *Connections with other areas* Some areas are near to others with similar characteristics; others are remote with no nearby connections; some have nearby areas with *different* characteristics. Some have good road links and public transport facilities, others have narrow lanes and infrequent bus services. Some are even small islands with limited connections with the mainland.

All these factors combine to give a locality a particular 'flavour', with its own needs for the products and services of the hospitality and catering industry.

The areas in Task 1.17 are all single villages, towns or cities. Some are very large, like London, some are very small, like Whaley Bridge. Some are so large that people live, work and spend their leisure time all within that

Task 1.17

Make a table showing the characteristics of the following places. You may need an atlas to help you with some of the places. If in doubt, have a guess and then check with your tutor to see if you are right.

	Population size	Population background	Job opportunities	Social grouping	Nature of area	Connection with other areas
London (inner)	*Very large*	*Ethnic/mixed*	*Many*	*Mixed*	*Built-up, Inland*	*Good*
Whaley Bridge (near Buxton, Derbyshire)						
Blackpool						
Birmingham						
Tenby, Wales						
York						
Belfast						
Macclesfield, Cheshire						

place. In London, for example, the city is so large that some people spend all their lives in just one part of it – they never need to travel outside that part (or perhaps they have not the time or money to do so). That part of London is their *locality*. It contains everything they need for most of their lives – houses, shops, schools, a college, a hospital, small hotels, perhaps a large hotel, cafés and restaurants of various types, a leisure centre, and so on.

Some places are so small that people need to travel outside them for some activities. The majority of people who live in Whaley Bridge work outside the village. There is no college or hospital in Whaley Bridge; the shops cater only for basic everyday needs; there is a couple of small restaurants, and plenty of pubs, but no large eating places, or foreign restaurants. There is no leisure centre either; the nearest large hotel is several miles away. People living in Whaley Bridge travel to other towns such as Buxton, Stockport and Manchester for work and other activities. This is their *locality*.

In-between places, like Macclesfield, have a wide range of facilities for the residents. There is ample work of different kinds available; good shops, with restaurants and cafés of different types; several small hotels, with larger ones within a few miles; a leisure centre; a college; a large hospital, and even a prison nearby. Although some people do travel outside the area for special requirements, most people are able to fulfil their needs within the town This is their *locality*.

Task 1.18

Look at your own locality. *What sort of area does it consist of – is it just your town or the area where you live, or does it contain nearby towns and cities? Write down the places which your locality consists of, and list the things which can be done in each place. Use the examples above to guide you. Tick the ones which you or your friends and family use regularly.*

Sources of information on outlets in a locality

There are several sources of information on the products and services available in a locality. You need to become familiar with these in order to perform some of the tasks in this chapter. The sources include the following.

Guides and handbooks

These are published by various organizations and individuals, such as:

- Motoring organizations (e.g. the AA and RAC). They include basic information on hotels, guest houses, restaurants, garages, etc. for each town in the country. There are also motorway maps with service areas marked. The hotels and restaurants are graded by the organization as a guide to the quantity and quality of facilities available.
- Associations of hotels and guest houses. These are groups of hoteliers who combine to publish information about their establishments throughout the country.
- Camping and caravanning organizations, such as the Caravan Club and the Camping and Caravanning Club. These publish data on caravan and camping sites. They also are responsible for the running of some sites, so can control the level of quality and service provided.
- Various handbooks of a specialist nature, e.g. places to visit or places to stay on walking holidays, bird-watching holidays, cycling holidays, etc. For example, the National Trust publishes a list of its properties which includes other places of interest to visit nearby.
- Guides to eating places, written by experts such as Egon Ronay.

Local information services

- Tourist information offices publish guides to hospitality and catering establishments throughout their area. Many offer their own rating system to grade and classify establishments.
- Local libraries provide information on places to visit, stay in or eat in, in the area.
- Telephone directories such as *Yellow Pages or Thomson's* offer lists of establishments in the area, with advertisements for some giving additional information.
- Local newspapers carry articles and adverts for local establishments.

Publicity material from outlets

The outlets themselves publish material advertising their goods and services. These may be in the form of leaflets or 'fliers' handed out in the street or delivered to people's homes, or inserted into the local paper. Or they may be in the form of posters displayed in public places such as the car park, the town hall, the market place etc.

Task 1.19

What sources of information are available on hospitality and catering outlets in your area? Keep a record of adverts which you come across over the next month, e.g. through the door, in the street, outside college, etc. Look in Yellow Pages *and* Thomson's *and record the establishments which advertise there. Obtain a copy of the AA or RAC guides and pick out the adverts which refer to your locality. Look for posters in the town centre. Visit your local library and tourist information office for details of outlets advertised there.*

Compile a table of outlets and their method of advertising (make a note of where you found each advert). Produce a graph or chart showing the numbers which use each method of advertising.

The scale and scope of hospitality and catering outlets in a locality

The products and services provided

The hospitality and catering industry is regarded as mainly as *service industry.*

Definition

- *A* ***service industry*** *is one which provides services to its customers rather than* products.
- ***Products*** *are items which are sold by an organization, which may be made by the organization or bought in ready-made for sale.*

The industry does in fact provide *both* products and services, but the products are only there to accompany the services provided. Apart from take-aways, where the product is the prime item for sale, other areas of the industry rely heavily on the service they provide, as well as any product which is offered. For example, a restaurant is providing not only the meal (the *product*), but equally important is the attitude of the staff, the speed of serving the meal, the comfortable chairs, the decor, the general atmosphere, etc. (the *services*). Good food which is served by impatient staff, delivered late, in a dingy nearly empty room with poorly laid tables, is not acceptable to most people, and would not be providing the service they require.

Task 1.20

Think of the last place you went to for a meal or snack. Make a list of the products and services it provided. Were there any you were not happy with, or any you felt were particularly good? Were there any services provided which you did not need?

Customer target groups

The range of products and services in a locality depends on the characteristics of that locality. Each area, and indeed outlet, has its own *customer target group*.

Definition

- *A **customer target group** is the type of customer which that outlet is seeking to encourage to use its goods and services.*

Few outlets have a target group so wide that it includes 'everybody'. Some outlets have several facilities within them which target slightly different groups. For example, a hotel may provide goods and services for a particular type of guest (perhaps the businessperson), but also have a coffee shop selling pastries and light snacks to local shoppers. These are two different 'target groups'.

Some organizations have different outlets targeting different groups. These may be spread throughout a town or the whole country. An example is the Forte group. They have large hotels for business clients, resort hotels for holidaymakers, 'Happy Eater' restaurants on main roads for travelling visitors (particularly with children), and Travel Lodges for motorists wanting an overnight stay near to the motorway or main road, at a competitive price.

Some outlets target according to age group, aiming for the teenager, the elderly, the family with children, etc. Some target according to price and level of luxury, aiming for those in the higher *socio-economic groups*.

Definition

- *A **socio-economic group** is a classification given to groups of people according to their education, background, qualifications, lifestyle and (partly) income.*

These outlets need to look carefully at the class of person living in their locality. Some areas of the country have a greater proportion of people in the higher groupings than others. The South and South-east of England have higher proportions than the North-west, for example. There is obviously no point in opening a high-class establishment in an area of low socio-economic grouping or in one with high unemployment.

A seaside area will require hotels and guest houses, caravan parks and self-catering establishments. If the nearby towns consist of affluent (well-off) people, the hotels will need to provide greater choice of meals and a higher standard of luxury than resorts with poorer visitors. The latter will probably have more take-aways and pubs.

A city area will need a wide range of outlets, providing all kinds of products and services. There will be a greater variety of customers and customer needs to be satisfied, from the expensive and high-class to the cheap and cheerful.

Some cities are tourist attractions, such as London with its diverse population and business centre, or Chester with its historical background. Both cities attract home and overseas visitors, and must cater for their needs. There will be a wide selection of hotels, restaurants of English and ethnic origin, fast-food outlets for the people who live and work there, etc. In such large centres there will be national and international hotel chains, providing standard levels of service, as well as local hoteliers.

Some establishments cater for the mass market, i.e. the general public; others cater for special types of customers such as the disabled. Many offer special types of holidays with activities included, such as sporting activities or walking weekends. Cities with buildings of architectural or historical interest, such as Nottingham, offer special holiday breaks which combine a guided tour of the town with a quiz or similar activity. In other words, they cater for a specialized market – people who require particular activities.

Task 1.21

Obtain information about your locality, or a nearby locality if necessary, and find out what special products or services, holidays, activities, etc. are provided. Make a list of those you find, and the types of customers who might be interested in them. Local newspapers and leaflets from tourist information offices may help.

Timing and frequency of products and services

Some establishments provide some products and services at all hours of day or night. A large hotel, for example, would be expected to provide room service for drinks and snacks until very late, and perhaps all night. A sandwich bar would probably close in the mid-afternoon.

Some products and services are provided daily – pubs, for example, are open every day. Some products and services are supplied only on weekdays – business lunches, for example; others only at weekends – Sunday roasts, for example. Fish and chip shops are rarely open on Sundays, and restaurants often choose to close on Monday due to lack of business.

Some products and services are seasonal – ice-cream stalls along the canalside in the summer, Christmas puddings and rum punches at Christmas.

Task 1.22

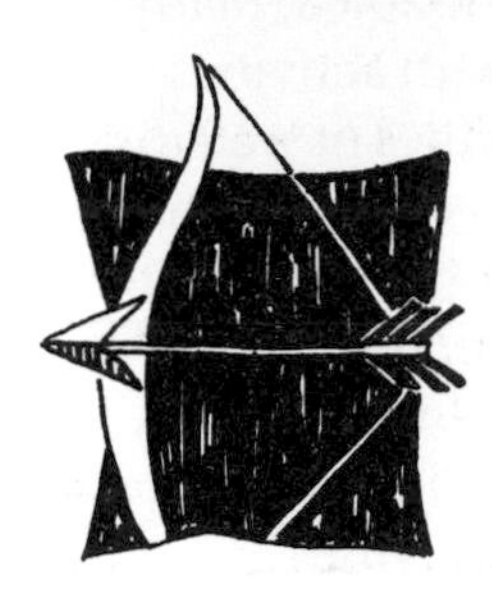

Look at your own locality again. Draw up a table of the days of the week, and show which facilities are available on each day, for a variety of establishments. Choose a facility from each of the following categories:

- *A school or college*
- *A hospital or prison*
- *A hotel*
- *A good-quality restaurant*
- *A take-away, fish and chip shop or sandwich bar*
- *A works canteen*

Task 1.23

Survey your local take-away or fish and chip shop for an hour on a normal day. Don't go at night without your parents' permission. Make a note of the people who go in and out. Look inside (discreetly!) and see who is already there. You should find that there are employees, suppliers and customers. You may also find a VAT inspector! If you join with other members of your class, you can take it in turns to 'cover' the premises for a whole day, and combine your findings. If you do this, you should obtain the permission of the owner of the establishment first. See also Task 1.22.

Task 1.24

While you are surveying your local take-away for Task 23, note the age group of the people who use it. Produce a table or graph showing the number in each age group.

Cultural background of customers

Customers come from many different cultural backgrounds. Britain has many ethnic groups among its population, and they have many similar needs to other groups. Some of those needs are special to their group.

Restaurants supplying Indian and Asian foods supply the needs of those nationalities (although many are too expensive for the people from those backgrounds to use). Ordinary English restaurants are often slow in adapting to meet the needs of people from other backgrounds. Vegetarian dishes now appear on many English menus, but choice is poor. Dishes for vegans and other types of 'vegetarians' are few.

Britain has a sizeable immigrant population and yet the everyday establishments are only just starting to cater for their needs. Jewish people, for example, do not eat meat with dairy produce, but few sandwich bars would offer a roast beef sandwich without butter. Catholics do not eat meat on Good Friday, yet many fish shops are closed on that day, and many restaurants have meat-only menus.

Task 1.25

Look at the restaurants in your locality. Make a note of any which offer dishes suitable for people from particular cultural backgrounds.

Customers with special needs

Some customers have needs which others do not have, because they are in some way different from the majority of people. They are described as customers with 'special needs'. These differences may be very minor, and require only slight adjustments to menus or methods of service. Other differences may be substantial and require special access arrangements, special diets, special furniture and so on.

Physical disabilities are the special needs which often spring to mind, and some of these are expensive to accommodate. Nevertheless, establishments are starting to realize the importance of customers with physical disabilities, and are making special arrangements for their needs and comfort.

Task 1.26

Imagine you are a person in a wheelchair, unable to get in or out of it without help. What special facilities or needs would you have if you were staying in a hotel for a week? Together with the rest of your class, write to a selection of establishments in your locality (not just hotels), and ask if they provide the facilities and needs you have identified.

Task 1.27

What kinds of help would you think the following people might need in a hospitality or catering outlet?

- *A blind person*
- *A deaf person*
- *A non-English-speaking guest*
- *A person suffering from tennis elbows or a frozen shoulder*
- *A confused, elderly guest*

Task 1.28

Find adverts in your locality for hospitality and catering establishments offering special opportunities to groups of people. What particular facilities do you think each group might require? You may need to visit your tourist information office for ideas.

Task 1.29

Match the following facilities and customers:

Customer 1 – a single mother with two small children on a week's holiday
Customer 2 – an executive salesperson
Customer 3 – a student in a flat
Customer 4 – an elderly lady

Accommodation types:

A Six single bedrooms in a large house, with a communal lounge, two shared bathrooms and a shared kitchen.
B Self-catering chalet with two bedrooms, a swimming pool and take-away on-site. Communal launderette and children's play area.
C A guest house with comfortable upright chairs, quiet lounge with TV and card table, plainly decorated rooms with en suite bathroom, dining room serving plain English food at set times.
D A large hotel with two bars and a late-night restaurant serving a variety of dishes. Bedrooms with en suite facilities, direct-dial telephone, video-channel, mini-bar and room service; telex and fax facilities on request.

Conclusion

In this section, you have looked at the scale and scope of the industry in your locality. You will have discovered some of the sources of information on outlets and examined them to determine the local position. You have looked at the different types of customers which use the industry, and how to match the products and services available with individual customers.

Test your knowledge

1 What factors determine the extent of a *locality?*
2 What is the difference between *products* and *services?* Give six examples of each which you might find in a hospitality and catering facility.
3 Where would you find information about the products and services of the hospitality and catering industry which exist in your locality?
4 How does an outlet decide on its target customer group?

▪ EMPLOYMENT OPPORTUNITIES IN THE HOSPITALITY AND CATERING INDUSTRY ▪

Employment opportunities in the hospitality and catering industry are many and varied. Some are specific to the industry and attract staff who particularly enjoy the contact with the public which exists in such an industry; others are general opportunities which exist in other industries, such as finance, maintenance and administration jobs.

The main job roles in the hospitality and catering industry

First, let us look at the various *operational areas* which exist in the hospitality and catering industry.

Definition

- *An **operational area** is one where particular activities or operations are carried out.*

In other words, these are the areas where people work in an organization. The operational areas can be divided into the following:

- Reception and reservations
- Accommodation operations
- Food preparation (kitchen)
- Food service (restaurant)
- Beverage service (restaurant and bars)
- Concierge (portering)
- Administration (e.g. Sales and Marketing, Finance)

The last area, that of Administration, can be very wide indeed. Those employed in this area could well require experience of the other areas in order to do their jobs properly, especially if they are involved in personnel and training, or purchasing of food and beverages.

The above is not a complete list, and is only very general. In different establishments the operational areas might be organized differently. In smaller establishments, for example, Food and Beverage service might be combined with Room Service. In a fish and chip shop, Food Preparation is combined with Food Service, Reception, Cashiering, and probably all other areas too!

Task 1.30 ****

Choose two *different hospitality and catering outlets with which you are familiar (e.g. your college restaurant, where you work, a hotel which you have visited, etc.). For each one identify which operational areas are separate and which are combined.*

Job roles in hospitality and catering

Different establishments also have different needs for the staff who work in each area – they might have very different job roles from those who work in other establishments in a job with the same title. In most areas there will be several levels of staff. These might be as follows:

1. *Management* These people will be responsible for the overall running of the operation. Senior managers or operational managers will manage everything to do with that operation – not only the staff who work there but also other things connected with that operation, such as materials used, the paperwork involved, methods of doing things, preparing reports on the activities of the department, solving problems and so on. They will be responsible for hiring and firing employees, ordering goods, etc. An example of an operational manager might be the Food and Beverage manager. Junior managers, perhaps responsible for a small area or operation, will take their instructions from senior managers who might be responsible for the whole outlet. However, many junior managers are able to make their own decisions for certain things, and simply 'report back' to senior management on anything which goes wrong or needs further advice. A duty manager is an example of a junior manager – he or she is responsible for the decisions which are needed while on duty. Managers are likely to be responsible for the medium-term running of the operation, taking decisions which affect the near future.
2. *Supervisors* These will be people who assist the management in a particular task or section within the department. There might be several supervisors under each manager. Supervisors are usually responsible for a small number of employees, dealing with minor problems themselves. They will also make some decisions by themselves, or may be instructed by their managers. Supervisors are likely to be responsible for the day-to-day activities of the area in which they work. Decisions which affect the longer term are usually referred to management.

3 *Operatives* These are the people who perform the everyday tasks within the operation. They are usually instructed by supervisors or managers, although some are well trained in their jobs and need little regular supervision except when there are problems.

There are usually more job opportunities for staff at the lower, operative levels than at the higher levels. Over three-quarters of the employees in the industry are in operative and craft positions, with only about 10 per cent in the supervisory roles.

Task 1.31 ****

Using the two outlets from Task 1.30 identify how many staff at each of the three levels (i.e. operative, supervisory, management) are employed in each one.

We will now describe a selection of job roles available in the different operational areas.

Reception

The receptionist is often the first person a guest (or potential guest) speaks to or sees. A large establishment will have several receptionists, and, as we saw earlier, some staff their reception desks 24 hours a day. There will probably be a senior or head receptionist in charge of each shift, as well as junior receptionists and trainees. In smaller establishments, the receptionist may well do other jobs when not needed in the reception area. This provides variety for the employee as well as being economical for the hotel owners.

The receptionist does not deal only with visitors. Other duties might include allocating rooms to guests, making sure that rooms are ready for occupation, notifying the Housekeeping staff when a guest has left so that the vacant room can be prepared for the next guest, and so on. The receptionist might be involved in preparing summaries of bookings taken and analysing the types of guest using the facilities. Handling different methods of payment would also be required, perhaps involving some calculations if the cashiering system is not fully automatic. In addition, the receptionist might be responsible for ensuring the clean and tidy appearance of the reception area, replacing flowers, displaying literature etc.

Task 1.32 ****

Using two different outlets of your choice (perhaps the two you used in the previous task), identify the duties of a receptionist. Compare the two outlets, and compare your lists with those of your colleagues, to make a complete list of all the duties you found.

Accommodation operations

Jobs here are connected with preparing rooms and other areas for guests to use. It might include the laundry operations as well as room servicing. In a large establishment, there might be a Head Housekeeper over all the areas requiring cleaning, and a separate Floor Housekeeper for each floor of bedrooms. Some establishments might offer butler and valeting services. Facilities which have banqueting and function suites might have a separate accommodation operations staff for that area alone.

Accommodation operations conjures up the vision of bed makers and cleaners, and these types of job are often regarded as being of low merit. In fact, any visitor to a hospitality and catering establishment requires a high standard of cleanliness at all times, and indeed this area is often top of the list of the things most important to a visitor. It is also an area which attracts a great number of complaints, and hence the job should not be regarded as unimportant. The bedroom is the area of a hotel in which guests spend most time, and which often makes a lasting impression on them.

The role of Head Housekeeper or Floor Housekeeper is a supervisory or even managerial role, and is of extreme importance to an organization. The Head Housekeeper will be responsible for scheduling the housekeeping operations to ensure that rooms are cleaned and prepared in the right order and in the most efficient manner.

Remember that the majority of a hotel's income, and its profit, comes from its room sales, and therefore clean and orderly rooms, available when required, contribute very greatly to the profitability of a hotel. Every person staying in a hotel will require the use of a bedroom, but not every guest will need to use the restaurant, the bar or the leisure amenities.

In large hotels there will be hundreds of rooms to service each day – top priority is given to this task, and its importance cannot be stressed too much.

Food preparation (kitchen)

Again, different establishments have different job roles, but it is wrong to assume that, even in the smallest kitchen, only cooking is carried out. In fact, although cooking is important, it is only one of many jobs involved in running a successful kitchen. Other jobs might be connected with nutrition, menu planning, food costing and purchasing.

There may be an overall Kitchen Manager, or Catering Manager. This person may also be in charge of the restaurant generally or may be solely concerned with the kitchen. There will be several chefs in a large kitchen, each responsible for different types of foods. These are:

- The Head Chef (Chef de Cuisine), who is responsible for the whole of the kitchen operation
- The Assistant Chef (Sous Chef) will assist the Head Chef, and take over in his or her absence. The Sous Chef may be responsible for some of the ancillary kitchen staff, such as the porters and storekeepers
- There will be separate chefs (Chef de Partie) responsible for each of the main food areas, such as fish, meats, sauces and pâtés, vegetables, starters, pastries, and puddings
- Assistant chefs (commis chefs) may be needed for each food area
- Kitchen assistants, porters
- Storekeepers

The staffing structure of a large kitchen such as the one described above is called the kitchen brigade. Each of the senior chefs will have assistants, and they will be responsible for the design and manufacture of dishes.

The kitchen staff does not consist only of chefs and cooks. There are also staff involved in nutrition and analysis of food. These are particularly important in hospitals, in prisons, and in the school meals service. There may also be a separate group of staff involved in food purchasing and the control of stores of food. In smaller kitchens, the Head Chef might perform all these tasks, with the aid of a commis chef, and perhaps a kitchen porter and cleaning/washing-up assistant for support.

In college halls of residence and boarding schools there might be a Domestic Bursar who is responsible for the provision of food to the students as well as a variety of other domestic arrangements.

In some establishments (e.g. McDonald's) staff are encouraged to undertake different job roles so that they can cover for absent colleagues and help out at peak times.

Task 1.33 ****

Choose a medium-to-large kitchen, and draw up a chart to show the various job roles of those who work in it.

Task 1.34 ****

Choose a medium-to-large outlet with a restaurant and bar, and identify the different job roles which exist.

Food service (restaurant and room service)

The Restaurant Manager will be responsible for this area, supported by various waiting staff. The type of job role will depend on the nature of the establishment. A self-service restaurant will require a different employee to a Silver service restaurant or a banquet. There is often a Head Waiter, with several assistants.

Room service requires another set of skills and procedures to deliver food and drink to guests in their rooms.

Beverage service (restaurant and bars)

The job title in this area will depend on the type of establishment. In a hotel restaurant, the job will be that of Beverage Manager/ess. In a bar, it might be a Bar Manager/ess. In a public house it is a landlord, a tenant or a pub manager. In specialist bars, there might be staff who deal with special types of drinks (for example cocktails).

Concierge

There might be a Head Porter, as well as room porters and luggage porters. Some hotels refer to the porter as a 'concierge', but in such establishments the porter's job consists of much more than carrying luggage – the concierge is an important person who looks after the wellbeing of new arrivals and departures in a professional manner. Concierges are often dressed in distinctive uniforms.

Administration

The list of jobs in Administration is almost endless. Many are similar to those which could be found in all types of businesses, such as finance, costing, purchasing, training and personnel, house security, stores manager, maintenance engineer, and so on.

Many of these jobs do not involve meeting the customer, and so could be transferred easily to other vocational areas. On the other hand, staff with experience in the practical skills of hospitality would be more likely to be recruited for administrative jobs than people without those skills.

Task 1.35

Look in the latest copy of Caterer & Hotelkeeper *and count the number of jobs advertised in the operational areas you have just examined. Make a list showing each operational*

area and the number of jobs. Ignore jobs which do not fit into any of the areas mentioned.

Progression routes between job roles

We have already described the various job roles which can exist in the hospitality and catering industry. Progression routes generally follow the theme of the main type of job role, because of the practical experience which is gained along the route. For example, if you are keen on housekeeping you might first find a job as an Assistant Housekeeper. In time you might become a Floor Housekeeper and later on become an Executive Head Housekeeper.

The movement between job roles in the industry is very general, and it is unlikely that short-term trends will produce any interesting information about job progression.

Who gets the job?

Some jobs are filled by employees with no previous experience – perhaps straight from school or college, or by people who have worked in other types of jobs. These are usually the lower-paid operative jobs, or the junior management positions which might be filled by recent graduates from university with degrees in the right subjects.

Senior positions tend to be filled by junior managers who have proved themselves able, perhaps transferred from other facilities within the organization or even from outside it. These positions require good qualifications and considerable experience of management as well as of the hospitality and catering industry.

Perhaps the most flexible level of job is the supervisory level. Many of these are filled by operatives who have gained practical experience in the skills required, and who show that they are capable (perhaps with further training) of supervising other members of staff. But many opportunities also exist at this level for recruits from college, particularly with GNVQ qualifications at Advanced Level. The GNVQ qualification combines general business knowledge with knowledge specific to the hospitality and catering industry, and so is very valuable.

How staff progress

Most progression is done stage by stage. For example, if you are working at operative level you might progress first to supervisory and then to junior management. However, do not assume that all good operatives progress upwards. Some remain as operatives for long periods, perhaps all their working life, for various reasons. For example:

- Some prefer to stay as operatives
- Some want to progress but do not have the right attributes for the next job (e.g. the skills, the experience, the patience)
- Some want to progress, and have the right attributes, but there are no vacancies
- Some require extra training or qualifications which they are unable to achieve

'Specialist' progression

Progression is not always 'upwards'. Some staff progress by becoming specialists in a particular area, rather than moving into a supervisory role. This is particularly obvious among kitchen staff, where a chef can specialize in particular dishes or techniques such as pastry or sauces. You may find this type of employment boring as it often involves repeating the same tasks every day, but many staff think it rewarding to become an expert in a particular area, especially if it is one which they enjoy.

Specialist progression might also occur in other areas. A member of the bar staff may become an expert on cocktails or whiskies; a person in the marketing department might specialize in banqueting or television advertising. Again, additional training might be needed in the specialist area.

Progression within other organizations

You might progress within your own organization or even within the same outlet. This has obvious advantages:

- You know the other staff and they know you
- You already know the methods used and the house rules
- You have no problems with finding a new home
- Your family can remain in its present location
- The organization already knows your capabilities

On the other hand, there can be disadvantages to progression within the same outlet:

- Some staff may be resentful of your success, and you could lose friends
- You might find it difficult to exert influence on staff previously on the same level of job
- The organization does not receive the benefit of new ideas from other organizations
- The progression might not be possible if there are no suitable vacancies

Some employees, therefore, might need to move to other organizations in order to progress. This might seem daunting if you have never worked away from home, but most people adapt quite quickly to a new environment, and often the new job can be used as a 'stepping stone' to another similar job in your original locality in the future.

Remember that the hospitality and catering industry is diverse. Skills learnt in a hotel kitchen can be transferred to a hospital kitchen or to a top specialist restaurant.

Some employees might move 'sideways' rather than upwards. This means that they move into similar grade jobs in a different area of the organization. For example, an assistant restaurant manager in a large facility might become bar manager in a smaller one. The two grades might be paid the same salary, but the position of manager has more authority and prestige, and may enable the employee to move into a larger bar later.

Task 1.36 ****

Interview three people in different job roles within any area of hospitality and catering who have changed their jobs in the last five years. Find out what sort of job they do now and what they did before. Ask them how they came to get their current job and whether they needed to move house. You can add other questions as you like.

Sources of information on job vacancies

Job vacancies appear in a variety of places. Some are regular sources, providing daily or weekly information on situations. Others are one-off sources, including word of mouth. Some of the sources are as follows:

- Job advertisements
- Advertisements of outlets and their goods and services
- Reports of developments in the industry
- Reports of changing local circumstances
- Employment agencies

Job advertisements

Jobs may be advertised in various places including:

1 Local newspapers
2 National newspapers
3 Trade journals
4 Advertisements located in the outlet

Those in *local newspapers* are likely to cover the lower-grade operative and supervisory jobs at outlets in the locality. They are often small in size and give only brief details of the job description. You will probably need to telephone or write for an application form or to ask for further details. If you are prepared to work outside your locality, your newsagent could arrange to get copies of other local newspapers with details of similar jobs.

In addition to your local newspaper there might be a newspaper covering a wider area, perhaps based on the nearest city or large town. In Derbyshire, for example, there are several local newspapers covering small towns and villages, with separate newspapers for the larger towns, and if you live in north Derbyshire the *Manchester Evening News* might include jobs nearby. All these should be available from your local newsagent.

Those in *national newspapers* will cover the higher-grade jobs, such as supervisory and managerial. Adverts may contain more detail about the duties of the job and the salary payable. Some state that the salary is 'negotiable', which means that it will be discussed at the interview, if you get one.

Adverts in *trade journals* also cover the higher-grade jobs, many of which will also appear in the national newspapers. The most popular trade journal is the *Caterer & Hotelkeeper*, which you might find in your college library as well as at your newsagent.

There are other journals for particular parts of the industry such as for pubs and fast-food outlets. Jobs in hospitals will be advertised in the journals for hospital staff.

Some jobs are advertised on the premises of the outlet itself, particularly where the outlet is in a busy area such as the main street of the town. It is worth looking in the windows of any outlets in your locality for such adverts.

Advertisements for outlets and their goods and services

Some jobs can be obtained by finding out which outlets operate in the area in which you are prepared to work, and by making contact with them, even if you are not aware that they are advertising for the type of job you want. You might be lucky in enquiring about a job which has just become vacant and has not yet been advertised. At the very least, the personnel department might take your name and address and put you on a list of possible employees to be contacted if a suitable vacancy arises in the future.

Reports of developments within the industry

If you read all you can about the hospitality and catering industry you might be able to see opportunities which have not yet been recognized. For example, if you read that new legislation is to be passed which states that all people serving food to the public must have a formal Food Hygiene Certificate, and you have one, you can offer your services to outlets which you know will not have such trained staff.

Reports of changing local circumstances

As in the section above, you should keep abreast of local developments in the hospitality and catering industry. You might hear of a new hotel to be built, or a health club being opened in a large hotel. Or a nearby town might be 'twinned' with an overseas one. These events might lead to increased job opportunities for a range of staff, including a 'healthy-eating' specialist or someone who speaks a foreign language.

As well as looking at your locality, you should also be aware of national changes which might affect your locality. If there are large increases in airfares, or a national disaster in a major overseas holiday location, this could mean increased trade for the UK.

If unemployment in your area suddenly worsens, or improves, people's eating habits will change. If you are aware of these events, you can plan in advance and take advantage of the situation for yourself, at the same time helping to provide the goods and services which are going to be required in the future.

Employment agencies

There are many good employment agencies, some of which specialize in the hospitality and catering industry, others more general. If you have been looking for a job for some time, or want a job in another area, these agencies can be a very good source of information. They will register your details, including your experience and qualifications, and notify you of jobs which arise which might be suitable. They might also offer careers guidance services to make sure that you know what you want to do.

Some agencies charge a fee based on the amount of time you are registered with them; others charge a fee if they are successful in finding you a job. This might be worth while if you find a job which you enjoy. These agencies advertise jobs in local and national newspapers, and you might get their addresses from your local employment office.

Task 1.37

Draw up a table to show the various sources of job vacancies, and use them to find a job for each of the following people:

- *A restaurant waiter*
- *A receptionist*
- *A commis chef*
- *A restaurant manager*

Qualifications, experience and skills needed

Every job in the hospitality and catering industry, and indeed in all industries, requires certain qualifications, experience or skills, or some combination of all of these. The lower-paid, operative jobs require mainly skills; the semi-skilled or craft jobs, skills and experience; the supervisory jobs, qualifications and experience, and sometimes skills; the managerial jobs require qualifications and experience. Supervisors will also need to organize staff, prepare rotas and other staff information, and deal with minor staff problems.

These guidelines are very general. Often the best person for a job will be someone with all three of these attributes – qualifications, experience and skills. Equally often, there are no applicants with all three relevant to the job, so employers have to weigh up each applicant individually.

Qualifications are mainly of two types:

1 Vocational qualifications
2 Academic qualifications

Vocational qualifications are those which are specifically required by the hospitality and catering industry, and cover the skills and knowledge required by that industry. Many of these qualifications are based on practical skills, and these are covered by NVQ qualifications (NVQ stands for National Vocational Qualifications), but it is also recognized that there are theoretical elements which are needed in the hospitality and catering industry, hence the development of the GNVQ qualifications (General National Vocational Qualifications). These are *vocational* qualifications, which means they are geared towards the needs of particular industries.

Academic qualifications are those which are not specifically designed for a particular industry, but cover general theories and knowledge which might apply to many industries and business situations. A good example of an academic qualification is that of Accountant. Hospitality and catering establishments require qualified accountants, but they are not specifically trained in such a narrow area. Instead, their qualification covers all areas and types of business, and their skills are transferable between different types of organization. We now look at the main job roles and the attributes needed for each.

Reception

The Reception operation might include the following job roles:

- Greeting and dealing with guests, face to face
- Room allocation
- Cashier duties
- Telephone enquiries from potential guests
- Telephone queries from guests already in-house
- Administrative duties
- Reception area organization
- Administering first aid to guests

It follows that a receptionist needs a range of skills in order to cope with the job. These might include:

1. Good communication skills for all types of guests
2. Knowledge of rooming systems
3. Accuracy in performing arithmetical calculations, including the conversion of foreign currencies
4. Ability to use a telephone system and communicate effectively
5. Neat handwriting and the ability to complete documentation
6. Flower-arranging skills, display skills, etc.
7. Ability to perform first aid

Experience will be gained while performing the job, particularly in how to handle difficult situations and awkward or upset guests. A degree of patience is required, and the receptionist must always appear calm and polite in front of the guest.

A pleasant appearance is required, although this does not mean that the receptionist should have any particular physical attributes. He or she should be clean, neat and fresh-looking at all times.

Qualifications might be necessary and are certainly an advantage. A GNVQ at Intermediate Level in Hospitality and Catering would be useful. Other qualifications might be an NVQ in Hotel Reception, if you are certain that Hotel Reception is the area in which you wish to work. Many hotels still ask for qualifications which have been largely replaced by NVQs, such as the City and Guilds Diploma in Hotel Reception. A Head Receptionist might require higher qualifications, such as a GNVQ or NVQ at Advanced level, plus significant experience of reception duties.

Task 1.38

*Find three different advertisements for jobs as a receptionist. What qualifications, experience and skills does each one ask for? Do they all ask for the same ones? (*Note: *this and the following five tasks all ask you to find advertisements for jobs – you might like to read through the rest of this section until Task 1.41, and complete all the tasks together.)*

Accommodation operations

Accommodation operations duties might include the following:

- Preparation of bedrooms, to include cleaning, bed making, flower arranging, provision of toiletries, etc.
- Cleaning of corridors, reception areas, toilets and other public areas
- Preparation of function rooms and banqueting suites

- Laundry and linen provision (e.g. towels, bathrobes, etc.)
- Cleaning of stains on fabrics and furnishings

The skills needed are mainly practical, but occasionally the employee will come into contact with the guest and will need to be able to communicate politely. If the guest has a complaint or query which the employee cannot answer, it must be reported back to the supervisor.

The supervisor will need additional skills, such as dealing with people (particularly employees), report writing, form completion, compiling rotas and timetables, keeping holiday charts, etc. It will be the Head Housekeeper's job to choose the most efficient method of room servicing (e.g. whole floor or vacant rooms only). He or she will also need a knowledge of fabrics and their treatment, cleaning agents and use of equipment. The supervisor or Head Housekeeper will also be involved in room design and choice of furniture and furnishings. A knowledge of health, safety and security requirements is also needed.

Qualifications are not so important for room-servicing staff, who are supervised at all times, but they would benefit from holding an NVQ qualification in Housekeeping. For the supervisory positions, an NVQ at a higher level or a GNVQ in Hospitality and Catering would be an advantage. These are particularly important following the introduction of new health and safety legislation which insists that staff are properly trained.

Task 1.39

Find three different advertisements for jobs in Accommodation Operations. What qualifications, experience and skills does each one ask for? Do they all ask for the same ones?

Food preparation (kitchen)

Food preparation is largely a craft activity, skilled or semi-skilled, but there are also jobs available in the theoretical areas of menu planning, kitchen organization, dish and menu costing and so on.

A person joining the kitchen staff will need skills in the areas of food handling, food preparation and cookery, but will also need skills in working with people. A busy kitchen is a model built around teamwork. A large number of skilled people working in a relatively small space works only if everyone respects each other; rules must be adhered to; work areas must be kept tidy and clean; people must not intrude on each other, but must be prepared to help out where necessary.

GNVQ qualifications are useful in these areas. In food-preparation jobs, practical qualifications are essential. These will cover the actual preparation and cooking of foods, dishes and menus, and will include working as part of a team as well as on your own. There is a wide range of NVQ cookery courses available. All these include general topics such as hygiene, safety and security in the kitchen, handling of equipment such as knives, the storage of food and cleaning methods. In addition, students can choose from a selection of cookery subjects, such as meat and poultry, pastry, vegetable, fruit, and special cookery areas such as pulses, pasta and vegetable protein dishes.

There are special units which cover particular types of food preparation, such as fast-food cookery, sandwich and snack preparation, cook–freeze systems, etc.

Many students enter the catering area of the industry because they enjoy cooking and preparing food, and while that is important, you should also realize that the *theoretical* aspects of the subject must also be covered. Do not expect, therefore, to spend all your time at college in the kitchen.

Task 1.40

Find three different advertisements for jobs in Food Preparation. What qualifications, experience and skills does each one ask for? Do they all ask for the same?

Food service (restaurant and room service)

The activities which take place in this area include the following:

- Preparing the restaurant and tables
- Presenting menus and explaining dishes
- Taking orders and notifying the kitchen of requirements
- Recording orders
- Serving the dishes ordered in a proper manner
- Clearing the tables and other areas
- Preparing and presenting bills for payment
- Removing debris and tidying the restaurant areas

The staff responsible will need a variety of skills, such as:

1. Serving food properly
2. Dealing with customers
3. Working as part of a team
4. The ability to describe dishes and their contents to customers
5. Bill preparation
6. Dealing with various methods of payment
7. Maintaining health, safety and hygiene standards
8. Restaurant layout and design

Qualifications might include City and Guilds or BTEC qualifications, particularly NVQs or GNVQs at Intermediate level in Hospitality and Catering. More senior staff might require higher qualifications such as NVQ Level 4, or the Higher National Diploma in Hotel, Catering and Institutional operations. A restaurant manager might need the qualifications of the Hotel, Catering and Institutional Management Association, or even a degree in the larger establishments.

Task 1.41

Find three different advertisements for jobs in Food Service. What qualifications, experience and skills does each one ask for? Do they all ask for the same?

Beverage service (restaurant and bars)

The skills required in this area are very similar to those for Food Service. In addition, a knowledge of wines and spirits is needed as well as of speciality drinks such as cocktails. Knowing the correct method of dispensing drinks is important, as well as the correct quantities to use. In addition, you need to know which type of glass is used for the different types of drink – you may be surprised how many there are! The employee might need a knowledge of legislation connected with alcoholic beverages, such as which guests should be refused service.

Cellar work involves a knowledge of the correct storage of drinks, including beers and lagers in kegs or barrels, and the essential cleaning routines for such drinks. Proper long-term storage of wines and liqueurs is a separate skill required.

Qualifications might be general, such as NVQ or GNVQ, but, in addition, the Wine and Spirit Educational Trust qualification might be an advantage.

Task 1.42

Find three different advertisements for jobs in Beverage Service. What qualifications, experience and skills does each one ask for? Do they all ask for the same?

Concierge

This area involves dealing with customers' luggage in different situations, such as transporting it into the hotel, from the hotel lobby to the guest's room, and back again. The porter might also be asked to provide safekeeping for luggage when a guest has vacated his or her room but is not yet ready to leave the hotel. Porters might also assist with finding taxis for guests and making sure that the guests and their luggage are properly despatched.

Porters are also expected to provide guests with information on various matters such as the location of the hotel's facilities, nearby facilities or tourist attractions, travel information, etc. They may be expected to book external and internal services on behalf of guests, and deal with the relevant paperwork.

It follows that the porter must be extremely courteous and efficient. The porter might be the first or the last person a guest has contact with, and such impressions last for a long time.

Administration

As mentioned earlier, the list of jobs in this area is quite long and varied. The skills required depend on the exact nature of the job, as do the qualifications. In many general administrative areas a GNVQ qualification would be very useful, together with GCSEs at grade C or above in Maths and English. In international hotels, or even UK hotels with a significant proportion of overseas visitors, the ability to speak a foreign language is invaluable. For jobs in finance and accounting, the qualification of the Association of Accounting Technicians is extremely useful, especially for supervisory and junior management positions. For jobs in personnel or training, qualifications in Personnel Management are important.

In many jobs the ability to use computers and computer packages is required, thus training in the use of information technology is useful, perhaps in general areas such as word processing, or in industry-specific areas such as booking and billing systems. Those wanting jobs in purchasing departments might need a knowledge of computerized stock control systems.

Task 1.43

Find three different advertisements for jobs in Hotel Administration. What qualifications, experience and skills does each one ask for? Do they all ask for the same?

Means of gaining the training, experience and skills required

There are many different ways in which the training, experience and skills can be obtained. Often the best method depends on whether the area is specific to the hospitality and catering industry or whether it is a more general area.

On-the-job training

Much training is done 'on the job', which means that the trainee is supervised and trained by another member of staff, perhaps senior to the trainee, or perhaps on the same grade but with the skills needed. There are many advantages of 'on-the-job' training. These include:

- The trainee is working for the organization while being trained
- The trainee is trained in the *exact* methods of the organization
- The person providing training is being paid a normal wage while training, which is usually much lower than the cost of a professional outside trainer
- The trainee does not have additional travelling or tuition costs to find
- The trainee does not have to settle into a strange environment in college
- The timing of the training can be chosen to suit the organization

There are also many disadvantages. These include:

- The trainee picks up the bad habits of other members of staff
- The person training might be very good at his or her job, but might have no particular knowledge of training techniques
- Two members of staff are involved in the training process, instead of just one if the trainee attends college or a special training course
- The trainee might be embarrassed to make mistakes in front of colleagues

Many of the large organizations rely heavily on 'on-the-job' training, particularly in the craft areas. Remember that it is not only hotels and restaurants which provide such training facilities, but also other large organizations such as the armed forces, the Health Service, and large employers like the Post Office, British Telecom, etc.

Task 1.44

Working in teams within your class, write to a selection of large organizations and ask for details of their 'on-the-job' training schemes for people working in hospitality and catering. Ask which types of jobs it covers, and how many employees take advantage of the training offered.

Off-the-job training

'Off-the-job' training might be done in school or college, perhaps one day per week, or in a special training centre. This might be run by your employer, if it is large enough. This method also has advantages and disadvantages – most of them are the opposite of those just mentioned for 'on-the-job' training. The two main disadvantages are the cost and the commitment to a fixed period of absence by the employee from his or her normal job.

Off-the-job training might be offered on a day-release basis, or as a block course (say, for a week).

Open learning

Other courses are offered on a flexible basis – the student attends between certain hours of the day, but can choose to 'drop in' at any time between those hours. Some centres are even more flexible and have their open-learning workshops open at all times of the college day so that students can come and go as they please (or as their employers please). This works well for larger colleges who can afford to staff the centre at all times even if the number of students using it at certain times is low.

Distance learning

As an alternative to attending college or going on a training course, employees can study at their own pace by means of a 'distance-learning' course. This means that study materials, often a 'work pack', are sent to the student by post. The student is allocated a personal tutor, who is there to give guidance and support, both in the subject and in general areas such as how to study, how to revise, etc. The student works through the work pack at his or her own pace and completes assignments or tests periodically which are sent off to the personal tutor for marking and comment. Many students succeed by this method, but many find they have not the self-discipline needed to study regularly. Some students miss the contact they have with other students on traditional courses. Some find it difficult to learn from textbooks rather than from a teacher in front of a class. However, the system is flexible; students can work at their own speed without undue pressure. It is, however, quite costly. Distance-learning materials cost a great deal of money to prepare, and the marking of the periodic assignments and tests is time consuming and expensive.

Choosing a training course

Your choice of training course depends on many factors, perhaps the main one being the restrictions which your employer might place upon you. You are going to need the support of your employer, if you are in work, so it is wise to involve him or her, or your personnel department, at an early stage.

Do not expect support for a course which will not benefit your employer. It is better to choose something which you both agree on, and build on it. If you are not employed, then you have more freedom. Try to decide what you want from a course – it might be to improve the skills you need for your *present* job, or to obtain skills and knowledge to help you *progress* into a different job or even into your first job. Try to choose something you will find interesting. Studying is hard work, and if you do not enjoy the subject you will find it much more difficult to succeed.

To find a suitable course, you could start by asking your colleagues, and your supervisor, for advice on courses they have attended or know about. Your personnel department or careers adviser will also help.

Look at job advertisements to see what qualifications employers are looking for, for the types of job you think you would like.

Next, find out what is on offer. Make your enquiries in plenty of time. Although colleges are much more flexible these days, and are changing rapidly, the majority of full-time and day-release courses still start in September, and places are often filled in the summer term. Write to your local college, and those in nearby towns, to ask for a *prospectus*. Look in the local newspapers. If you are prepared to travel or move away from home, look further afield. Visit colleges on their 'open days'. There you might meet present students with whom you can chat, and some of the lecturing staff.

You can also obtain information from the bodies which award certificates and diplomas, such as BTEC (Business and Technician Education Council), City and Guilds, RSA (Royal Society of Arts), the HCIMA (Hotel and Catering Industry Management Association).

Entry qualifications

Many courses now have flexible entry requirements, and students may be considered without the standard qualifications. Always enquire if you could be acceptable. This particularly applies if you have other qualifications in a different subject, or if you have experience, or if you are a *mature student* – i.e. a few years older than most other students taking such courses.

However, do be guided by the entry requirements. A course which requires five GCSEs at Grade C or above is likely to be too demanding if you struggled to get three grade Es. Many courses ask for GCSE in English and Maths, but often what is really required is a reasonable ability to read and write clearly and maturely, with correct spelling and punctuation, and the ability to perform basic arithmetical calculations such as percentages, simple fractions and decimals. You might be able to take an 'aptitude test' in these two areas if your grades are not quite good enough.

Grants

If you are under 19 you should be entitled to free tuition on most full-time courses. If you are over 19 grants are often available for higher-level full-time courses. Some grants are 'mandatory' which means that you cannot be refused, others are 'discretionary', which that means it is up to the education authority to decide if you should get one.

Some grants cover the cost of your tuition only; others include an allowance for travelling costs and books; some provide you with income while you are studying. Many grants depend on the income of your parents or guardians, or on your own income, and may be reduced quite substantially.

Which jobs suit you?

This question is extremely difficult to answer for most people. A few know from a very early age exactly what job they want to do, but most of us are not like that. We have a few ideas of things we like and don't like, and things we are fairly good at. Few of us are superb at anything, and most of us have to choose a job, or a career, without really knowing what we are choosing. You only really get to know if you like a job when you have been doing it for some time. Often, a job is enjoyable because of the people you work with, but again, we don't get to know that before we start. Therefore, it is wise not to expect too much from your first job, other than the chance of gaining experience which will help you in the future.

Another difficulty is that many of the skills needed in certain jobs are skills that we have never used before, so it is hard to know whether we will be any good at them or like them. However, you should still try to analyse the things you can and cannot do, or like and dislike, to help to identify the general areas in which you would feel most comfortable.

Task 1.45

Working in groups within your class, contact a selection of educational establishments, such as colleges, inside and outside your locality, and find out what types of course in hospitality and catering are on offer. Each group could take a separate area to investigate (e.g. craft courses, supervisory courses, management courses). Identify the entry qualifications, the length of the course, the method of study (full-time, day-release, open-learning, etc.) and produce a chart of your findings.

Task 1.46

To do this, make a list of all the things which you like doing (your strengths) and all the things which you dislike (your weaknesses). The lists can be as long as you like, but you might include things such as:

- *Working with figures*
- *Cooking from recipes*
- *Working to a deadline*
- *Helping people*
- *Telling others what to do*
- *Speaking a foreign language*
- *Working in a team*

- *Thinking logically*
- *Designing things*
- *Solving problems*
- *Creating new dishes*
- *Obeying instructions*
- *Meeting new people*
- *Writing reports*
- *Listening to people*
- *Making own decisions*

Think also about your personality as well as your skills. Are you shy or outgoing? Do you find it easy to complain if something is not correct? Do you make new friends easily, or do you wait for others to approach you? Are you reliable? Do you like to find the quickest way to do something, or do you prefer to take your time and get it just right?

Task 1.47

After you have listed your own strengths and weaknesses ask someone else in your class to say what they think they are, compare their answers with yours – and then discuss any differences.

Matching the main job roles with your own interests

When the time comes for you to choose your first job, or to plan your career, you need to look again at the main job roles and decide which area might suit you best. Then you will need to look for job vacancies in those areas. You might not get exactly the job you want, you may have to compromise with something similar, but you should aim for a job which is in the right area to suit your interests and abilities.

Let us remind ourselves of the main job roles:

1 Reception
2 Accommodation operations
3 Food preparation (kitchen)
4 Food service (restaurant)
5 Beverage service (restaurant and bars)
6 Concierge
7 Administration

Some of these might not appeal to you at all. For example, you might have joined this course because of your love of cooking, and the idea of portering or a job in administration fills you with horror. On the other hand, you might have enjoyed learning about food purchasing and costing and have decided you would prefer that kind of job to one involving shift work and the heat of the kitchen.

This section has introduced you to the various types of job available and the qualifications, experience and skills needed for them. It has shown you how to go about finding out more information, and the tasks you have completed will have helped you learn a lot more about the job roles.

Re-read the sections which tell you about the jobs, and then attempt the final task.

Task 1.48

Make a list of all the jobs which you might consider. Alongside each job make a note of the particular tasks which a person in the job might need to perform. Bearing in mind your own strengths and weaknesses from Tasks 1.44 and 1.45, give each task a score out of 5, according to whether you would love *to do that task or whether you would* hate *it. Give a 5 to those you would love and a zero for those you would hate, with a 3 for any you would quite like or are not sure about.*

1, 2 and 4 can also be used where necessary. Then total up the scores for each job. If one job has a much higher total than the others, then that might be the one to try for. It is quite likely that two or three jobs will have similar scores, but you might be able to see whether they are in the same general area, e.g. all concerning food preparation and service or with accommodation operations.

Conclusion

In this section we have looked at the different job roles in hospitality and catering and the skills, experience and qualifications needed for each of them. We have diminished ways of progressing within the industry and have concluded by looking at our own strengths and weaknesses, our likes and dislikes, and have attempted to match them with suitable jobs.

Test your knowledge

1 What are the main job roles in hospitality and catering?
2 Approximately what percentage of employees in the hospitality and catering industry are in operative jobs?
3 What job roles might you find in the kitchen brigade of a large restaurant?
4 What job roles might you find in a fast-food outlet?
5 What are the main sources of information about job vacancies?
6 What are the advantages and disadvantages of 'on-the-job' training?

Assessment: Investigating the industry and job opportunities

Scenario

You and your friends are looking for careers in the hospitality and catering industry. You all have different skills, experience and qualifications, as well as your own ideas as to the type of career you would like, and you have decided on the following main areas of employment:

- Food preparation
- Accommodation operations
- Food and drink service
- Reception
- Administration

Your tutor has advised you all to seek jobs which will enable you to progress to supervisory level or even beyond, at an early stage in your careers, but more than one of you is hesitant about doing that. You are also anxious to choose employment in an outlet and sector which is likely to do well in the future, so that your jobs will be secure. You are aware that some areas of the industry have more opportunities than others, and some are meeting the needs of their customers well, while others are less successful.

You have decided to investigate the current situation within the industry, both nationally and locally, in order to get a full picture of what the industry does and the employment opportunities available.

Assessment details

Working in small groups, research the industry, both nationally and locally, to obtain as full a picture as possible of the industry, the goods and services it provides, the customers who use it, and the employment opportunities available. You should retain all the information you collect, including copies of letters, written details of interviews, copies of newspaper or magazine articles, etc. Obtain copies of information collected by your colleagues to include with your submitted work, and note the name of the colleague who supplied it. Make a note of the source of any statistics or other data which you find. All your information should be organized and filed properly.

Activity

Prepare a report in three sections, outlining the hospitality and catering industry and its employment opportunities, to contain the following areas:

Section 1: The hospitality and catering industry nationally

- A description of the sectors of the industry and the outlets which each contains, choosing three outlets from each sector
- A description of the economic significance of the industry, and its connections with other industries
- A description of the classification systems used in the industry, and an explanation of how they apply to your chosen outlets

Section 2: The hospitality and catering industry in a locality

- A description of the scale and scope of two outlets (one from each sector), in your locality
- A description of the products and services which each outlet provides and an explanation of how it meets the needs of different types of customers
- A directory of sources of information on outlets in the locality, to include details of the information which each source provides

Section 3: Employment opportunities in the hospitality and catering industry

- An outline of the main job roles in the industry, together with a description of the qualifications, experience and skills, and the common progression routes within each main job role
- A directory of sources of information on job vacancies
- A detailed description of four job roles of your choice, with details of the means of gaining the training, experience and skills required for each role. At least one job should be chosen from each sector of the industry.
- An analysis of one of the jobs you have chosen, which is most suited to yourself, with a discussion of the reasons for your choice

Assessment coverage

Elements 1, 2 and 3 *Performance criteria – all*

Core skills:

Communication – 2.2 (all), 2.3 (all), 2.4 (all)

Information Technology – 2.1 (all), 2.2 (all) 2.3 (all), 2.5 (all)

Application of number – all are possible

CUSTOMER SERVICE

For any outlet to function effectively all staff must realize the importance of satisfying customer requirements as efficiently as possible, in a manner that meets with the outlet's standards and procedures. Your customers are the most important people in your outlet and if you know the types of customers who are attracted to it you are better able to offer a service which meets their needs. Good customer service can increase income through repeat business, often by word of mouth. Therefore, customer service is the key to the success of any business, and any business requires customers. If customers are not happy with the service we offer they will vote with their feet and go elsewhere. This unit covers:

- Types of customers
- The importance and purpose of customer service
- Customer requirements
- Customer needs and expectations
- The assistance available to customers
- How to deal with differing customer needs
- The benefits of customer service
- Methods of monitoring, assessing and recording customer service

Recognizing our customers

Who are our customers?

We are all customers in some way. So are our friends and relatives, our neighbours, our employers and our lecturers. They may be:

1 Male or female
2 Of a variety of ages
3 Single, partners, married couples or families
4 In differing occupations
5 At different income levels

Customers may be the people in residential homes, the sick in hospital and the disabled, the rich and the poor. In other words, customers can come from every walk of life, be of any nationality or religion. All sorts of people will use the hospitality and catering industry every day. They even have a variety of names. You may hear them being referred to as guests, clients, consumers or, as in this unit, customers.

No customer is unimportant, every customer has needs and expectations to be fulfilled. Some of these needs and expectations are shared by other customers, or even by all customers (such as the need for courtesy); some needs and expectations are different for different groups of people. Customers are individuals with likes and dislikes. No two customers will ever want exactly the same service.

External and internal customers

We all think of the customer as being someone who comes into an outlet to use facilities or amenities or purchase products. If you buy a milk shake and a meal from the school/college refectory or go into a fast-food outlet with your friends at weekends for a burger and chips you are one of those important people who are so important to the hospitality and catering industry, a *customer.*

When purchasing your milk shake from the school or college you are known to be an *external* customer. If purchasing your burger from a fast-food outlet on the high street you are also referred to as an *external* customer. Let us examine in more detail the different customer types.

External customers usually pay for the facilities, amenities and products they use. If they are disappointed they will not come again and will not recommend our establishment to other people. Remember: We cannot exist without our customers – they are our best form of advertising. Without customers we have no jobs.

Some customers are already *in situ,* they may be patients in hospital or a residential home, they may be ill and in need of short- or long-stay care. They may be convalescing or in need of a long-term home.

Within a university or college our customers may be living on a temporary basis in a hall of residence, attending a conference or, as is now a popular option, taking a holiday.

Task 2.1

Can you think of any locations of universities or colleges in the country which would be popular venues to book accommodation for a holiday? What customer services do you think these customers would expect?

In a hotel customers may be

- Travelling on business or for pleasure
- Touring as an individual or having a holiday as an organized group
- Attending a meeting, conference or interview
- Attending a banquet or function
- Visiting an event in the area or looking for property to purchase

Customers may be local or from overseas.

Within the outlet there are our colleagues who are also customers, they may work in another area of the outlet or even come from head office. This category includes all employees and suppliers of materials and services and are known as *internal customers*. They have less opportunity to choose whether or not to come again, but a disgruntled employee can cause a lot of ill feeling and difficulty by being awkward, unhelpful and working without much interest in the job. An unhappy employee spreads doom and gloom and unhappiness to others in the workforce. The morale of the team drops, making colleagues inefficient and ready to leave.

Task 2.2

Look around your school or college and try to identify a typical customer. It might be someone visiting the refectory or the restaurant.

Describe on a sheet of paper a typical customer. Write down what you think your customer might spend money on and approximately how much. Are there different types of customers using your outlet? Do different customers spend their money in different ways?

Task 2.3

Survey your local hospital. (It is wise to seek permission of the establishment first. You should also have your parents' permission if going out at night.) Make a note of the people who go in and out of the outlet. You should find there employers, suppliers and customers. If you join with other members of your group you could take it in turns to 'cover' the outlet for the whole day and combine your findings.

Age groups of customers

Differing types of outlets will attract particular age groups. Teenagers and young adults go to clubs, as well as to school, college and fast-food outlets and cafés. Pubs are visited by all age groups. Businesspeople in the age group 30 to 55 are more likely to use hotels on a daily basis. The elderly will use residential homes, while all age groups are likely to frequent hospitals and restaurants. Families will make use of resort hotels and holiday camps.

Task 2.4

While you are surveying your local hospital note the age group of the people who use it. Produce a table or graph showing the number in each age group.

Cultural background of customers

Restaurants providing Indian and Asian foods supply the needs of those nationalities. It is not the aim of this section to cover all dietary needs but it is useful to be aware of the client groups who visit your outlet and have a basic knowledge of their cultural background and dietary requirements. Islam requires similar restrictions to those of the Jewish people in that they also do not eat pork. Their meat is prepared by a method known as Halal, while those of the Hindu religion do not eat beef and tend to be vegetarians. Those who do eat meat eat goat's meat, chicken or fish. Sikhs are also vegetarians and any meat they eat tends to be lamb. Their method of preparing meat is known as Jhatka. Britain has a sizeable immigrant population, and yet everyday establishments are only just beginning to cater for their needs. Some of the London hotels now incorporate ethnic restaurants as part of their policy in place of the traditional restaurants to which we have become accustomed.

As well as dietary needs we should also take account of the importance of recognizing the differing customs associated with religion and culture. For example, some cultures do not permit women to circulate or eat in public places. When observing Ramadan Muslim customers will observe a fast from sunrise to sunset and may require food outside of normal service times. Sometimes the room may need the furniture rearranged to satisfy religious observance so customers may pray facing Mecca.

Many of our customers may speak in a foreign language and it is therefore considered an asset for staff to have key phrases and knowledge of at least one other language. This enables you to communicate with the customers and make them feel welcome. General information about the outlet, instructions relating to fire and safety and menus are also printed in several languages as well as English to help the customer.

Ordinary English restaurants are often slow in adapting to meet the needs of people from other backgrounds. Vegetarian dishes now appear on many English menus, but choice is often poor. Speciality restaurants have thus begun to become popular and are to be found more easily in the cities and where a strong ethnic community resides.

Task 2.5

Working in small groups investigate the client groups who have particular needs relating to their religion or culture. When you have completed this look at the restaurants or fast-food outlets in your locality. Make a note of any which offer dishes suitable for people from particular cultural backgrounds.

Task 2.6

As a group you may prefer to write to or visit your local restaurants and gather some specimen menus and compare them to see if they cater for customers from differing cultural backgrounds.

OR

You could visit your local supermarket to investigate if they stock a variety of commodities suitable for differing cultural communities.

Customers with special needs

Some customers have needs which others do not have, because they are in some way different from the majority of people. They are described as customers with 'special needs'. These differences may be very minor, require only slight adjustments to methods of service or menus (e.g. a diabetic). Other differences may be substantial and require special access arrangements, special diets, modified furniture or complete privacy and so on.

Physical disabilities are the special needs which often spring to mind, and some of these are expensive to accommodate. However, different sectors of the industry are beginning to realize the importance of customers with physical disabilities, and of their spending power, and are beginning to make special arrangements for their needs and comforts. To this effect, many outlets when refurbishing are modifying their accommodation and new projects are incorporating especially designed accommodation. The Forte Travel Lodges are now providing bedrooms designed for people with special needs and many other outlets have facilities and amenities which allow access for these people (e.g. widths of doorways to allow for wheelchairs, the height of reception desks which allows the customer to be seen).

Task 2.7

Imagine you are a person who is blind. What special amenities or needs would you have if you were staying in a hotel for a week? Together with others in your group, investigate other outlets in your locality, and find out if they provide access to the facilities and amenities to satisfy the needs you have identified.

It is necessary that we are aware of the need to be sensitive to those who have sensory impairment. Difficulties can arise with notices and steps. All facilities in an outlet should be clearly labelled, signposted, coloured, well lit and placed at appropriate levels to be recognized. Many large buildings now have speaking lifts. Customers may have needs associated with health. For example, a customer with a heart complaint may not wish to have to climb too many stairs, a customer who requires dialysis treatment will have differing needs but both may wish to stay in a hotel or both could be patients in a hospital. Whatever the need of the customer, it is important to recognize they have a need. Be sensitive to the need, and offer support without becoming intrusive.

Task 2.8

Choose an outlet of your choice. What kind of help would you think the following customers might need?

- *Mother with toddler twins*
- *Deaf person*
- *Person with a broken leg*
- *Confused elderly customer*
- *Person in a wheelchair*

Task 2.9

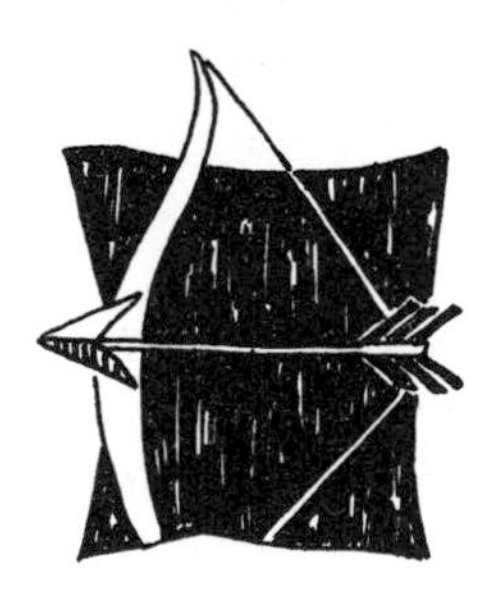

Compare your list with those of others in your group. Arrange as a group a visit to a nearby hotel, guest house or restaurant (not a take-away). Using your list of items which you compiled in the previous task, identify how many of those needs would be met by the outlet you have chosen.

Special requirements

Special request and requirements required by the customer can also be seen to be a special need. Usually these requirements would be arranged in advance and sent on an internal memorandum to the various facilities within the outlet. For very important customers the head office of the organization may become involved. These needs might include security arrangements, personal acknowledgement by the management or complete privacy away from the media. A foreign diplomat may require confidentiality as to the itinerary and whereabouts, royalty may need strict security measures to be enforced. These customers are often referred to as very important people (*VIPs*) or commercially important people (*CIPs*).

Definition

- ***VIPs***: *These could be a celebrity, member of a royal family, foreign diplomat, president of another country, prime minister, etc.*
- ***CIPs***: *These are internal customers (e.g. a supplier or senior manger from the organization, chairperson, managing director of a large company).*

The attention bestowed on VIPs and CIPs is not to assume that they are in any way better than our other customers and the quality of service we offer, but generally they pay a higher price for the additional service they receive.

Task 2.10

Why do you think management give extra attention to VIPs and CIPs? Can you think of any VIP or CIP who may have visited your school, college or place of employment? What special attention or needs were provided and why?

Task 2.11

Discuss with some of your group and make a list of ten VIPs or CIPs and how you would correctly address them. Arrange to role play this with the group. should they decide to visit your school or college.

Individuals or groups

Individual customers are generally fairly easy to accommodate. Their needs do not put any strain on the resources of the outlet and they often well satisfied with the services they receive. In larger outlets it is not always possible to remember every customer, especially if there is likely to be greater movement of staff. It is custom and practice for there to be a customer history card and, if nothing else, it impresses the customer when special requests, favourite rooms or tables are reserved. It is these small considerations which make our customers feel special and valued.

History records

These may be kept manually or on computer and contain information about the customers' preferences and requirements so their needs may be met next time they visit your outlet. Business customers are usually travelling at their companies' expense and out of necessity rather than pleasure. Time will be important, therefore quick, efficient service is required.

Task 2.12

A businessperson arrives late at your hotel. The restaurant is closed. The customer wishes to check out speedily for an early start to the day. What services might this person request?

Women travellers often require additional services such as a hair dryer or an iron in their room. Seating locations within a restaurant are often planned with the single woman in mind. The attitude of staff to women travellers is also important so that they are not humiliated in front of other guests. Groups of customers are more difficult to accommodate due to the numbers involved. A single customer requiring a room or a table overlooking the sea is easier to arrange than a group of 24 who all want adjacent single rooms or to be seated together on one table overlooking the sea. Groups and tours bring in substantial income to many hospitality and catering outlets, and therefore should be considered as a special group as regards their requirements. Special arrangements are generally made to receive these customers on arrival. They may have an itinerary which needs to be kept to. Many hotels offer favourable terms to larger groups and even advertise special facilities and entertainment programmes to encourage their custom. Customer history records are also kept, as often these groups will return, especially if they have enjoyed their visit.

If you wish customers to return, all must be treated with respect and courtesy. *Remember*: a friendly smile can make all the difference.

Classifying customers

The hospitality and catering industry provides a service to its customers and, as such, every customer is special and will require some slightly different service and have a different perceived need. It helps therefore to have a broad understanding of different types of customers and their groups. By classifying customers it is possible to match customers closely to a particular type or segment. This is very useful for marketing purposes, because they can target new customers through different forms of advertising campaigns, and brochures relevant to the classifications.

We have already discussed the different customers who might visit a hotel. They may be customers on business, some will be on expense accounts and others will be paying their own bill. This information is useful in deciding what the customer will expect. For example, a businessperson who is on company expenses will probably require speedy check-out, as it is likely that the company will be invoiced for the accommodation and expenses.

This classification assists in providing a suitable service, facilities and amenities. Some outlets take a conscious decision to attract different markets to make use of their facilities.

A classification or categorization of customers, by age, sex, occupation and culture assists us in giving the best possible service and provision of facilities and amenities according to their needs.

Your outlet will have a preferred house style and procedures guidance, often referred to as the Procedures Manual. In this manual you will probably find all the help you will need to guide you in your contact with the different types of customers.

Task 2.13

List the likely needs of a customer attending a two-day conference wishing to register in a hotel. Compare these needs with those of a customer about to be registered into a short-stay convalescent home.

Design the procedures for receiving a visitor to the Reception of your school or college in keeping with college style.

Customer service

When offering a service to our customers it is necessary to be polite and courteous at all times. You should treat the last customer as if they were the very first, even though it may be late in the day and your feet are aching. As far as the customer is concerned they are the very first and they will not know how long you have been on duty.

Customers need to know that they are valued for their custom, and it will be expected that every member of staff, including trainees, will be prepared to put customers first. In order to succeed, every member of your team must want and believe it to happen, and understand how to achieve customer satisfaction by the standard of service they offer.

Customers may be *regular, occasional* or *chance.* You and other members of the staff will form a relationship with them. This may be:

1. *Directly*
   Face to face – as part of your work in a fast-food outlet such as Burger King.
   By telephone – receiving an enquiry for a restaurant booking or dealing with a complaint.
2. *Indirectly*
   By offering a service which the customer receives but does not come into direct contact with the member of staff providing the service (e.g. cleaners, linen keeper, chef)

Willingness to assist

The customer expects that you will be willing to assist and give prompt service and a good impression to the customer. In carrying out customer service it will be necessary for you to identify each customer's requirements. In some cases you may be required to put something right for a customer that was beyond your control. We call this 'remedial action'.

Task 2.14

How would you deal with the following incident? A new member of staff in the restaurant informs a regular customer that the place usually occupied is reserved for someone else. The customer is somewhat upset and asks to speak to you. What remedial action would you take?

Figure 2.1 Exceeding customer expectations

Customer perceptions and requirements

This means that everything you do should be seen from the customer's point of view. It is how the customer perceives you that determines whether the level of service you provide is acceptable.

What makes your operation better than others is the 'value added' by you and the staff of your outlet. One well-trained member of staff in customer care is worth more than five or six performing at a low level of service in front of customers.

Levels of service

- Rude – which is unacceptable
- Indifferent – often referred to as impersonal
- Value added – considered to be the most favourable level of service

The customers want you to:

1. Pay attention and listen
2. Show respect
3. Show concern
4. Take responsibility for problems
5. Find solutions to problems
6. Be accurate with information
7. Attend to the basics
8. Remember it's their time and money – without them we have no job
9. Give prompt service

The customer expects to receive value for money. They do not like to see waste or extravagance, and they realize that you need to operate a cost-effective outlet. They do not expect inferior service or poor-quality products.

Remember: it takes, on average, five times more effort to attract a new customer as it does to retain an existing one.

Customer requirements within the hospitality and catering industry

The customer has many points of contact to form impressions – e.g. in a hotel the Linkman, Reception, Concierge, Restaurant, Housekeeping, to name a few. The impressions which are generally favourable are:

- Attention to detail
- Caring, friendliness and courtesy

- Dealing efficiently with requests for information
- Physical help when required (e.g. with luggage)
- Ability to resolve problems quickly
- Taking ownership of problems
- Cleanliness

A customer's perceptions may be altered by the impressions they receive. For example, if they see a dirty kitchen, they might then wonder how clean the staff are and whether the food is hygienically handled. They may then consider whether they wish to give you their custom. The seeds of doubt have been sown, such as is the food fresh? Is it good enough to eat? Do they really wish to stay?

Importance of prioritization

It is expected that you can prioritize and 'do it now' when there are urgent requests made and respond effectively (e.g. emergencies, security alert or accidents) and limit disruption to other customers within your outlet (e.g. telephone calls). This may sometimes mean that you will have to reschedule other tasks; it is important to do tasks in the right order. If this is not done efficiently the customers gain a *negative impression*. Negative impressions come when, for example,

1. You have no opportunity to explain something to a customer on the telephone, but you can to a customer waiting to be attended to at the Reception desk
2. A customer is kept on hold on the telephone without explanation
3. There are long queues
4. You do not have information at your fingertips
5. Items are out of stock
6. Promises are forgotten
7. Surroundings are dirty
8. The customer is ignored
9. There is a failure to offer physical help

If customer perceptions of you or your outlet are poor you are fighting a losing battle and customers will not wish to return. Create a positive perception and exceed customer expectations. Always try to deal with customers' problems as if they are the most important tasks you have ever had – try to see the problem as if you were in their shoes. You don't win the battle by being right and clever unless the customer feels better and the problem is resolved.

The level of personal attention should be the same for all customers. You never know who your customers are. All deserve the same level of attention and service. You cannot rely on their appearance and often VIPs travel under an assumed name for security reasons.

Remember to meet their expectations and perceived needs. Serve them quickly on their terms.

Putting customer service into practice

Earlier we discussed the need for a system in order to develop procedures which could have clear standards by which we could operate. These procedures need to be monitored against the practices that actually take place in an outlet. If the outlet ignores the procedures the service offered to your customers is likely to differ according to who operates it and the standards will be noticeable. In the next section we will look at how these procedures can be monitored.

Task 2.15

Arrange as a group to visit several different outlets. Design a checklist suitable to be used for all the visits. Arrange to visit one outlet each and observe the customer practices of part of the outlet. Ask to see if it is possible to look at the procedures manual. Make a comparison between what you recorded and what should happen. Exchange your findings among the rest of your group.

You should now be able to identify

- The requirements of customer service
- The facilities required by customers
- The need for procedures in hospitality and catering outlets
- The benefits of good customer practices

Quality

This should be seen as a total experience. You should put yourself in the customer's shoes and try to visualize how the customer would react. Some organizations actually allow their staff to experience being a customer so than they appreciate what the customer needs and expects. The standards are set by the customer, they will decide whether they return to give you their custom again. In other words, the customer influences the standards by which you are expected to operate. This is brought about by having a customer service policy which is derived from what the customer expects. Later in the unit you will be finding out about the value of customer feedback.

In planning your operation you should ask yourself:

1. How well am I performing?
2. Which things are important for my customers?
3. Do I get the right things done first time?
4. How can I improve?
5. What am I doing wrong?
6. How can I help to make the service better?
7. What appropriate changes and improvements do I need to make?
8. Am I responsive enough to customers, do I respond within the agreed time?

As an individual it is important that you follow the procedures set by your outlet. There will be many practices which have been tried and tested, and you will find these in the standards manual previously discussed. All the procedures should be made into a regular routine, with various members of the team being allocated jobs to ensure that procedures actually happen. If no one is asked to this then nothing happens. Sometimes checklists are used to ensure that the procedures are being followed. If all the guidelines are followed and you work with your team it is likely that you will be well on your way to providing a quality service.

Customer requirements

The hospitality and catering industry, like every other, is becoming very keen on quality. De Vere Hotels was one of the first to become quality orientated and achieve Investors in People. This is a benchmark by which customers can judge the standards and quality of the organization and in future, those organizations who fall short of this benchmark may well find that customers will be attracted elsewhere and they will go out of business.

Quality is about identifying the defects in the policy, the products and services we sell and taking appropriate action to eliminate them. Remember: we identified earlier that prevention is better than cure?

Quality criteria

Cost

Customers look for value for money, and the outlet needs to consider cost when deciding how best it can give this to the customer. Customers do not mind paying a little extra if they can see the benefits. Very often they are willing to pay more because of the value-added service, politeness and willingness of staff to assist.

Time

The time taken to provide a good service relates to cost both to the outlet and to the customer. Prompt attention is required by those paying for a service. For example, a group of businesspeople in your restaurant may need to return to work and are therefore likely to require a more speedy service than some pensioners on a reunion outing. How you use your time will also have a cost factor and will determine how quickly you get things done. Quality is also measured by the benefits gained from standard procedures and an agreed conformity to operate to those standards.

Staff

In any outlet there needs to be available resources. Without adequate resources the quality of the service suffers. The main resource is that of *staff*, properly trained and well motivated to serve and exceed customer expectations. You need to be flexible, able to adapt to a variety of situations, have a positive attitude, be energetic and enthusiastic. In addition, you need to know your outlet inside out and keep up to date on the products and services you sell.

The hotel and catering industry operates all day long every week of every year; it is a continuous operation. While you may be feeling tired at the end of your working day, some of our customers may be just arriving. To become a really shining light you need to maintain all these characteristics all day long, despite the aching feet, the stress and the pressures that come with the job. The present customer will not necessarily be aware of the problems created by the previous one. One thing for certain is that the customer requires personal, friendly service.

Procedures for customer service

There could be several reasons why an organization or outlet needs to have a customer service policy; for example:

1 To maximize customers
2 To increase profitability
3 To increase customer loyalty
4 To create a reputation for being customer orientated, to have the edge over competitors and to be the very best.

Each organization will have its own aims and objectives of how to appeal to its customers, and these must be compatible with the culture of the outlet and will be turned into targets or goals for the outlet to achieve. In order for this to happen the outlet or organization will need to have procedures and standard practices in place so that everyone knows what is acceptable to the outlet.

Standard practices are derived from having an agreed system in place. It is of little use asking staff to provide a service to customers if we do not specify exactly what we expect of them in delivering this service.

Developing a system

The whole system needs to be developed with the customer uppermost in your mind. It needs to be designed around the customer and not to suit you. It should be customer friendly and provide what the customer wants. For example, have you ever been on a overseas holiday and found that you are herded back to the airport hours before your flight because it suits the tour operator to gather all the tourists onto one coach to make the journey from the resort to the airport? You probably did not wish to leave quite so early and would have preferred to depart later.

You need to study carefully how the system you operate will affect your customers. Try to put yourself in their place and imagine the effect your system would have on you. If you find it unacceptable, there is every chance that your customers will.

Imagine cutting your finger very badly and seeking assistance from your lecturer or teacher, only to be told that, according to the system they have to follow, an accident form must be filled in first. In this case the system is not very helpful to you in distress and needing emergency attention. For this reason, it is necessary to have procedures in place and to define the standards of performance.

Procedures

These need to be supported by management and written in such a way that they are easy to understand. Every facility within the outlet needs to have a copy and referred to on a regular basis. All new staff should be inducted and trained according to the procedures laid down by the outlet in order to ensure good-quality service to customers.

Administrative procedures, while important as in the case of your cut finger, need to be minimized and prioritized. In this case it was more important to stop the bleeding and look after your wellbeing. The accident form could have been filled in later. The personal touch is much preferred by customers to the necessity of form filling and documentation. By having procedures in place they will become the regular routine, duties and responsibilities will be allocated and the standards can then be adopted and monitored.

The procedures need to be broken down into manageable items and a standard set against each. What your organization or outlet aims to do in order to actively pursue good-quality practices will lead to customer satisfaction and the measures by which it judges if it is successful.

Benefits of customer service practice

It is not only the customer who benefits from customer service by receiving genuine smiles, eye contact and a willingness to help but the organization or outlet that you work in. This is achieved by the standards and procedures set by the outlet for the staff. Increased business will come by being competitive, that is, by offering better services than your competitors. Customers who are satisfied will come back, and this is known as repeat business. They will inform others. Research suggests that one satisfied customer tells four or five others, whereas a dissatisfied customer will talk to ten or more, in fact anyone who will listen. This information is not helpful in increasing custom. Even competitors will refer trade to your outlet when they are not able to assist a customer. This is acceptable by a customer as it still means that the customer's needs can be met. However, your competitors will be reluctant to do this if they think your standards are not comparable with their own because they would hope that their recommendations would not be a disappointment. They would also hope that the customer might return to them on a subsequent visit. In other words, the reputation of the outlet as seen from a customer's point of view.

Standards

These are a level of quality or achievement at a level thought to be acceptable, an agreed target to aim for. If there is more than one outlet then the policy for that outlet is probably based on the standards set by the organization, so that consistency is upheld (e.g. McDonald's, Little Chef, Nuffield Hospitals). The branding of very large organizations such as Forte Crest hotels into Travel Lodges, Post Houses and Prestige categories may also set different standards within the same organization. Customers exercise their right of choice but would still anticipate, for example, the same degree of friendliness from staff even though all the services are not the same. Customers would therefore acknowledge that there are differences in what each brand offers and that these differences are often reflected in the tariff or price.

Customer service standards

What your organization or outlet aims to do in order to actively pursue good-quality practices will lead to customer satisfaction and the measures by which it judges if it is successful.

In order that these standards can be carried out there will need to be guidelines provided for staff on how to do things. These are usually to be found in Standard of Performance manuals or operational specifications. Each facility within your outlet usually has a copy written for their operations. They are often referred to, especially when new staff are being inducted into the job or for training purposes. These specifications influence customer service when they become visible or affect the customer (e.g. noise from the kitchen, an unanswered telephone ringing) or if something fails to meet their expectation (e.g. being told there is a sauna and finding it is out of order). The specification or standard does not really affect the customer, it is the impact that it has upon the customer that is important.

The impact on the customer

The customers are only interested in how the quality of your service standards affect them. For example, they may not be concerned that they do not have a linen napkin but would notice if there was no napkin at all, or be too bothered whether the guest towels were coloured or white but would be concerned if they had been used or indeed found none in the bathroom

Holiday Inns provide specifications and standards in a manual for all its outlets 'called *Together We Care*'. It is designed to help managers and heads of facilities train their staff in customer care standards, and each outlet customizes it to meet its own operational needs.

Customer-care training in isolation will have little lasting effect unless the performance of staff is monitored, the necessary action taken when it is not up to standard, and all new staff trained in customer care as part of their basic job training. To improve and maintain standards of customer care it is necessary to review and take corrective action on:

1 *Quality of staff care.* If you are cared for and provided with good conditions of work you are more likely to be happy and offer a good service to customers
2 *Quality of systems for identifying the level of customer satisfaction and customer needs.* If the standard procedures are clearly defined and are owned by you, in other words, you have contributed to the development of these procedures, you are more likely to follow them. You should consider how well you are performing against the procedures of the outlet. These should have been produced from the points customers have made about what they find important.
3 *Matching of the product and service to customer needs.* You need to be aware of why the products and services of the outlet are offered to customers. You also need to be given feedback as to what customers say they want. It is important for you to learn to recognize, interpret and act upon clues and comments that customers give about the standards of your organization or outlet. In addition, you should know the action that you can take and the mechanism for reporting back and to whom.

Examples of specifications from a standards manual

The standards may be divided into three parts:

- The Key Point or primary consideration
- The standard
- The specific requirement for the outlet

Let us look at some examples:

Key Point Uniform,
Standard Free from stains and odours, well pressed and in good state of repair (e.g. no missing buttons, dropped hem).
Specific requirement Bow tie and winged collar to be worn. Name badge to be worn when on duty.

Key Point Communicating with customers in the bar.
Standard Do not stand so close to customers to make them feel uncomfortable.

Specific requirement Disabled customers. Do not assume physical disability. Do not 'talk down' or shout. Talk to the disabled person, not to the companion.

Generally the specifications are placed under headings such as:

- Appearance
- Behaviour
- Service to be offered to customers
- Special situations

Task 2.16

Try to think of some standards which would apply regarding:

- *The appearance and standards of dress required by a chef working in a kitchen*
- *When answering a telephone*

Once it has been decided what standards need to be in place in your outlet and appropriate training given, it will then be possible to monitor if the customer-care policy is working. We will examine this in the next section.

Telephone skills

In communicating with customers and in order to offer a service it is often necessary to deal with customers on the telephone. When answering the telephone, be polite, smile with your voice, introduce your organization and identify yourself. A phone call should be answered within three to four rings.

Standard expressions are used as they save time for you, the receptionist or the switchboard operator and, most important, line time. This costs money both to the customer and to the outlet. How you answer the phone is important. Reasons for answering the telephone are:

1. To obtain custom by selling your product or service
2. To ensure income
3. To be efficient and offer a service

The three cardinal points for good telephone manner are:

C. A. S.
Courtesy
Accuracy
Speed

Remember these points and you will be on your way to success.

Every organization will have its own style and procedures for answering the telephone (e.g. 'Good morning, Aylestone Restaurant, Samantha speaking, how may I help you?'). This evokes a response from your customers, they are assured they have connected correctly and have a point of contact should they need to call again. Next time they will have a name to refer to, and this avoids the caller repeating themselves as you already have some background information.

Avoid, if possible, keeping the caller on hold. If this is necessary it is probably because you need to transfer them to someone else or seek information. Always ask if the caller minds holding and wait for a response. Never hold for more than 45 seconds without coming back to the caller. Remember, the customer cannot see what is happening. Impressions are formed from your tone of voice, the words you use, and the delay in response to their questions. You should always stay on the line and introduce the caller. Never transfer if the other member of your outlet is not available. This leaves the caller in limbo. Customers do not like being transferred, they feel that they are being passed off. Avoid the use of the word 'transfer', it makes the customer feel powerless. If you need to transfer the customer bear in mind that a lost customer is one lost forever. If they are disconnected or passed off they may not call back.

If you cannot help, state what you *can* do, not what you cannot. Be positive (e.g. Let me connect you... I can help you by putting you in touch with') or take their name, telephone number and offer to call them back. Be positive and give an indication of when. It is better for you to do the legwork. Keep your promises, even if you have not obtained the information. Return the call. The customer will then have a level of satisfaction to know that you have tried to help.

An answerphone, while taking the pressure off you, leaves the caller feeling processed rather than being given personal service. It is better to take the transfer call. If you have been introduced by the receiver you are able to give positive feedback and improve the customer's satisfaction by mentioning the customer's name and recapping the query example (e.g. 'Hello, Mr Jones, this is Amanda, I understand you have a query...').

Task 2.17

Practise taking messages, or role playing dealing with customers and with their queries. You might find it easier if you have a pair of dummy telephones (even better if you have the opportunity to practise on an extension line).

Active listening skills

Customers want to feel welcomed, important and understood. They wish to command your respect, concern and understanding. In order for this to happen you need to *listen* to your customers.

Hearing what the customers say is not sufficient. Hearing is listening to sounds (for example, a fire alarm, a crying child). Active listening is trying to understand the meaning of the words used and the unspoken message behind what is said. The tone of voice, emotion and the context of the situation as well as evaluation of the facts contribute to active listening. In listening we try to understand and appreciate the customers. We respond by letting them know we are listening, by verbal reinforcement, using words such as 'I understand', 'All right', 'I see'.

Ways to active listening

1 *Be prepared*. Have paper or notepad and pen. Have the computer cleared and ready for the next contact. If answering the telephone let the customers know if you take notes. Show you are listening. Use attentive words such as 'OK', 'I see', 'I understand'
2 *Ask questions*. These should evoke a response (e.g. 'How may I help you?'). Get the customer to talk to find out what they really want
3 *Show understanding*. Repeat the message in your own words (e.g.if I understand correctly, Mr Smith, you require...? Can I conclude that...? 'Am I right in thinking...? Only repeat the main points.
4 *Silent pauses*. Invite the customer to correct you if you have misunderstood before proceeding

Task 2.18

Form a group of three. Tape the conversations. Take it in turns to listen to these conversations and then repeat what you think you heard. Play the tape back to check if you heard correctly.

▪ THE METHODS OF ASSESSING CUSTOMER SERVICE ▪

This section investigates methods of assessing customer services. It involves looking at the quality of the service we give to our customers. It shows how we assess the service we give. We also need to identify relevant methods of reporting customer feedback and what we do with the information we evaluate in order to deliver better quality. We look at the methods of responding to customer feedback and the follow-up procedures which you can adopt. Finally, we describe health, hygiene and safety criteria expected by customers.

Assessment

This is an examination of how we are performing against the agreed standards which should reflect customer needs. You need to know:

- The reasons why we assess customer service
- How to collect data effectively from different sources
- How to formulate an ongoing monitoring system against reliable and valid data
- How to make recommendations for improving customer service
- How to examine the methods for recording and follow-up of customer feedback

Monitoring

This is the method used to measure and check that the quality and standards relating to customer service are being met.

The need to monitor customer service

There could be several reasons why an organization or outlet needs to monitor customer service:

1. To check that the agreed procedures are being maintained
2. To improve the manner of service
3. To ensure value for money
4. To check that the physical environment is clean, hygienic and in good repair
5. To investigate complaints
6. To rectify errors in the service
7. To acknowledge good practice
8. To receive compliments

The benefits of monitoring are:

- To maximize customers
- To increase profitability
- To increase customer loyalty
- To create a reputation for being customer orientated
- To have the edge over your competitors

Each organization or outlet will have its own aims and method of appealing to its customers. These must be compatible with the rest of the business plan and will be turned into targets or goals like those listed above. Given *criteria* such as quality of service, attitude of staff and standards will need to be established so that the targets and goals can be monitored and measured.

Definition

- ***Criteria****: a set of guidelines or directions that indicate quality services, products and facilities in an outlet.*

Before you can assess a customer-care policy you need to have some standards to monitor against and you must to be able to give answers to such questions as:

1. What level of service do we wish to provide for our customers?

2 How many complaints do we get and why?
3 What staffing levels do we require?
4 How much time do we need to spend on customer service?
5 Do we require training?
6 Do we manage time effectively, and offer a timely service to our customers?
7 How is the outlet perceived in the marketplace?
8 Is the outlet considered to be clean, hygienic, safe and offering a secure environment?
9 Is business increasing or decreasing?

Task 2.19

Look at your own school, college or workplace and see if you can answer the questions above. You may need to ask your colleagues or request an appointment to speak to someone who works there.

You have probably established by now some interesting viewpoints from the people you have spoken to together with your own ideas. Ideas and comments such as you have gathered are used to form the standard by which a customer service policy operates. This information is known as feedback.

Customer feedback

The reason for assessing customer service is to extract information that can be used to provide the outlet with effective feedback. Feedback may be obtained from a variety of data sources. It may be *subjective*, in other words, expressing the customer's feelings:

- I really wanted to
- We are looking for
- I would really like
- Could we have

or the feedback may be *objective*, giving facts and figures about the customer service:

- The food is cold
- The bookings are up by 5 per cent on last week's figures
- The takings are down
- We have been waiting for a table for 20 minutes

Types of feedback

As you can see from the above comments, the feedback can be either positive or negative. That is, it can be in the form of either complaints or compliments. Obviously, compliments are what we wish to receive because then we know that the customers are happy with the service they get from us.

Feedback can be solicited or unsolicited. It may be originated from using your initiative or through consultation with others. The ideas and views of others could assist in establishing the ways in which you can obtain feedback from customers. The feedback may be formal or informal.

Oral feedback

This is usually given by the customers directly to staff in face-to-face situations, or it may come from your colleagues. Staff who have contact with customers have the opportunity to chat and listen to customers' comments. Customers do not always respond objectively when asked their views about a service to someone involved in providing that service (e.g. customers in a college restaurant do not like to complain because they know students are training).

Some outlets will telephone customers to obtain feedback. Important customers who provide regular business are sometimes visited to check that everything was to their satisfaction. Through monitoring the operation in the outlet it is possible to see where corrective action needs to take place. Prevention is always better than cure.

Observation

By observing our customers it is possible to obtain feedback on their reactions to the service we offer. Facial expressions, comments to other customers in the vicinity, how they behave towards you and the other staff are all indicators of customers feeling satisfied. It is often easier to resolve problems which appear through observation before they become complaints. By walking the floor or by being present in the area you can quickly spot potential problems which could give rise to customer satisfaction well before they arise.

Task 2.20

You have been asked to observe the lunchtime service in your college/school restaurant. What action would you take on observing the following?

- *Lipstick on a wine glass*
- *Spilt food on the cloth of a newly laid table*
- *A knife missing from a place setting*
- *Two customers standing at the entrance to the restaurant*
- *A customer who keeps counting the change presented with the bill*
- *A customer who has left most of the meal on the plate*

Explain how by observing the above and taking remedial action you could avoid customer complaints.

Written feedback

This may be in the form of:

1 Letters
2 Comment sheets
3 Questionnaires

Letters

Customers often write letters to either the head office or the manager of an outlet. Sometimes it is to express dissatisfaction or to clarify a point before raising a complaint, but frequently when a customer puts pen to paper in the form of a letter it is usually to congratulate the outlet and offer praise. Some outlets actually display such compliments on a notice board for everyone to see. It not only acts as a morale booster to staff but also allows other potential customers to see what previous customers thought. Have you ever visited a hospital and seen the correspondence thanking the staff for their care? Outlets that specialize in special functions such as weddings often display letters of thanks either on a notice board or in a record book.

Comment sheets

These may be single pieces of paper which allow the customer to comment or similar to the postcard size used by Novotel. Comments can also be in the form of a simple comment in a book similar to those used by Little Chef restaurants. Most hospitality and catering outlets will use some form of in-house customer survey, which may be in the form of comment cards placed in coffee shops, restaurants and cocktail lounges to measure the outlet's performance. Some organizations also use them to grade management and to compare one outlet with another.

Questionnaires

When more detailed feedback is required questionnaires are generally used. Each outlet will have its own particular questionnaire designed to obtain the feedback specific to its

STAKIS
COUNTRYCOURT
HOTELS

PLEASE GIVE YOUR ASSESSMENT OF THE FOLLOWING:

RECEPTION

	EXCELLENT	GOOD	AVERAGE	FAIR	POOR
MAKING YOUR RESERVATION	☐	☐	☐	☐	☐
RESERVATION ACCURACY	☐	☐	☐	☐	☐
CHECK IN	☐	☐	☐	☐	☐
CHECK OUT	☐	☐	☐	☐	☐

SEASONS RESTAURANT

	EXCELLENT	GOOD	AVERAGE	FAIR	POOR
VARIETY	☐	☐	☐	☐	☐
SERVICE	☐	☐	☐	☐	☐
QUALITY	☐	☐	☐	☐	☐
VALUE	☐	☐	☐	☐	☐

COURT BAR/LOUNGE

	EXCELLENT	GOOD	AVERAGE	FAIR	POOR
VARIETY	☐	☐	☐	☐	☐
SERVICE	☐	☐	☐	☐	☐
QUALITY	☐	☐	☐	☐	☐
VALUE	☐	☐	☐	☐	☐

CLUB TROPICS

	EXCELLENT	GOOD	AVERAGE	FAIR	POOR
SERVICE	☐	☐	☐	☐	☐
FACILITIES	☐	☐	☐	☐	☐
GYMNASIUM	☐	☐	☐	☐	☐
ATMOSPHERE	☐	☐	☐	☐	☐

BUSINESS COURT

	EXCELLENT	GOOD	AVERAGE	FAIR	POOR
SERVICE	☐	☐	☐	☐	☐
FACILITIES	☐	☐	☐	☐	☐
VALUE	☐	☐	☐	☐	☐
OFFICE SERVICES	☐	☐	☐	☐	☐

BEDROOM

	EXCELLENT	GOOD	AVERAGE	FAIR	POOR
DECOR / FURNISHINGS	☐	☐	☐	☐	☐
CLEANLINESS	☐	☐	☐	☐	☐
BATHROOM	☐	☐	☐	☐	☐
LIGHTING	☐	☐	☐	☐	☐

1	2	3	4	5	6	7	8	9	10	11	12	13	14	15	16	17	18	19	20

PLEASE RATE US IN TERMS OF OUR HOSPITALITY AND EFFICIENCY:

	EXCELLENT	GOOD	AVERAGE	FAIR	POOR
RESERVATION STAFF	☐	☐	☐	☐	☐
RECEPTION STAFF	☐	☐	☐	☐	☐
SEASONS RESTAURANT STAFF	☐	☐	☐	☐	☐
COURT BAR / LOUNGE STAFF	☐	☐	☐	☐	☐
CLUB TROPICS STAFF	☐	☐	☐	☐	☐
BUSINESS COURT STAFF	☐	☐	☐	☐	☐
HOUSEKEEPING STAFF	☐	☐	☐	☐	☐

DID ANY ONE MEMBER OF OUR STAFF PROVE ESPECIALLY HELPFUL ?

NAME ______________________

GENERAL:

HAVE YOU STAYED HERE PREVIOUSLY ? ☐ YES ☐ NO

HAVE YOU STAYED AT OTHER COUNTRY COURT HOTELS ? ☐ YES ☐ NO

IF IN THE AREA, WOULD YOU STAY HERE AGAIN ? ☐ YES ☐ NO

	EXCELLENT	GOOD	AVERAGE	FAIR	POOR
OVERALL HOW WOULD YOU RATE THIS HOTEL ?	☐	☐	☐	☐	☐

COMMENTS ______________________

PLEASE PROVIDE THE FOLLOWING INFORMATION:

ROOM No. ______ ARRIVAL DATE ______ DEPARTURE DATE ______

NAME ______________________

ADDRESS ______________________

TELEPHONE No. ______________________

Figure 2.2 A customer questionnaire

own environment and what it wishes to know about the service it offers. It may only wish to know whether you enjoyed the high-quality service or it may enquire about the standard and quality of the food and drink, the cleanliness of the environment, the accommodation and a little about you, the customer. These questionnaires usually require a response by either ticking a box, giving a yes or no answer or rating the service in some way (for example, 1 to 5). Often there is a small space for you to add your comments.

The information gathered from feedback can yield valuable information. It must, however, be valid, authentic, current, reliable and readily interpreted. When surveys meet these requirements they can be powerful tools for management action to improve customer service for future planning and measuring staff performance (see Figure 2.2).

Monitoring customer feedback

Any of the feedback methods above can be used to obtain feedback. There are, however, some essential points to consider:

- Identify customer satisfaction determinants
- Consider the relative contribution of the determinants and establish their importance for your outlet
- Develop a system that can be calculated and measured on a percentage basis

The system should be:

Easily administered and capable of being analysed to indicate efficiency and effectiveness of customer service. If using a survey:

1. It should not be too long or wordy
2. The language should be clear and precise
3. The questions should not prompt the answers expected
4. It should be appropriate for your target market
5. It should be comprehensive and be capable of statistical analysis

Satisfaction determinants

These are the variables of satisfaction and dissatisfaction that are important to customers. They may have to be categorized if there are too many to put into the questionnaire or survey. For example, instead of referring to (1) cleanliness of room and (2) cleanliness of bathroom as two questions, these could be combined as (1) cleanliness of room and bathroom. Reception and cashiering could be combined as reception services. Other variables might include:

- Price
- Restaurant
- Professionalism of staff
- Prestige and aesthetic appeal of property
- Sports and leisure facilities
- Room service
- Accommodation

These variables form the criteria to determine quality of services, availability, quality of facilities, quality of products such as food, and the health and safety and security of customers. In addition, the attitude of staff towards each other and to the customers.

Weighting the responses

It is useful to know the weighting that customers place on the satisfaction determinants. This can be established by asking them to rank the order of importance they place on the variables. For example, the customers may decide that the cleanliness of room and bathroom is 25 per cent more important than Reception services.

Market segment

Another important finding available to you is a simple addition to the questionnaire or survey of one or two demographic or purpose-of-stay questions which will allow you to determine the satisfaction of a particular market segment.

Task 2.21

Your coffee shop attracts shoppers mainly between 10 a.m. and 3.30 p.m. You want to know how well you are satisfying a small but growing group of business executives who have started to use your outlet at lunchtime. What demographic and purpose-of-visit questions might you consider asking?

The questions you ask of both groups visiting your outlet can be compared between both customer groups and you can obtain a quick measure of overall satisfaction or dissatisfaction. The results you obtain will be valid and reliable. The questions asked could be used to determine:

1 Current *patterns* and *trends*
2 Operational mistakes
3 What your customers need (e.g. good quality food)
4 What your customers want (e.g. prompt service)
5 The market segment who visit your outlet
6 To measure improvements over time

Definition

- ***Patterns and trends***
  Documentation about products and services, or customer feedback that portrays a fashion, tendency or direction.

Who gives feedback?

Any customer should be able to give feedback about the service they have received. Many outlets leave feedback sheets in prominent places for customers to fill in. Sometimes when left to customers the response rate is very low unless there has been a particular incident which has provoked a response. However, sometimes you may wish to carry out a survey or questionnaire to obtain specific feedback (perhaps you want to refurbish and change the style of service you presently offer). To do this you may decide to use a *representative sample* of customers or potential customers.

Definition

- ***Representative sample*** *This is selected from the market mix to represent a cross-section of your customers or potential customers.*

Monitoring within the context of hospitality and catering

In the hospitality and catering industry precise knowledge of our products and services is essential. A large part of our product is service, and it can fluctuate widely within an organization, from outlet to outlet and even within an outlet. The facilities within an outlet will want to have feedback and this may well be incorporated into a full-scale questionnaire or may just involve a response form or indeed observation or oral feedback.

Special events such as conferences and party bookings may wish to ask different questions and have their own methods of monitoring feedback as the customers to these events have differing expectations (see Figure 2.3).

Task 2.22

Look at the example of the conference questionnaire in Figure 2.3 and the questionnaire usually put in a hotel guest room and see if you can spot the difference.

novotel coventry

CONFERENCE QUESTIONNAIRE

Welcome to the Novotel Coventry. We do trust that you find all aspects of the Hotel and Conference facilities to your satisfaction. We are always looking for ways to improve on our standards and service, so I would be grateful if during your conference you could fill in this questionnaire. If you have any queries or questions or require any business services, please do not hesitate to contact myself or the Duty Manager.

Name: ....

Address: ....

....

Function Room: ....

Date of Conference: ....

ADMINISTRATION	YES	NO
When making your booking, was this dealt with in a professional and helpful manner?	☐	☐
CONFERENCE ROOM		
Easy to locate?	☐	☐
Correct temperature?	☐	☐
Good standard of cleanliness?	☐	☐
Was the room correctly set up?	☐	☐
Was the lighting satisfactory?	☐	☐
Equipment in good working order?	☐	☐
CATERING		
Coffee/Tea on time and hot?	☐	☐
Lunch on time and hot?	☐	☐
Dinner on time and hot?	☐	☐
Good quality of food?	☐	☐
Good food service?	☐	☐

Figure 2.3 A conference questionnaire

GENERAL	YES	NO
Staff smartly dressed and in uniform?	☐	☐
Helpful and efficient staff?	☐	☐
Good bedroom facilities?	☐	☐

How often do you hold events like this? ....

Where do you hold them? ....

Have you any future events you would consider holding at the Novotel Coventry? ....

If yes, please give details ....

....

....

Can we send you any further information? ....

COMMENTS

....

....

....

....

....

Thank you for taking the time to fill out this questionnaire and I look forward to welcoming you to the Novotel Coventry again in the future.

Robbin Leftwich
Conference & Banqueting Co-ordinator

A customer's full satisfaction is essential for repeat business. Knowledge of our product and service and what the customer expects is crucial to the feedback you obtain, especially if it yields information you need to ensure success.

Customer service data

Whenever you gather information, be it written or verbal, this is known as data. Data can be presented in various forms:

- Tables
- Graphs
- Text

The methods of collecting may be both formal and informal using some of the suggestions previously discussed. Some establishments also make use of the mystery guest who will use the service and facilities that your outlet provides to test their quality. Boddington's Village Hotel Group operate this system to test out their own customer-service policy. Before making recommendations to the public other outside agencies will often visit an outlet as a mystery guest for the same reasons, only revealing who they are before leaving.

Whatever data you have and no matter the source, they are of little value if not acted upon. Remember, data can come from:

1 Customers
2 Colleagues
3 Staff
4 Management
5 Mystery guests

Techniques of data collection

Methods of data collection have been discussed previously. Data may be written, verbal or experienced. In any event, data must be reliable and valid. By putting yourself in the place of the customer and thinking the way the customer would can often help you in deciding whether the course of action, the comment or the suggestion is appropriate. This way you can often avoid giving rise to customer dissatisfaction.

Reliability and validity

By monitoring, measuring, assessing and reviewing repeatedly over a period of time it is possible to ensure that the data we use are reliable and valid. This means consistent and dependable, covering all the processes for getting things done right and checking to see that they are done correctly. Different methods of collecting evidence may prove to be valid but unreliable. For example a banquet is held for 100 customers and only two customers complain about the meal. The complaint is valid in the eyes of the customer but not reliable evidence insofar as a major rethink on the menu is necessary before it can be used again for future banquets. In this case the two customers had every right to complain if the meal did not meet their expectations, apologies should be given as well as an offer of alternative food and a possible refund. There should have certainly been an apology. In future it would seem to be good practice to enquire if any customers had any special dietary requirements. Other *variables* such as the time of year, weather and world crises such as war can alter the data being analysed. If custom is normally very busy but due, for example, to a heavy fall of snow it is very likely that many customers decide not to travel resulting in a large number of cancellations, it would therefore be wrong to assume that there is a problem with the outlet's reputation. By careful monitoring a pattern should emerge if there is a problem.

Definition

- ***Variables***
  The components of the service which affect the expectations of the customer service (e.g. price, value for money, comfort, time, atmosphere, flavour and appearance of food, temperature and cleanliness).

'Er, I'm afraid your room isn't *quite* ready yet. Would you mind taking a seat in the lounge for a couple of days. . . ?'

Task 2.23

Read the following case study and try to identify which of the above variables affected the expectations of Mr and Mrs Day.

On arrival at the Gables Hotel Mr Day struggles with the baggage while Mrs Day joins the long queue at the Reception desk waiting to 'Check-in'. While waiting Mrs Day notices that there is only one receptionist on duty and the hall porter is sitting behind the porter's desk reading a newspaper. Meanwhile, Mr Day finds his way to the bar, but there is no one there to attend to him. Disappointed, he joins his wife. The receptionist is very pleasant and helpful and offers to make a booking for the Days in the restaurant for that evening.

Mr and Mrs Day arrive at their room. They are late arrivals and, on entering, find that their room has not been serviced, the bed not having been made up. Mrs Day telephones reception, but they are still very busy and do not answer for some time. Also, the housekeeper has long since departed for the day.

The duty manager suggests that Mr and Mrs Day visit the restaurant while their room is made ready. After all, they do have a table booked. On entering the restaurant they are greeted by the head waiter and shown to their table.

Some 40 minutes later a waiter appears with a menu. The soup is served promptly but the main course is delayed and, on arrival, is cold and lacks flavour. Mr Day complains to the head waiter who says that it is not the fault of the waiting staff and will report the complaint to the kitchen.

Mr and Mrs Day decide to leave the restaurant and return to their room. Noticing a customer questionnaire, Mrs Day fills it in not yet having unpacked. They 'check-out' of the hotel feeling very dissatisfied. Their expectations have not been met.

No doubt the customer evaluation form would give rise to concern by management and these data would need to be analysed along with other questionnaires handed in.

Task 2.24

What comments and feedback do you think the Gables Hotel will have received from Mrs Day's questionnaire?

Follow-up procedures

Data need to be sorted in such a way that they are easy to interpret and organized into categories or headings. This makes it easier to monitor the responses from the data. Comments given directly by customers will have more value than those from *indirect* sources. Improvements and changes should be based on facts and customers' requirements, not on what we think customers want. Any evidance should be sufficient, current and authentic (i.e. valid).

Basic statistics such as frequency counts, mean, mode and median are used together with measures of probability in interpreting information for monitoring purposes. Any gaps or deficiencies need to be recognized and acted upon. However, it may be your organization's or outlet's policy to inform management, so the issues can be raised at appropriate meetings.

Information gathered from monitoring customer service needs to be filed and stored. It may be referred to in order to check whether progress has been made and targets for improvement have been met.

Unreliable data

Inconsistencies will show up regularly in unreliable data. Subjective comments should be avoided. Correct analysis of data cannot be undertaken if the data have been tampered with in any way or are incomplete. Sometimes data are spoilt.

Indirect sources

These could be records which can provide customer information, customer letters, complaints book or compliments, all of which should be acknowledged and, when necessary, a follow-up letter indicating the solution or action taken. Reservations and profit and loss accounts are other indirect sources.

Secondary sources

This is information collected from other outlets (gossip, the media and information for other purposes).

Methods of recording feedback

Whatever method you choose to monitor feedback, the information will need to be stored in a safe and secure place until it is required for further analysis. Customers are usually requested either to post their comments in the box provided in the outlet or to send them to the manger of the organization or outlet. Often a prepaid envelope is provided. If observation or oral feedback is used to monitor customer service then it would be useful for you to make notes and put them on file.

If records are kept in a record book or customers' log the manager will look at these comments on a regular basis, responding as appropriate to the customers who made an entry.

Within the organization the management may require written reports to be submitted from each outlet and within each outlet, the manager may require the section heads of the facilities also to provide written reports.

Taking action on feedback

The feedback will need to be looked at on a regular basis and priorities determined. It will fall into two categories:

1 *Urgent.* That which needs immediate attention in order to satisfy the customer, reduce damage and satisfy health, safety and security requirements.
2 *Non-urgent.* Matters which are still important but can be dealt with more slowly.

Some of the feedback may require information from the staff within the outlet before a response to the customers can be given, and this is known as referral. Sometimes feedback needs to be referred to senior management for a decision or advice on the action to be taken. Usually it is the manager's responsibility to respond to a customer who has given feedback to the outlet, but you may well be asked for your comments before this takes place. Remember, not all feedback that is monitored is negative or bad. Often customers are complimentary about the service they receive.

Urgent and important criteria will need to be dealt with much more quickly and this will usually take the form of an oral response either to the customer or to the member of staff to whom it relates. For example, a customer may complain about the language being used by a member of staff, and this will need to be addressed quickly. A customer may be about to leave because of the long queue at Reception, and telling them that another assistant is about to serve may persuade the customer to stay.

When the organization or the outlet arranges for a monitoring exercise such as a survey or questionnaire to take place the responses will need to be recorded and logged. Analysis of the data will be needed and a written report outlining the findings, conclusions and recommendations prepared.

Discussion on the feedback will usually take place at management meetings, quality meetings and section meetings, and any new procedures and standards put into operation after management have fully considered the issues. The procedures to be implemented will usually be introduced to staff when appropriate and directions placed in the standards and procedures manual.

Follow-up procedures

The most important question you should ask yourself is: Is the customer satisfied or dissatisfied and will the customer return? If the answer is no then you must ask yourself why the customer would not return and whether you or the outlet can do anything to reverse the customer's decision.

It is only polite to acknowledge receipt of any letter or feedback you obtain from a customer, whether it be a compliment or a complaint. Never promise anything you know you or the outlet cannot deliver. For example, if a customer complains about a meal, the procedures of the outlet must be followed. It would be wrong to offer a complimentary meal if a refund is the acknowledged procedure.

Investigate the cause of complaints, apologize and explain what has happened. Equally, you should rectify any deficiences in your organization's or outlet's policy.

It is good practice to report any incidents to your supervisor or manager and to make a file note for future reference. If a written communication is being dealt with it is also good practice to file the response with the correspondence in case it needs to be referred to again. Always thank the customers for their co-operation with questionnaires and surveys and offer complete confidentiality.

It often helps if an explanation as to why you require the feedback is given before conducting the questionnaire or survey. Some organizations and outlets offer a reward for completion and return of questionnaires as an incentive. This may include a free drink at the bar or a free Continental breakfast. This obviously has a cost factor, but it is considered a small price to pay for reliable, current data that yield a large enough sample to be valid. The results of a survey that satisfy hospitality and catering needs and results in the customer's return, is well worth the money spent on the investment.

Health, hygiene, safety and security requirements

Whatever the needs and expectations of customers, staff and others, they must be fulfilled with regard to health, safety and security, and hygiene standards as appropriate. Customers need to know that they, their family, friends and belongings are in a safe and secure place. They also expect to be served in a clean and hygienic environment. Every member of your outlet needs to be aware of the need to care for our customers and offer a service which conforms to statutory and regulated legislation. Every facility within your outlet will have appropriate legislation and codes of practice to follow and these are mentioned in each unit of this book.

We need to care not only for our customers, both internal and external, but also for their belongings. You must know which legislation applies to you (for example, hygiene laws, health and safety at work). In addition, it is necessary to be aware of the laws relating to the premises in which you work and offer a service to the customer.

Don't forget that it is not only *customers* who need a healthy, safe and secure environment, but also those who work in the establishment and those who visit for other reasons (e.g. inspectors, sales representatives, those delivering goods, etc.). Therefore you need to know that all customer services offered by you are consistent with hygiene, health, safety and security requirements.

Health

Health requirements are to do with the cleanliness of the establishments, and the hygiene standards which are necessary to ensure that no one becomes unwell as a result of visiting the establishment. This means that proper procedures should be in force to ensure that the following areas are kept clean and hygienic:

- Kitchens and work surfaces
- Cooking equipment
- Serving equipment
- Staff cleanliness, both personal and of clothing
- Table equipment
- Bedding
- Toilet and washroom areas

In addition to cleanliness, it is important to ensure that staff are free from disease or infections, and if they temporarily contract any of these, they are removed from areas which might affect the health of customers, other members of staff and other visitors to the establishment, such as suppliers, sales representatives, etc.

Hygiene

It is important that a high standard of hygiene is maintained in all hospitality and catering service areas of the outlet. Equally, it is important that staff also maintain a high standard of personal hygiene. The relevant sections of the book cover this in detail but it is important to note that as well as contravening legislation, outlets and staff who do not have the highest of hygiene standards are not likely to attract customers to return and give you their custom.

Safety and security

Procedures in the event of a fire or security alert.

1 Every customer, whether a conference delegate, a resident or a short-stay guest, should be made aware of the evacuation procedures in the event of a fire or security alert.
2 In the event of a fire the alarm should be raised immediately.
3 Firefighting equipment should be used in accordance with the laid-down procedure.
4 You should follow the correct evacuation procedure of your organization or outlet in a calm and orderly manner. On no account should you allow a customer to re-enter a building until the all-clear has been given. You should indicate to the customer how to get to the assembly point should it be necessary.

Measures should be taken to ensure the safety of customers and others. This includes the following:

1 Providing facilities for the safe storage of customers' property
2 Preventing unauthorized people from entering the premises
3 Preventing unauthorized people from entering guests' rooms
4 Ensuring the safe operation of all equipment in the premises, such as lifts, electrical equipment, machinery, etc.
5 Installing efficient fire-prevention methods, coupled with early fire-detection systems and methods of firefighting and safe evacuation
6 Reviewing safety and security measures regularly

Task 2.25

Look at your own college or school, or place of work if you have one. What areas or items are subject to regular health, safety or security checks? What security measures does it employ to ensure that the above measures are complied with?

Suspicious items or packages

In offering a customer-care service you may be requested to look after packages or items belonging to a customer. It is necessary to be on constant alert and any suspicious item, package or luggage should be reported in accordance with the laid-down procedures of your outlet and remain untouched. Sometimes items are forgotten or left unattended, but if it appears that they have been left for no apparent reason then safety procedures need to be adopted.

Accidents

In any area where people meet there is likely to be at some point in time an accident or emergency that will require your attention. Minor accidents may, for example, be a spillage on a customer's clothes in a restaurant or a cut finger suffered by a member of the staff. More serious accidents could require medical attention. It could be a customer having a heart attack or one in need of medication. In the event of a death the management should call for a doctor who will in turn inform the police. After initial enquiries the body will be discreetly removed from the area. You may need to care for the relatives or friends of the customer. This situation calls for a lot of tact and discretion, without fuss. Details such as the bill would tend to be dealt with at a later date or not mentioned.

If you are not a first-aider then you should know who to contact immediately. You should also know the appropriate action to take to ensure the safety of injured and non-injured customers and be able to reassure them that assistance is on its way. As far as possible, you should try to make any injured person comfortable without running the risk of making the injury worse. Any accident should be reported or documented in accordance with the procedures of your outlet.

It is important that when carrying out your duties that you ensure that you work in a safe environment. It is also important that if you spot any potential hazards they are reported through the appropriate channel and that you take immediate preventative action to safeguard your customers. Notices and warning signs should be erected to alert your customers to the dangers or you could be deemed to be negligent should an accident occur.

Security

Every outlet exists to provide a service to its customers. You have a responsibility for the security of your customers and their belongings. If customers feel insecure or under threat they will not give you their custom. When there are airline disasters, or unrest in particular countries it affects the hospitality and catering industry. The Lockerbie air crash in 1988 deterred many American customers from visiting the UK and reduced trade for some time.

There are four aspects to security:

- Loss of possessions
- Personal damage
- Damage to the building and its furnishings
- Fraudulent damage

Unfortunately, not all customers are honest, and some may leave without paying their bill or may help themselves to the belongings of others. This is deemed to be theft. If, however, a person enters a building without permission, such as breaking into a guest's room this is classed as burglary. You should assist your outlet in being alert at all times and know the correct procedures to follow in the event of a breach of security.

Section 1 of the Theft Act 1978 defines theft as dishonestly appropriating property belonging to another with the intention of depriving them of it. A person is guilty of burglary if entering a building as a trespasser intent on committing such an offence. Deception, that is dishonestly obtaining services, is also an offence. Personal security is also important especially when dealing with VIPs. Bomb threats and other forms of terrorism cannot be taken lightly. Usually your outlet would be expected to liaise closely with the local police for advice when high-risk customers are visiting your outlet. Unfortunately, the hospitality and catering industry has many outlets which are vulnerable to undesirables masquerading as *bona fide* customers.

Telephone threats are a cause for concern and while many turn out to be hoaxes, they should not be ignored. You should be aware of the procedures to follow so that important information is not lost. It could save lives. Confidentiality is important when dealing with customers – some require complete privacy and do not wish to be disturbed. You may be given information in confidence that the customer does not wish you to repeat. Customers' property can often be a security problem. Money and valuables make them obvious targets for muggers, thieves and confidence tricksters. Sometimes the customers themselves lose their belongings and suspicion could then be directed at you and your colleagues.

How to avoid a breach of security

- Constant alertness and reporting of any suspicious activities
- By having a blacklist of unwanted customers or those who are not creditworthy. Often banks and finance companies will issue these
- Having a security person at the entrance to the building and regular patrols of the area to ensure that anything suspicious is noticed. It is often good practice to limit the number of unlocked entrances and exits, providing there is no breach of fire regulations
- Anyone looking suspicious should be politely questioned
- Burglar alarms and pressure pads will alert you to an approaching intruder
- Keys and other unlocking devices should be carefully monitored. You should not hand over security keys to anyone without being signed for, nor should they be left lying around
- The use of safety deposit boxes or strong-rooms is recommended. If customers decline to make use of these facilities they are deemed to have accepted responsibility.

Task 2.26

A customer books into your hotel for the night and decides not to use the safety deposit box. While taking clothes from a suitcase the jewellery wallet falls to the floor. The customer picks it up, puts it on the dressing table and leaves the room for a while. On returning, the customer finds some jewellery missing and reports this to the management, indicating that it has been stolen. You are very concerned and decide to investigate.

- *What would you say to the customer?*
- *Who else would you speak to?*
- *What action might you take?*
- *If missing jewellery is subsequently found by the accommodation staff the day after the customer has left, what action would you take?*

In this section you have looked at the provision of customer service. It is hoped that you now have the knowledge to be able to put customer-service into practice. To test your knowledge you will find some questions at the end of this unit. All the answers are to be found in the text.

▪ ASSIST CUSTOMERS IN HOSPITALITY AND CATERING OUTLETS ▪

Provision of customer service

Following on from previous sections where we defined customer care service, identified our customers and evaluated their needs and wants, you now need to know:

1. How to provide the best possible service to your customers according to their requirements
2. How to prioritize your customer needs
3. The measures to be taken to deal with different customers' behaviour
4. How to deal with dissatisfied customers and the remedial measures you might take
5. Finally a possible checklist you might use when assisting customers

Why do we offer customer service?

Services are required by our customers to satisfy their requirements and within the hospitality and catering industry it is generally accepted that this includes a personalized contribution by staff which distinguishes it from the products you may well sell. In order to do this you need to:

- Be considerate
- Impress your customers
- Exceed their expectations

Services are required for our customers for many reasons:

1. To provide a need (perhaps business traveller requires clothes to be valeted)
2. Security of self or belongings
3. Comfort such as the provision of an extra pillow
4. Pleasure (services such as the provision of a newspaper)
5. Fear (the loan of an umbrella for fear of getting wet or a patrolled car park service to avoid theft of a car)
6. Habit: many customers will require a service out of habit, you need to know your regular customers so that you can provide for the service they require. History cards are a good way of keeping records on customers' habits
7. To satisfy a need: the customer realizes that you offer a service such as a courtesy bus to the airport and decides to make use of it

Services are different from products in that they are less tangible. They are usually offered to match customers' needs and are often tailored to individuals, therefore the customers' presence is an essential element. The services you give your customers may be offered in a slightly different way to that of your colleagues. It is therefore not always easy to establish the standards and even more difficult to ensure that the standards have been met.

Unlike a product which you may purchase, find faulty and thus return, if the service is found to be lacking your customer is less likely to return. Therefore this means that the quality of the services you offer depends very much on how you and your colleagues behave while providing the services on behalf of your outlet.

Requirements of good customer service

You need to:

- Be accessible and able to be contacted. For example, the reception desk must be located near to the entrance so that on entering the building customers can easily locate Reception staff.
- Communicate. There is a need to keep your customers *informed*. In a previous section we looked at the methods of communicating. However, there is a need to *explain* to customers how to access facilities (e.g. operate the minibar or air conditioning). There may need to be an explanation of an increase in charges or the reason for the restaurant being out of use. Communication is a two-way process: it is also important to *listen* to what customers are saying.
- Be competent. You must have the necessary skills and knowledge about your outlet, standards and procedures and the tasks you are responsible for in order to carry out the job to the customers' satisfaction.
- Be courteous. This means being polite, even when a guest is being difficult, inconsiderate or even rude and offensive. It means being friendly without being familiar, calm and positive.
- Have credibility. This means being trustworthy, dependable, reliable and putting the customer first. Any suspicion that the customer is being exploited (e.g. overcharged) will be counterproductive and the customer will become dissatisfied.
- Be reliable. You need to be consistent and dependable, to work according to your outlet's laid-down standards, to be punctual and prompt. An example might be to deliver an early-morning alarm call on time.
- Be responsive. Service should be available as and when the customer requires it and not when you wish to provide it. It includes being prompt in answering the telephone or providing a drink requested from the bar. It is *not* acceptable to continue a conversation with colleagues and keep a customer waiting.

Some matters may be urgent and need immediate attention.
- Understand. You should make every effort to appreciate the differing requirements of your customers. Customers need to be treated and received as if they were the first.

Dealing with a challenging customer

Some customers are going to get upset, complain or be downright awkward and challenging. The situation is not helped if you are also challenging or discourteous. Once dissatisfied, a customer is more than likely to find fault and complain throughout the duration of the visit to your outlet. It is therefore important for you to acquire the skills through practice to know how to deal with such situations.

Society is made up of all kinds of customers and they have the right to be challenging but not offensive. From time to time you will be faced with a customer who is not completely satisfied and in such cases the policy of the organization or outlet should always be adhered to, particularly in relation to refunds, exchanges, discounts or hospitality.

Task 2.27

You are approached by customers. Decide to which of the following you would give a refund, exchange, discount or hospitality and explain why.

- *A telephone call is charged to the final bill which, you are informed, has not been made.*
- *A customer complains that a wine glass is dirty.*
- *The manager has invited the customer to have a drink on the house.*
- *A customer wishes to claim a special offer on weekend breaks.*

The following are guidelines on how to keep a customer satisfied. However, the policy of the organization or outlet should always be followed.

- Take the lead, the customer is giving us the opportunity to get it right for them. The complaints and concerns and even good feedback is very valuable information and can only serve to improve your service and products.
- Always remain calm.
- Apologize, but do not keep saying 'Sorry'.
- Listen attentively to customers. Let them vent their feelings.
- Do not interrupt them. They will begin all over again.
- Deal with the emotions first, acknowledge how upset they are and make them feel valued.
- Repeat. Let the customers know you understand the nature of their concern.
- Show concern and interest (this does not mean that you agree with the customer).
- Do not make excuses.
- Do not pass the blame.
- Thank the customer from bringing the issue to your attention.
- Take the necessary action by solving the problem immediately, or inform your line manager or supervisor.

Why, then, do our customers get upset? It really has to do with the perceptions, how a customer feels at the time and what they expect. For example, a family books a weekend break at your hotel because it has a leisure club with an indoor swimming pool. They check with the hotel before making the booking that they can have use of the pool as guests of the hotel. The family arrive expecting to be able to use the pool at all times as no restrictions appear in the brochure. After they have checked into their room the family visits the leisure facility and are informed by the receptionist that the pool is only open for children up to 4 p.m. because, being a leisure club, it has times when only adults and members may use it. The family were very angry. In other words, the customers did not get what was promised. Expectations were not fulfilled.

Other reasons why customers get upset are:

- You are rude to a customer
- You are indifferent to a customer, having excuses such as 'I can't do this' or 'It's not my job to do that'
- No-one listened to the customer – this is a waste of feedback that can help you to improve your service

How to handle a customer complaint

1. Listen to the customer
2. Give your apologies, assure the customer that you are sorry and want to help
3. Show sympathy and understanding
4. Never disagree or agree
5. Accept the blame, do not make excuses
6. Advise the customer how you will help
7. Take the customer away from public view
8. Refer to your supervisor or line manager if you cannot deal with the problem
9. Record any awkward situations by logging them in the diary or handover book and make sure that others in your team are updated in case the problem or complaint arises again

How to deal with an enquiry

1. Acknowledge the customer's presence promptly
2. Greet the customer with a friendly smile, be courteous but not too casual or familiar
3. Apologize for any delay which may have occurred, show concern
4. Listen to the customer, do not interrupt
5. Identify the customer's needs
6. Give the information required or refer the customer to the appropriate section or person
7. Never refuse to help, always make an alternative suggestion

Customer referrals

On occasion it is not always possible for you to assist the customer and there is a need for you to pass them on to someone else. This is known as a referral. In order to do this you need to know who the staff are in your outlet and in some cases the organization of which you are a member. In addition, you need to know the roles and responsibilities of these staff. Many outlets have an organizational chart, the in-house directory may also give you this information and, failing this, personnel could inform you. It is obviously much preferred if you become aware of the product knowledge of your outlet and try to get to know the staff with whom you work.

If there is a need to refer a customer you should explain why and give as much direction on how to find the new person as possible. It is a good idea to escort them if you can, or to ask them to be seated while you locate the new contact.

Customer service

Customer service is central for our organization's survival. Whether we deliver is not an option in the hospitality and catering industry. It is a customer service industry and consists of providing a service on behalf of your organization or outlet. You are the face and voice and exhibit the personality which signifies what your outlet stands for. You are expected to give a total service so positive that the customer cannot wait to return. You are expected to:

- Create customer satisfaction
- Identify customer perceptions and requirements
- Maintain their wellbeing

In order to do this it is necessary to understand customer needs and expectations.

The whole purpose of customer service is to maintain and increase for your organization the market share through increased customer satisfaction. This means having more satisfied customers who will buy more of your products or use more of your services repeatedly.

Customer needs and expectations

Different people or 'client groups' have different needs and expectations.

- A businessperson entertaining an important potential customer will want a high-class meal served in a quiet restaurant with full table-service and a large range of wines. The service must be swift and courteous. The bill must be accurately calculated, and there must be a convenient method of payment available
- A soldier returning from a day's exercise wants a hot shower, a satisfying meal and a drink in the bar before retiring to bed
- A patient in hospital wants clean sheets, a warm room, nutritious food, the ability to buy snacks and magazines, and a quiet environment while recovering
- A student taking a break from classes wants a cheap meal served quickly, with a selection of fizzy drinks, and a stool at the bar to perch on

All the above customers require both products and services. They also expect a certain standard of courtesy, efficiency and cleanliness. *All* customers are important, young or old, big spenders or not. The difference between them is that they require different products and services, dependent on their needs and expectations.

Task 2.28

Look at your own locality. Identify a single outlet or facility for each of the following:

- *An elderly person needing residential care*
- *A young person wanting food, drink and entertainment in the evenings*
- *A middle-aged businessperson wanting an evening meal with a client*
- *A mother with young children wanting a quick lunch*
- *A traveller on a long car journey, needing an overnight stay*

When you have your list, identify the products and services which each outlet or facility provides.

Meeting customer needs

The needs for assistance will, in the main, be for information and physical help. For the most part, the customers will require:

1. Advice (e.g. security and fire drill procedures, times of meals)
2. Information on local amenities, the outlet's facilities
3. Physical help (with baggage if necessary, car parking)
4. Assistance (e.g. valeting, room service, food and drink, shower facilities, sundry items)

Task 2.29

A customer arrives at a hotel too late for the evening restaurant enquiring if it is possible to obtain a meal. The hotel offers room service. The receptionist, in offering 'added value' not only offers to contact room service, but arranges for them to contact the customer to discuss the menu and determine if any beverages are required. To which of the customer needs – advice, information, physical help or assistance – is the receptionist responding?

Culture

The services provided by your outlet for your customers help to meet their needs and expectations. It will depend very much on your type of outlet as to the services you provide. The culture of your outlet will also determine the type of service. Is the enrichment of the outlet, and the services on offer in the outlet, over and above the norm which the customer expects? Usually this incurs extra costs to the customer.

A Travel Lodge will provide basic accommodation with a hospitality tray in the room but not a direct telephone, for this the customer needs to go to the lobby. However, a four-star hotel is very likely to have a direct phone in the room and may offer many other services as well. The increase in the accommodation tariff reflects this as well as the increased telephone charges.

If, for example, you were to visit the Simpson's-in-the-Strand restaurant in London, you would be expected to be formally dressed. No man would be allowed into the restaurant without a jacket and tie and women would be expected to wear a dress or skirt. This being the culture of the establishment, you would also expect the waiting staff to be formally dressed. The beliefs and the customs of the outlet as to how you behave and respond to customers form the basis of a code of practice, i.e. the guidelines which enable everyone to work within a culture to the standards that the outlet has set in order to provide good customer service. The traditions of the establishment are considered to be good custom and practice and give added value which customers identify with your outlet (e.g. in Fortnum and Mason in London all the male staff wear pinstripe trousers and tail jackets).

Task 2.30

Discuss in a small group the different traditions and customs that are celebrated in December. Outline the considerations that you would need to be aware of in planning events in a hospitality and catering outlet of your choice.

Satisfying customer needs

Every outlet aims to give the customer good service and to give this good service involves social skills. If you display these skills, the guests will leave with the feeling that they have received value for money. To succeed in doing so, it is important to identify what customers want and how you can best satisfy this want.

Give a warm welcome as in Figure 2.4. Motorway service stations actually use 'Welcome Break' as a logo to promote their business. Establish a rapport. A warm and friendly manner, a spontaneous smile, eye contact are all important in making the customers feel safe and comfortable in possibly strange surroundings. Greet the customer with 'Good morning' – 'Good evening', by name, if possible, *even when serving someone else at the same time*. Customers then know that you have seen them and will deal with their requirements as soon as possible.

Good personal appearance creates the right 'first impression'. Personal hygiene is of utmost importance. You should be neat and tidy, but never severe in personal appearance (e.g. clothes, make-up or body lotions). Customers want to feel they belong and can depend on you.

Adopt a pleasant attitude. Consider customers by giving help and guidance without necessarily being asked. Make them feel that they can depend on you. Treat customers politely with tact, prompt attention and efficiency. Show interest in what they are doing or telling you.

Indicate that you have time for customers. If not, they may feel isolated or not accepted, and this can lead to complaints. Remember: never leave a customer waiting while you complete a conversation with another member of staff. If the telephone rings as a customer arrives, greet the customer before answering it.

Display tact and diplomacy. Customers go to a bar to meet people, i.e. for companionship. They may well drink too much but the social

HOLIDAY INN LONDON-KINGS CROSS/BLOOMSBURY
1 KINGS CROSS ROAD, LONDON WC1X 9HX
TELEPHONE: 071 833 3900 FAX: 071 917 6163/6164

Dear Guest

A very warm welcome to the Holiday Inn Kings Cross/Bloomsbury

My staff and I are here to help you enjoy your stay and should you require our services please do not hesitate to call myself or the Duty Manager by dialling "0".

On your desk you will find a Directory of Services which will help you to familiarise yourself with all the facilities available.

I would particularly like to draw your attention to our fine "Carriages" Restaurant located on the ground floor, which offers a superb choice of daily carvery or à la carte menus. Alternatively, our lounge provides light refreshments throughout the day.

Next to Reception you will find our "Charings" Bar where a wide variety of cocktails are available.

For your relaxation our excellent "Locomotion" Health Club, located on the lower ground floor, offers a swimming pool, sauna, steam room, solarium, whirlpool, fitness area and squash court. Also situated within the Club is the Hair & Beauty Salon where you can pamper yourself with our extensive range of hair and skin care treatments.

On a final note, please may I remind you to take all your belongings with you when you vacate your room.

Wishing you a very pleasant stay with us.

Yours sincerely

F A Kassam
Managing Director & General Manager

The Holiday Inn London-Kings Cross/Bloomsbury is owned and operated by Firoka (Kings Cross) Ltd., under license from Bass European Holdings N.V.
Firoka Registered Office: Firoka (Kings Cross) Ltd., 59 Sheldon Avenue, London N6 4NH. Registered in England No. 06540

Figure 2.4 A welcoming letter to the customer

skill required in handling them is tact and diplomacy, not an air of disapproval or reproach.

Customers want to be recognized as distinct from other individuals. In order to do this you need a good memory. Remember customers' names, favourite drinks, likes and dislikes. Customers will then feel important. The customer history card is useful for keeping this sort of information. Situations often occur when a customer is trying to impress an important client. You can help by welcoming the customer by name and giving efficient attention.

Customers who are unable to pay

- Never argue with the customer
- Discreetly refer the customer to the person in charge

Customers who are intoxicated

- Avoid becoming over-friendly
- Do not be reproachful

'I know we insist on you being courteous, Fosdyke, but don't you think you're taking it a little *too* far. . . ?'

- Refer the customer to the person in charge
- If the customer looks like causing a disturbance or trouble avoid getting involved, call for assistance

Dealing with children

- Treat them with equal amount of politeness as you would adults, but be a little less formal with them
- Do not get too involved with their activities. You are employed to work, not play
- Always suggest high chairs, cots, or baby-minding facilities where appropriate

Useful tips on your behaviour

In relationship with your customers the following tips apply. Do not:

1. Be over-friendly with customers
2. Get the reputation for being a moaner and weary the customer with your troubles. They would rather tell you theirs
3. Spend too much time in conversation with the same person. This gives the impression that you are favouring one particular customer above the rest
4. Listen to gossip or criticize one customer to another
5. Use Christian names unless invited to do so
6. Be patronizing to customers; treat all customers with equal regard
7. Be impatient with customers
8. Offer your opinion unless it is asked for
9. Discuss politics or religion
10. Be argumentative with colleagues in front of customers
11. Try to be helpful – it makes for good-quality service and relations
12. Talk too loudly to other members of staff when customers are present

Salesmanship

Once a customer has decided to buy a bedroom or a meal we must ensure that the experience justifies this decision. Remember, earlier we discussed that, above all, we want the customer to return or to inform others of a good experience. In order to do this you must impress the customer by

- Your attitude
- Your appearance
- Your knowledge of the customer's wants
- A tasteful display of literature and products

Task 2.31

Make a list of literature and products that you could display in a restaurant to impress customers.

Attitude

This plays a significant part in salesmanship. If your attitude is not right you will not be able to impress a customer and encourage a sale. Always ask if there is anything else that the customer requires before leaving the customer to pass onto someone else. Always use the opportunity to mention other alternatives and facilities (e.g. inform customers of other restaurants within the hotel or offer to book a table for them if they prefer to eat out). Offer a choice of rooms if they are available and, if possible, sell the most expensive ones first. This is called 'selling up'. Always enquire if the customer is satisfied, have they enjoyed their meal, visit, etc. Ask if you can make another reservation or put them on your mailing list. This way you can remind your customers to come back again. *Always remember*: a departing customer is as important as an arriving one.

Having the right product knowledge

Having the right product knowledge helps you to give the customers what they need. You should know:

1. The facilities of your outlet and, better still, of your organization if you are to recommend other outlets within the organization to your customers. This might include special menus, dinner–dances, baby-sitting services, car parking.
2. The layout of your outlet, the location of various rooms and the types of accommodation if a hotel.
3. The product (e.g. the restaurant's menu and wine list) and use phrases such as 'Which wine would you like this evening?'
4. Which dishes on the menu show more profit than others or which rooms need selling first. You should be able to describe them if questioned by a customer. The way in which you describe them can often persuade a customer to make a purchase. You must, however, tell the truth. You cannot say a soup is home-made if it came out of a packet or that strawberries are fresh if they come from a tin. Likewise, you cannot sell a room that is easily accessible if you have to climb five flights of stairs and walk a mile down a corridor to get to it.
5. The sales promotions in current use in your outlet (e.g. bargain breaks, two for the price of one).
6. The house brands. Sell these unless asked for other brands. This probably gives a better profit margin to your outlet and also promotes your outlet to the customer.
7. The procedures to follow when a customer wishes to make a block booking, conference or special event such as a wedding.
8. Your competitors and the range of products and services they offer. You are then aware of your unique selling propositions (known as USP).
9. The nearest outlet within your organization so that you can make recommendations to customers. This is particularly useful for travellers and business executives. Little Chefs and Travel Lodges have maps and guides that they give to customers indicating where other outlets are located around the country. Many organizations have company directories with details of all their outlets.
10. The changes taking place in your outlet that could have an effect on the customer. This may be the introduction of a new menu or some refurbishing that is taking place which prevents the customer using some of the facilities.
11. Local attractions and events in your area. These could have an effect on how busy you are likely to be. Customers may well ask you questions about the events or how to find the attraction. Sometimes you may be asked to recommend a chemist, hairdresser or florist. It is useful if you can give directions and a telephone number or address.

Task 2.32

What would be the USP of your college/school refectory or your training restaurant?

Task 2.33

Working in a small group, look at a menu and practise describing some of the dishes in irresistible ways to tempt your customer.

Task 2.34

In what ways could you promote your college/school refectory or restaurant?

Influences on customer behaviour

The impressions we give to our customers influence how our customers behave. At every point of contact we make with the customer we communicate. Unfortunately, we may not be communicating the right impression.

Your outlet will be only as successful as you allow it to be. You need to:

- Have a positive attitude
- Enjoy working with people
- Tune into what the customer expects
- Have a need to please
- Get things right the first time
- Let the customer know you care
- Be responsible
- Value the customer

In order to do these things effectively we need to watch our body language, our tone of voice, and the words we use, especially if face to face or over the telephone. The impressions we portray will seek either a favourable or a negative response from our customers. What we seek to do is to create a favourable impression that will last.

Poor impressions are given when our body language, tone of voice and the words we use are cold, unfriendly, impersonal and requests to assist are ignored. Good impressions are given when the customer has been served and valued, are given a warm reception, you try to understand and empathize with the customer, you smile and we don't forget to thank them for their custom. It costs nothing to be polite to our customers. *Empathize*: Customers want you to support, understand and respond.

Body language

What people say to you, or what you say to your customers, is often very different from what you or they feel or think. Customers' feelings need to be accurately gauged through observation of their behaviour and through sensitive questioning. Such feelings can include vulnerability, distress, anger or confusion. Your own behaviour needs to be adapted to the perceived needs and feelings of the customer.

The body language you use allows others to interpret your thoughts by your gestures. To customers it affects how you heard them and how you ultimately deal with them. If you shrug your shoulders you are implying that you do not understand. A thumbs-up sign could mean that you are OK, you want to hitch a lift, or a rude gesture if jerked sharply upwards. Scratching the neck indicates that you are not in agreement with your customer. We should therefore be aware of our own non-verbal signals and the effects they could have on customers.

Eye contact

Eyes can give clues to a person's thoughts. I am sure you have heard the phrases 'looked daggers at,' 'the evil eye', 'shifty eyes', 'gleam in the eye'. Can you think of others?

As a person's attitude and mood change from positive to negative thought so the pupils of the eyes will dilate or contract. The different ways you direct your gaze could have a powerful effect on face-to-face contact with a customer.

Tone of voice

When speaking to a customer the tone of voice relays a signal and evokes different responses depending on your manner and the emphasis placed on the spoken word. It's how we say it, not what we say that matters (e.g. raising the voice).

Treatment of customers should always be courteous and helpful even when we are under stress. We should treat our last customer just as we would the first and be consistently friendly. It is not easy in the hotel and catering industry after long hours of duty not to feel tired and let it show by our tone of voice and manner. How often have you said

'It's time I went home!'
'Not another one, it's time we closed!'
'Here they come again!'

Practise the way we say 'have a nice day', 'next'. It can be more friendly and positive if we add 'please' after 'next' and smile.

Customers' wellbeing

It is not difficult to deal with people who are pleasant, friendly and cooperative, but from time to time occasions will arise when intelligence, care, understanding and common sense will be needed to handle awkward situations caused by customers' behaviour. It takes self-discipline to deal with such customers without putting yourself or your outlet in the wrong, or at risk.

Often a customer may be over-tired, showing impatience or displaying aggressive behaviour. The influence of drink may alter a customer's behaviour. Drunkenness and disorderly conduct is an offence on licensed premises, and if permitted, could lead to the licensee losing the licence. Likewise, the influence of drugs, or lack of them, can cause customers to behave differently. Customers are often taken ill and require medical care. Sometimes you may have to contact a customer to deliver bad news and you should inform them as early as possible and in person. Get to the point quickly by saying 'You are not going to like hearing this' or 'I have some sad news', and be prepared for a reaction to this news.

If a customer displays unacceptable or odd behaviour it is best to accompany them to a more private area, such as an office or lounge. This then removes any scene which may occur from public view, gives privacy to the customer and allows for further assistance to be called or first aid to be administered, without the customer feeling embarrassed or suffering loss of face. Remember: the customer may have to face you, other members of staff or other customers again.

Good 'value added' service practices can have many benefits to the customer. If guests feel welcome and receive friendly service with a smile they will return. Their perception is favourable and we have satisfied customers. This increases business, involves repeat sales of products and services, your reputation as an outlet increases, and encourages staff to set and keep high standards of working. In addition to benefiting the outlet, customer service practice gives satisfaction to us to know that customers are happy and we have been able to brighten their lives.

Assist customers in hospitality and catering

This final section on customer service is intended to provide you with ideas for developing a checklist for recording your experiences when assisting customers. Any evidence you acquire should be gathered for inclusion in your portfolio. If you subsequently decide to aim for an NVQ in customer service this evidence may serve to contribute to this qualification.

Dealing with customers

Have you been able to observe or assist in the procedure with regard to the following task?

Task 2.25

	Where	When
Dealing with enquiries		
Dealing with ethnic minorities		
Receiving customers		
Giving information to customers		
Liaison with internal customers		
Dealing with letters		
Acquiring sufficient local information		
Receiving and caring for a VIP, CIP, a business person, special needs, an elderly person or a child		
Using a telephone correctly		
Receiving and sending a message		
Writing a simple report		
Listening to and dealing with an enquiry, or a complaint		
Asking questions and giving appropriate answers when dealing with a customer		
Taking part in a fire drill/security alert or having received instruction		
Knowing the security measures for your outlet with regard to:		
Keys		
Cash		
Mail		
Reception of articles and parcels		
Theft		
Lost/found property		
Care of customers' belongings		
Dealing with and receiving enquiry agents, police and official inspectors		
Taking action in the event of illness, accident or death of a customer		
Participating in a security alert involving local emergency services		

In this section you have looked at the provision of customer service. It is hoped that you now have the knowledge and understanding to be able to put customer service into practice. To test your knowledge you will find some questions below. All the answers are to be found in the text. To complete customer service there is a unit assignment which will provide evidence for your portfolio.

Test your knowledge

1 How can you provide the best possible service to your customers?
2 What is meant by the term 'personalized contribution'?
3 How would you distinguish between a product and a service?
4 List the main reasons why customers require a service?
5 What are the requirements of good customer service?
6 Explain how you would deal with an angry customer.
7 A customer complains about an overcharge on the bill. Explain how you would deal with this.
8 A customer complains that soup has been spilt on their clothing by a waiter. What would you do?
9 Give three possible reasons why customers get upset?
10 What is the purpose of customer service?
11 What do customers require in order to meet their needs?
12 Why do you need to have knowledge of the culture you work in?
13 What is a code of practice?
14 Why do customers require a warm welcome?
15 A customer is unable to pay for a meal taken in the restaurant. What would you do?
16 Why is self-image and personal appearance important?
17 Give three tips on how you should behave when dealing with customers.
18 What is meant by
USP?
Selling up?
Product knowledge?
19 How does your body language affect your customer's behaviour towards you?
20 What is meant by added value?
21 What is meant by standards?
22 Why is telephone skill important in customer service?
23 What do we mean by monitoring customer service?
24 Give three methods of monitoring customer service.
25 What do we mean by
Valid?
Authentic?
26 Give examples of data which could be used in monitoring customer service.
27 What are the different kinds of customer who might use hospitality and catering facilities?
28 What particular needs might groups of customers have?
29 What areas of a hospitality and catering facility would need to be kept clean on a regular basis?
30 What types of safety and security measures should an establishment take, and why?

▪ ASSIGNMENT ▪

Customer requirements, provision and feedback

- Look around your school, college or place of work and identify the different customer groups.
- Identify a range of requirements and needs for assistance which are likely to be found amongst customers using the facilities avaiable. The facilities may be a refectory, shop, restaurant or leisure centre.
- Identify the characteristics of the service on offer within the facilities.
  What are the benefits of offering good customer service practice within your school, college or work place.

You receive the following customer feedback sheets (see Figure 2.5).

- Describe the follow-up procedure you would take for each.
- How would you record the receipt of the customer feedback?

- Make appropriate responses to the feedback sheets
- Elements 2.1 PC1 PC2 2.3 PC1 PC4
- Elements 2.3 PC2
- Elements 2.2 PC3 PC4 PC5
- Core Skills – see attached sheet
- Your responses to the feedback sheets should be word processed

TALKBACK

Customer Service Comment Form

Your comments are most welcome and will help us continually improve our service to you.

Customer comments/suggestions

Today I ate in the refectory and found my food to be cold, the food had little flavour and I felt was not worth the money especially as it cost more being a Christmas lunch. The refectory assistant was quite rude when I asked for a refund.

Date: *12/12/1994*

Thank you for completing this form. Please leave it with the College Reception. It will be passed to the Principal/Head Teacher/Manager

Please complete the details below if you wish to receive an acknowledgement:

Name: *Jenny Wren*

Address: *15 The Bank*
Anytown

Course (if applicable): *Mature Student Business Studies*

Figure 2.5

TALKBACK

Customer Service Comment Form

Your comments are most welcome and will help us continually improve our service to you.

Customer comments/suggestions

I would like to complain about the price of sandwiches sold in The College Shop. I can obtain the same type of sandwiches from the refectory. Can you explain why there is a difference in price.

Date: *10th November 1994*

Thank you for completing this form. Please leave it with the College Reception. It will be passed to the Principal/Head Teacher/Manager

Please complete the details below if you wish to receive an acknowledgement:

Name: *Sam Jones*

Address: *21 Marriott Close*
Sunnyside
Devon *Tel. 123789*

Course (if applicable): *Secretarial. PT Day Student*

TALKBACK

Customer Service Comment Form

Your comments are most welcome and will help us continually improve our service to you.

Customer comments/suggestions

The reception staff were very helpful today when I lost my spectacles and I would like to thank them for all their help and courtesy.

Date: *11 Jan. 1994*

Thank you for completing this form. Please leave it with the College Reception. It will be passed to the Principal/Head Teacher/Manager

Please complete the details below if you wish to receive an acknowledgement:

Name: *Joe Smith* *student*

Address: *12 Ford Road*
Kibworth Norton
Leicester

Course (if applicable):

PROVIDE FRONT OFFICE AND ACCOMMODATION OPERATIONS

Essentially, Front Office and Accommodation operations are practical tasks. This unit aims to give some background and underpinning knowledge of the types of operations involved in a number of different outlets to meet customer requirements. In order that you may practise your skills effectively the unit contains:

- Customer requirements and service needs
- Front Office and Accommodation operations
- Systems for recording bookings
- Receiving and registering guests
- Administrative procedures
- Methods of payment
- Methods of communication
- Importance of health, safety and hygiene
- Procedures for cleaning and materials used
- Skills needed in Front Office and Accommodation areas

▪ ESTABLISHMENTS PROVIDING FRONT OFFICE AND ACCOMMODATION SERVICES ▪

In this section we are going to concentrate on the Front Office and Accommodation services within the hospitality and catering industry. Establishments such as hotels, hospitals and hostels need to provide Front Office services to deal with bookings, registration and, where appropriate, payment for the accommodation and the services which they sell. They also need to provide accommodation for eating, drinking, sleeping and for personal hygiene. Establishments such as restaurants and leisure complexes which do not have sleeping facilities also require systems to manage their bookings and payments. They too provide accommodation for eating and drinking and for personal hygiene.

This accommodation needs to be cleaned, maintained and serviced to a standard which the customer expects. The customer may also expect some additional services depending upon the type of accommodation chosen.

What is a Front Office ?

This is the section of a hotel or other establishment which deals with the administrative aspects of caring for a customer. Generally, the Front Office looks after advance bookings for the establishment and the reception and registration of customers when they arrive. For some establishments, such as hotels, the Front Office also prepares and deals with the payment of the customers' bills. It is the place where customers can go if they have any queries.

When we spend time away from home we are *customers* and, as such, we have a number of basic needs and expectations. If we are away for a day or part of a day we will need *food* and *drink* and probably facilities for *personal hygiene*. If, however, we go away for an overnight stay we will need somewhere to *sleep* as well as facilities for *personal hygiene* and for *refreshment*.

Task 3.1

In your group brainstorm and make a list of the types of establishment you have used when you have been away from home during the day. Make a second list of the type of establishment you have needed to use when you have stayed away from home for one or more nights. Remember that you are studying aspects of the hospitality and catering industry and so you can leave out staying with family or friends.

When we decide that we want to or have to stay away from home for one night or more we first need to find a place to stay. We have a number of places to look for information:

- At advertisements in the newspaper or in magazines
- At a travel agent
- In a guide book published by one of the organizations such as the AA, the RAC or Michelin
- By contacting the tourist office of the area we want to visit
- By asking a friend or a relative

Task 3.2

Working in small groups, obtain information from as many of the sources listed about accommodation away from your home. You may need to telephone or write to some of the sources listed.

From an initial enquiry to one establishment we would probably receive a *brochure* and possibly a *booking form*. This will give us an outline of the establishment and the facilities which it offers. It will have been sent to us from the Front Office.

Task 3.3

In your small groups, select some of the establishments which you identified in the previous task. Telephone or write to these establishments requesting a brochure. Try to select a range of different types of establishment.

When we have decided which establishment we like, our next step would be to complete the booking form and send it to them. Alternatively, we could *telephone* or write a *letter* to see if there were accommodation available. Our enquiry would be received and dealt with by the Front Office and, if we wanted to go ahead and make a firm *booking*, then they would attend to this.

When we arrive at the establishment of our choice we will need some means of getting into and, later, getting out of the building. Some establishments have a number of *entrances* and *exits* which may be separate for staff and for customers.

Task 3.4

Look around your college or school. How many entrances and exits are there? Are any of them for exit only? Is the Reception or Enquiry Office easy for visitors to find?

Once inside the building, we will need to know where our room is and where the various outlets are. We would go first to the *reception* area where our booking would be checked and we would be asked to *register* our arrival. We would also be given a key to our room.

We will require ways of obtaining *information* and for this we may use an *enquiry desk*. We will also need at least one method of communicating with the outside world, by *telephone*, telex or facsimile machine (fax). All these services are provided by the Front Office.

When the time comes for us to leave we may have to pay for the accommodation and services we have received. We do this by seeing the *cashier* who will make up our bill and receive our payment.

Another of the tasks of the Front Office is to *sell* the accommodation of the establishment. The standard and type of *accommodation* and the level of *accommodation services* offered is often an important aspect of this.

What are accommodation services?

These are the services provided to care for the customers when they are visiting an establishment. The term usually refers to the services required by customers who have booked sleeping accommodation. They include the cleaning and maintenance of the building, the provision of clean laundry and supplies such as soap and toilet paper. In many establishments they also incorporate some provision for customers to be able to have food and drink in or near their room.

Task 3.5

Make a list of the different types of room you may use during the course of any day.

When we arrive in an establishment we are allocated appropriate *accommodation*. We will expect this to be in an area which is *clean*. If we have been allocated sleeping accommodation we will assume that the bed has been made for us with *clean linen*. We would hope that the establishment is kept clean during our stay. In some establishments we will expect to be provided with supplies, such as soap, towels and stationery, and services, such as someone to do our *personal laundry* for us.

Task 3.6

From the brochures which you received try to identify any services which the establishment offers to its customers.

We will need to be kept *warm*. The majority of establishments within the hospitality and catering industry are centrally heated and fuelled by electricity, gas or oil. Some operations, especially those in old buildings, may feature an open coal or log fire to provide atmosphere and effect.

We will need to be provided with adequate *ventilation* and, possibly, *air conditioning* to keep the air clean, at an acceptable temperature and with a comfortable level of humidity.

A supply of *hot and cold water* will also be required as well as *sanitation* for personal washing. We will also need to be provided with a system of *drainage* for clearing away foul water, waste matter and other debris.

Much of the time we will be able to go to a restaurant, coffee shop or bar in order to get *food and drink*. There may be other times, such as in a hospital, when we have to depend on having our food served to us in the place where we sleep. We will need to be kept *safe* and *secure* while we are in the building.

Task 3.7

Suggest ways in which customers and their belongings can be kept safe and secure while staying in any establishment away from their own home.

Special customer needs

It is now a legal requirement that new buildings for hospitality and catering establishments must provide facilities for people who are disabled or have other special needs. This includes people who

- Are confined to a wheelchair
- Can only walk with difficulty
- Are blind, partially blind or have hearing problems
- Are suffering from a temporary disability such as a broken leg
- Are elderly
- Are travelling with young children
- Are women in the late stages of pregnancy
- Have mental health problems
- Have suffered some form of brain damage

The Building Regulations, which refer to providing suitable facilities for people with a disability or special need, give minimum standards for access such as suitable car parking and the incorporation of ramps. Minimum standards for bedrooms refers to the width of the doorway, the provision of Braille room numbers and an emergency call system. Bathrooms should have WCs, baths and basins at the appropriate height and with space to accommodate a wheelchair.

Task 3.8

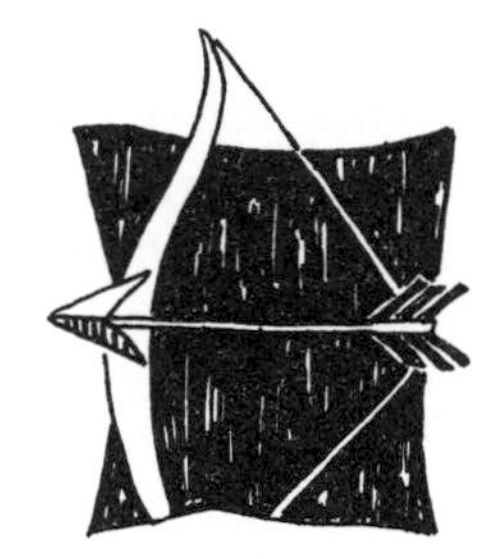

Investigate the provision made in public buildings in your area for people who have special needs such as those listed above.

Hotels

Hotels provide accommodation on a commercial basis. This means that they are selling sleeping facilities and places for consuming food and drink in order to make a profit.

The first area we will see when we arrive at a hotel is the Reception or Lobby area. In a purpose-built hotel we will probably find that this is a fairly large open area with lots of space for people and for their luggage. In hotels which started out as something else, such as a large house or a row of smaller houses, the available space for a Reception area may be more limited.

Large hotels divide the Front Office into a series of different desks. We may go to the Reception desk when we arrive where we will register our arrival and be allocated a room. In an increasing number of hotels we may be asked whether we would like a bedroom which has been designated as non-smoking. The room keys may be kept at the Enquiry Desk which will also distribute any letters or telephone messages which arrive for us. The Enquiry Desk will also arrange theatre or travel tickets and deal with any other queries which we may have. Our luggage will be looked after by the concierge or porter and, when the time comes for us to leave, we will pay our bill at the Cashier's Desk.

Smaller hotels do not have the staff or the space to have several different desks and so all the work is done from one desk, the Reception Desk.

After we have arrived and have completed our registration we then go upstairs to our room. We may have booked into one of the following rooms:

- *Single room* with one bed designed for one person
- *Twin room* with two beds designed for two people
- *Double room* with one bed designed for two people
- *Family room* with one bed for two people and with beds for one or more children.

Any of these rooms may be *en suite* (Figure 3.1).

Definition

- ***En suite*** *refers to a bedroom with a private bathroom forming one unit.*

In a luxury hotel we would also have the opportunity of booking into a *private suite*.

Definition

- *A* ***private suite*** *comprises one or more bedrooms, one or more private bathrooms and a private sitting room. There may also be a small kitchen for the preparation of hot drinks and snacks.*

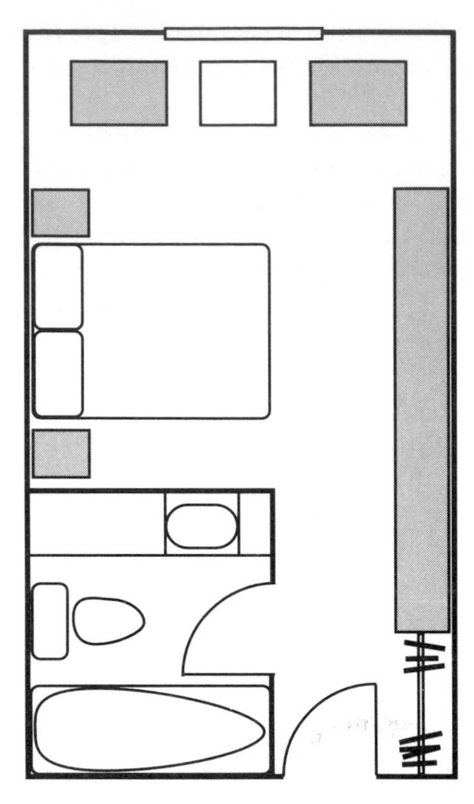

Figure 3.1 Plan of a typical hotel bedroom with en-suite bathroom

Our hotel bedroom and bathroom will be cleaned every day and our bed will be made for us. The bed linen will be clean on our arrival and will be changed regularly. In expensive hotels we may be given clean sheets and towels every day.

Should we require them we may be provided with extra pillows or blankets and many hotels supply these automatically by storing them in the wardrobe in the room. Facilities are offered for dealing with our personal laundry and dry cleaning. Rooms may be equipped with a hair dryer, a trouser or skirt press and we may request items such as a *bed board* or an ironing board.

Definition

- *A* ***bed board*** *is a flat board which slides between the mattress and the bed base to make the bed firmer. It is requested by customers who have a back problem.*

If we are travelling with small children we may require a cot or an additional single bed in our room and we may be offered a baby-sitting service. We may also wish to have some form of 'in-house' entertainment such as a television set. In some large hotels this includes satellite channels and in-house video programmes. In expensive, luxury hotels our room may be given a turn-down service in the evening (Figure 3.2).

Figure 3.2 Turn-down service

Definition

- ***Turn-down*** *is a service offered in a few luxury hotels. It is done in the evening. Bedspreads are folded back and the bedding is turned back to make it easier for the guest to get into bed. Any night clothes may be laid out neatly on the bed. The bedroom and bathroom will be tidied and the curtains closed. Before leaving, the room attendant may turn the bedside light on and leave a small box containing two or three complimentary chocolates on the pillow.*

Task 3.9

Arrange to visit a local hotel. Take note of the type of accommodation and accommodation services offered. If there are a number of you, in small groups arrange to go to different hotels. Compare the accommodation and services offered in the establishments visited.

After we have unpacked our suitcase we may decide to go back downstairs and explore the rest of the facilities. Close to the reception or lobby area we should find the *public areas*. They are known as public areas because they may also be used by customers who have not booked any sleeping accommodation.

1 *Restaurants* are provided for us to eat our meals. In large hotels we may have the choice of more than one restaurant each offering a different style of menu.
2 *Bars* are where we can buy and drink alcoholic and non-alcoholic beverages. There may be more than one type of bar in the hotel.
3 *Lounges* are provided for us to sit and relax. In small hotels we may find a television in the lounge but in larger ones it is usually in the guest's bedroom. In large hotels the lounge is an area where we can have morning coffee, afternoon tea or early-evening drinks.
4 *Function rooms*, sometimes known as banqueting suites, are where we may attend events such as formal lunches and dinners, conferences, meetings, receptions and dances.
5 *Cloakrooms and toilets* are provided for us if we are visiting the hotel but do not intend to stay the night. The cloakroom is a place where we can leave our outdoor clothing while we are in the hotel.

In many hotels we may expect there to be some service of drinks and meals in rooms or the provision of facilities for self catering such as a *courtesy tray* or a *mini-bar*.

Definition

- *A **courtesy tray** provides all the equipment and commodities required to allow us to make our own hot beverages such as tea, coffee or hot chocolate. This will include a kettle, teapot, cups, saucers, sachets of tea, coffee, chocolate, sugar and milk. We may also be provided with biscuits.*
- *A **mini bar** is a small refrigerator containing miniature bottles of spirits and appropriate mixers (tonic, soda, ginger), quarter bottles of wine and small bottles of fruit juice. Some mini-bars also contain vacuum packs of cocktail nuts or potato crisps. We help ourselves from the bar and this is later checked by hotel staff. We can then be charged for the items which we have consumed.*

In a large hotel we may be able to call on *room service*.

Definition

- ***Room service** is when food and drink is served to us in our room. We select our choice from the room service menu, telephone our order and, after a short time, the food is served. For breakfast service we are provided with an order form which we complete and hang outside our bedroom door before we go to bed. The menu is collected during the night and the meal is served at the time we have stated on our order.*

Some hotels have additional facilities such as a swimming pool or a *health club*.

Definition

- *A **health club** is like a small gymnasium with machines and apparatus for people to use for exercise. These are usually free of charge if we are staying in the hotel. If we are not staying but live in the neighbourhood we can choose to pay an annual subscription to join the hotel's leisure club which allows us to use both the pool and the health club.*

Task 3.10

Using hotel guidebooks such as the ones produced by the AA, the RAC, Michelin or the local tourist board find examples of types of hotel. Describe the different types of hotel listed. What features make them different?

Restaurants

There are many different types of restaurant for us to choose from but they all have one thing in common. They are all *providing accommodation where we can sit and eat a meal* which has been prepared on the premises for us.

The simplest of restaurants will include a dining area and toilet facilities. As they do not need to be booked in advance this type of restaurant is unlikely to require a receptionist but there may be someone to help us to find a vacant table during busy periods of the day. When we need to pay for our meal there may be a cashier or we may pay the person who served the food and drink to us.

Larger and more elaborate restaurants will have a separate reception area with a permanent receptionist responsible for taking advance bookings and receiving us when we arrive. There will probably be a bar with comfortable seating where we can wait until our table is ready.

This type of restaurant may also have a number of smaller dining rooms suitable for private parties. There may be a separate cashier who will prepare our bill and take our payment before we leave.

Task 3.11

Whenever you visit a restaurant of any type make a note of the reception arrangements and the method of payment for the food and drink.

Holiday camps

Holiday camps are also commercial establishments. Like hotels, they provide accommodation for sleeping, eating, drinking and for personal hygiene in order to make a profit. They are, not surprisingly, aimed at the holiday market, and in particular, the family market.

In recent years the companies who own holiday camps have spent millions of pounds to improve the accommodation and facilities and many have been renamed as *holiday centres*. Other holiday centres were specially built during the 1970s and 1980s as *activity centres* or *theme parks*.

On our arrival we would have to report to a reception office and we would probably find that this is very similar in appearance to the Front Office or lobby area of an hotel. We would also find a number of public areas similar to those found in a hotel.

Task 3.12

Make a list of the public area you would expect to find in a holiday camp or a holiday centre.

The accommodation where we would be expected to sleep will probably be an individual unit known as a chalet.

Definition

- *A **chalet** is a room or group of rooms which opens directly to the outside. There are very few chalets designed for single occupancy and most are designed to accommodate families or groups of up to eight people. There would be more than one bedroom and a private bathroom. The chalet may also have facilities for some cooking.*

Most holiday camps nowadays offer us a choice of restaurant. There is usually one which provides fast food as well as one which serves the food in a slower more relaxed manner. There will also be a choice of bars should we feel thirsty and possibly a nightclub for dancing.

As we would choose a holiday camp for rest and relaxation we will find sport and leisure areas such as swimming pools, tennis courts and table-tennis rooms as well as accommodation for outdoor activities such as horse riding, golf and walking.

Task 3.13

Visit a local travel agent and get copies of any brochures which advertise holiday camps, holiday centres, activity centres and theme parks. What are the special facilities provided? What are the differences, if any, between the different establishments?

Leisure centres are quickly replacing the standard swimming pool provided by local authorities. As well as a swimming pool, a leisure centre provides accommodation for some indoor sports such as table tennis and squash. There may also be a refreshment service area. Some are licensed to serve alcoholic drinks and others have extensive facilities which may be rented for birthday parties, wedding receptions and other types of function.

Task 3.14

Describe the special type of accommodation which may be required by a customer using a leisure centre.

Hospitals

Most of the large hospitals in the UK are operated within the National Health Service (NHS). There are also a number of smaller private hospitals. They both provide accommodation for us when we require medical assistance or treatment.

We need to be accommodated in a hospital for three basic reasons:

1 For a short period while we receive treatment or see a specialist doctor as an out-patient
2 For one or more days but spend the night in our own homes as a day-patient
3 For one or more nights as an in-patient

We may also need to be accommodated by a hospital if we are visiting or accompanying someone who is a patient. We may occasionally need to use the services of the Accident and Emergency department.

When we first arrive at the hospital, whether we are a patient or a visitor, we will probably need to ask the way. There is usually an information or reception desk which can give us all the help we need.

When we are out-patients or accident and emergency patients we first have to check-in or be checked in at the reception desk of the appropriate clinic. There may be a short delay before we can see the doctor and so we will need to sit in a waiting area. When it is our turn to see the doctor we will be accommodated in a consulting room which is private and has all the medical equipment the doctor needs.

If we have to go into hospital as a day-patient again, we will need to register at a reception desk. We will need somewhere to rest, perhaps a bed in a ward, and somewhere to receive the treatment we need.

As an in-patient we will probably be accommodated in a ward which means that we will have a bed in a large room which has six or perhaps twenty-six more beds for other patients with a similar illness. If we are very seriously ill or are in a private hospital we will be given a room of our own.

In hospitals the beds are made with clean linen but on a less frequent basis. This is usually done by the medical staff and not the accommodation services staff, especially if the patient is unable to get out of the bed. With one or two exceptions, hospitals do not provide a personal laundry service.

When we are in-patients we may not be physically capable of getting out of bed. We will therefore have to rely on someone serving our meals and providing us with something to drink at regular intervals. Meals and drinks may be served to us in bed. This is limited to the three main meals of breakfast, lunch and dinner with tea and coffee served at the appropriate times.

The Women's Royal Voluntary Service (WRVS) runs shops and tea bars in many hospitals which are used by out-patients and by people visiting patients in one of the hospital wards.

Some treatment is specialized and the hospital will have areas where this can happen such as

- *Physiotherapy* which involves using special exercise equipment
- *Hydrotherapy* is exercise in water and for this there will be a swimming pool. This pool is not for recreational swimming
- *Occupational therapy* is for people who have a temporary or recent disability and they need to relearn how to do basic domestic tasks. A section of this area is set up like a house with small areas to represent the different rooms.

Task 3.15

Look in your local hospital and identify other areas which a patient may need to use. Describe the type of accommodation provided for patients and visitors.

Residential homes

These are provided for people who, for one reason or another, cannot take care of themselves. The majority are for children, for people with a learning difficulty or for elderly people. Most of the children's homes, those for people with a learning difficulty and some of the elderly-care homes are run by the local council. These are not commercial establishments and are therefore not expected to make a profit. There are an increasing number of elderly-care homes operated on a commercial basis which are required to be profit making.

People stay in residential homes for a longer period than in the other types of accommodation we have dealt with so far. They do not have the need for a permanent reception desk but will have an office where a member of administrative staff will deal with bookings and will welcome new arrivals. The administrative office may also deal with the receipt of payment for the accommodation.

Some homes offer single bedrooms but many require their residents to share with one or two others. The rooms may be provided with a wash-basin with other sanitary facilities nearby. In residential homes for the elderly there may be a number of aids to mobility such as a stair lift, hand rails along the corridor or specially designed baths. There will be a dining room and a lounge for all residents to use. In some residential homes for the elderly there are facilities for residents to do some catering for themselves.

Task 3.16

What other special facilities might people in a residential home require?

Hostels

These are provided by universities and some colleges for students who have to study away from home. These are usually known as *halls of residence*. Hostels are also provided by some employers, such as the police, hospitals and some hospitality and catering establishments, to accommodate staff who are working away from home.

University halls of residence

These do not need a large reception area for the students as new arrivals are generally limited to the beginning of the academic year in late September or early October. At this time the Administration Department will need to make temporary arrangements to deal with the registration and the allocation of accommodation to students. A number of universities have decided to enter the tourist and conference market during the vacation periods in order to generate additional funds. These will need to provide a system for dealing with advance bookings and for the reception and registration of arrivals. The Administration Department may also need to provide a system to deal with the preparation of bills and the receipt of payment from students, tourists and conference delegates.

We will probably find that the sleeping facilities are very basic especially when we compare them with some hotels. We may find that those universities which are catering for the conference market may have rooms with more facilities. Rooms are usually for single occupancy and provide a bed, storage facilities and a wash basin.

Task 3.17

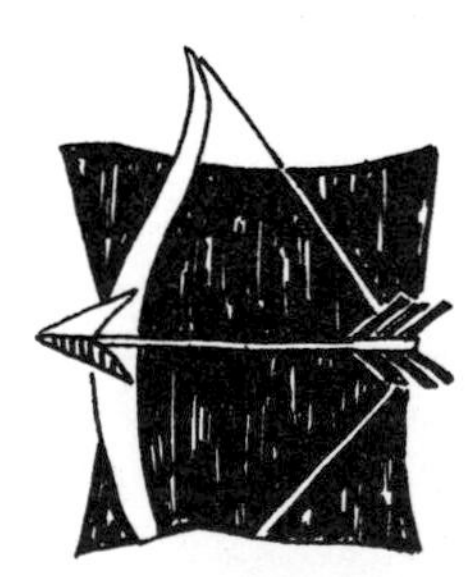

Describe the type of storage facilities required by a

- *Student*
- *Tourist*
- *Conference delegate*

accommodated in a university hall of residence

Toilets, baths and showers are provided in separate cubicles for everyone to use. Again some universities have rooms with en-suite bathrooms especially for the tourist and conference market. These are usually given, during the academic term, to postgraduate students who are older and generally more likely to look after them.

As students in a hall of residence, we may be supplied with clean bed linen on a weekly or fortnightly basis and we are usually required to make our own beds. In many universities we must provide our own towels. If we stay in a hall of residence as a conference delegate or as a tourist we will receive a service similar to that delivered in a hotel.

Utility rooms are provided for us to make our own hot beverages or to do any cooking.

Definition

- *A **utility room** provides facilities for storing milk and other perishables and appropriate equipment for cooking. There may also be limited facilities for students to do their own laundry and ironing. The utility room is often a place where students congregate while they eat and socialize.*

Some halls of residence have a dining room where we may be served with breakfast and an evening meal. Others are self-catering which means that we are provided with cooking facilities but have to supply and cook our own meals. Universities are well equipped with bars and these are frequently operated under the management of the Students Union.

Task 3.18

Arrange to visit a hall of residence at a nearby university. Note the standard and type of sleeping accommodation which is available for students. What facilities are available for eating and drinking? Is the university open during the vacation for customers other than students? Compare the facilities with those offered by the hotel which you visited.

Access

Most establishments will have a system of providing entry to the accommodation by both customers and staff. The most complex is the method used in hotels. This is based on a system made up of a number of types of key:

1. *The grand master key* – there are only one or two grand master keys in the system and these are carried by the Duty Manager and/or Security Officer. The key will lock and unlock any door in the system and will also *double-lock* any door.

Definition

- ***Double-locking** means that the lock can only be opened by using a grand master key. It cannot be opened with any of the other types of key.*

2. *The master key* is carried by Housekeepers and some others (e.g. Front Office Manager, Chief Engineer). It will open all doors in the system except those that are double-locked.
3. *The sub-master key* is carried by room attendants and room service staff and will open doors in one section of the building except those that have been double-locked.
4. *The room key* is the individual key which will only open the appropriate room unless it has been double-locked.

Many large hotels now use *electronic keys*. These are plastic cards linked to a computer system. They have a unique lock combination which is changed with the arrival of each guest. To maintain effective security of rooms:

- Keys should be secured to the holder by either a chain or a belt
- When not in use keys should be kept secure in a key cabinet
- Keys should be signed for when issued and signed back when returned
- Keys left in the key cupboard should be checked at regular times throughout the day
- If a key is lost the lock should be changed

Security

In any establishment this involves the security of the building and grounds, the contents including any cash and the security of the people who are using the building whether they are staff, residents or visitors. Many large establishments within the hospitality and catering industry employ security officers. They are responsible for making sure that everything is kept safe and secure by advising the management about security procedures and for making sure that staff follow those procedures.

Task 3.19

In small groups brainstorm and identify specific security problems which there may be in

- *Hotels*
- *Hospitals*
- *Halls of residence*

Maintenance

If you have ever been at home when the electricity has failed you will know what a nuisance it is. For problems like that to happen in a hospitality and catering establishment it is nothing short of a disaster. In a commercial establishment customers may be inconvenienced and may take their business elsewhere. In a caring establishment, such as a hospital or a residential home, the effects may be even more serious.

In order to maintain buildings such as hotels or hospitals many large establishments employ their own engineers, plumbers, electricians, carpenters and painters. These are organized as a Maintenance Department under the direction of the Works Manager or Chief Engineer. Smaller establishments may employ one or two general maintenance assistants and call in specialist help when required.

Task 3.20

Find out who is responsible for maintenance in your college or school. If possible, discover which specific maintenance tasks they are responsible for and which they have to contract out to a private company.

Health and safety

Why do we need to be aware of health and safety?

- Because the law requires it
- Because we have a moral obligation to take care of our customers
- Because customers would stop coming to an establishment if they thought it was not safe

Task 3.21

What will happen to an establishment if it allows its safety standards to drop in:

- *Customer areas?*
- *Non-customer areas?*

One of the things you should have identified in both areas is that there will be an increase in the number of accidents. Accidents are difficult to classify. Research indicates that all accidents are not one single, surprising, sudden event but are the end result of a series of events.

Some people are more at risk from accidents than others. People's sense of balance, steadiness of posture and walk, sight, hearing, sense of smell, sense of touch are all physical characteristics which vary between individuals. People with poor sight or hearing may be more at risk. Accident types may be related to the age of the victim – the young and old are at risk from certain types of accident.

Task 3.22

Which types of customer within the hospitality and catering industry would you identify as being more likely to be at risk from accidents?

Safety Audits (or safety checks) and hazard spotting are good methods of identifying health and safety problems. A safety audit is a careful check, item by item, department by department, of equipment, installations, procedures, rules and working practices. It is an organized exercise. Hazard spotting is the ability to recognize and take action on dangerous or possible dangerous places, systems or products which arise throughout the working period.

Task 3.23

Choose a hospitality and catering area such as a restaurant or an office and carry out

- A safety audit
- A hazard-spotting exercise

Some locations have more hazards than others. Kitchens may contain hot cookers, knives and slicers, stairs may be uneven, there may be no hand rail or the lighting may be poor.

Some products are more hazardous than others. Cleaning products such as toilet cleansers produce a toxic gas if mixed with sodium hypochlorite (household bleach) whereas substances for cleaning ovens are strong alkalis which are likely to damage the skin.

Task 3.24

Prepare a list of likely hazards within the Front Office and Accommodation Services areas. Are any more likely in one particular type of accommodation?

The Health and Safety (First Aid) Regulations 1981 cover the employers' responsibilities to their employees at work. They do not cover guests, visitors, customers, etc. The regulations require employers to make adequate first-aid provision for employees who are injured or fall ill at work. The Health and Safety Executive gives guidelines on this. It is dependent on such things as the number of employees, the nature of the work, degree of hazard and size of establishment. Employers must

- Provide sufficient numbers of first aiders
- Appoint people to take charge of an incident when first aiders are not available
- Appoint occupational first aiders wherever there are special hazards involved in the work
- Inform employees of the provisions

All businesses need to ensure that they have a suitable number of properly stocked first-aid boxes.

Task 3.25

Find out which items constitute a 'properly stocked' first-aid box. Are there any items especially designed for use in the hospitality and catering industry?

Accident reporting

There are more than 4000 injuries a year in the hospitality and catering industry. Many of these are slips, trips and burns and many could have been avoided if staff had been more cautious. Accidents are unpleasant but are always likely to happen even in the best-organized establishments. In the event of an accident if you follow correct reporting procedures then the information may be used to prevent similar accidents from occurring

All staff in the hospitality and catering industry should remember to record workplace accidents, employee sickness and absences. The records help to understand and prevent accidents and ill health in the future. There are also laws which require you to keep certain records and these may be used to provide essential evidence in the case of any legal action.

It is important that procedures are developed for dealing with accidents. If you are present when an accident occurs you should

1. Attend to the injured person
2. Remove or isolate the danger if this is possible without injuring yourself
3. Call a first aider, doctor or ambulance
4. Inform a higher authority or a safety representative
5. Make careful mental note of the accident area and of anything that may have caused the accident
6. Be prepared to make an accident report or assist in the accident investigation (see Figure 3.3).

Health and Safety Executive
Health and Safety at Work etc Act 1974
Reporting of Injuries, Diseases and Dangerous Occurrences Regulations 1985

Spaces below are for office use only

Report of an injury or dangerous occurrence

- Full notes to help you complete this form are attached.
- This form is to be used to make a report to the enforcing authority under the requirements of Regulations 3 or 6.
- Completing and signing this form does not constitute an admission of liability of any kind, either by the person making the report or any other person.
- If more than one person was injured as a result of an accident, please complete a separate form for each person.

A Subject of report *(tick appropriate box or boxes) – see note 2*

Fatality ☐ 1 | Specified major injury or condition ☐ 2 | "Over three day" injury ☐ 3 | Dangerous occurrence ☐ 4 | Flammable gas incident (fatality or major injury or condition) ☐ 5 | Dangerous gas fitting ☐ 6

B Person or organisation making report (ie person obliged to report under the Regulations) *– see note 3*

Name and address –

Post code –

Name and telephone no. of person to contact –

Nature of trade, business or undertaking –

If in construction industry, state the total number of your employees –

and indicate the role of your company on site (*tick box*) –

Main site contractor ☐ 7 | Sub contractor ☐ 8 | Other ☐ 9

If in farming, are you reporting an injury to a member of your family? (*tick box*) ☐ Yes ☐ No

C Date, time and place of accident, dangerous occurrence or flammable gas incident *– see note 4*

Date [ ] [ ] [19] (day month year) Time –

Give the name and address if different from above –

Where on the premises or site –

and

Normal activity carried on there

ENV

Complete the following sections D, E, F & H if you have ticked boxes, 1, 2, 3 or 5 in Section A. Otherwise go straight to Sections G and H.

D The injured person *– see note 5*

Full name and address –

Age ☐ Sex ☐ (M or F)

Status (*tick box*) – Employee ☐ 10 | Self employed ☐ 11 | Trainee (YTS) ☐ 12 | Trainee (other) ☐ 13 | Any other person ☐ 14

Trade, occupation or job title –

Nature of injury or condition and the part of the body affected –

F2508 (rev 1/86)

continued overleaf

Figure 3.3 An accident report form

E Kind of accident - *see note 6*

Indicate what kind of accident led to the injury or condition (*tick one box*) →

Contact with moving machinery or material being machined ☐ 1	Injured whilst handling lifting or carrying ☐ 5	Trapped by something collapsing or overturning ☐ 8	Exposure to an explosion ☐ 12
Struck by moving, including flying or falling, object. ☐ 2	Slip, trip or fall on same level ☐ 6	Drowning or asphyxiation ☐ 9	Contact with electricity or an electrical discharge ☐ 13
Struck by moving vehicle ☐ 3	Fall from a height* ☐ 7	Exposure to or contact with a harmful substance ☐ 10	Injured by an animal ☐ 14
Struck against something fixed or stationary ☐ 4	*Distance through which person fell ☐ (metres)	Exposure to fire ☐ 11	Other kind of accident (give details in Section H) ☐ 15

Spaces below are for office use only.

F Agent(s) involved — *see note 7*

Indicate which, if any, of the categories of agent or factor below were involved (*tick one or more of the boxes*) —

Machinery/equipment for lifting and conveying ☐ 1	Process plant, pipework or bulk storage ☐ 5	Live animal ☐ 9	Ladder or scaffolding ☐ 13
Portable power or hand tools ☐ 2	Any material, substance or product being handled, used or stored. ☐ 6	Moveable container or package of any kind ☐ 10	Construction formwork, shuttering and falsework ☐ 14
Any vehicle or associated equipment/ machinery ☐ 3	Gas, vapour, dust, fume or oxygen deficient atmosphere ☐ 7	Floor, ground, stairs or any working surface ☐ 11	Electricity supply cable, wiring, apparatus or equipment ☐ 15
Other machinery ☐ 4	Pathogen or infected material ☐ 8	Building, engineering structure or excavation/underground working ☐ 12	Entertainment or sporting facilities or equipment ☐ 16
			Any other agent ☐ 17

Describe briefly the agents or factors you have indicated —

G Dangerous occurrence or dangerous gas fitting — *see notes 8 and 9*

Reference number of dangerous occurrence ☐ Reference number of dangerous gas fitting ☐

H Account of accident, dangerous occurrence or flammable gas incident - *see note 10*

Describe what happened and how. In the case of an accident state what the injured person was doing at the time —

Signature of person making report ☐ Date ☐

Case study

Every day between 3.30 p.m. and 4.30 p.m. one of the floor porters at the Station Hotel is responsible for clearing the rubbish sacks from the room maids' trolleys. The sacks are collected in a trolley and taken to the large dustbins in the loading bay area. Depending on the level of occupancy and the amount of rubbish collected, it is sometimes necessary for the porter to make more than one journey.

On the day Ron Bush was responsible for clearing rubbish from the room maids' trolleys the hotel had been fully occupied the previous night. It was his last job for the day and, as it had been a busy day, he was late starting. By the time he had collected from the fifth and sixth floors his trolley was very full and he had to make a trip to the loading bay before continuing with the lower floors.

There appeared to be less rubbish to collect from the remaining floors but, nevertheless, Ron's trolley was nearly full by the time he reached the second and last floor. It was getting late and so, to avoid making an extra journey, he balanced the last two sacks on to the top of the pile and made his way to the loading bay.

As he arrived at the dustbins the top bag wobbled and fell to the ground, bringing with it a further three sacks. One of the sacks burst open on impact, scattering its contents over the floor. As Ron collected up the pieces he came across a number of pieces of broken glass. In his haste when trying to pick these up he cut his hand badly.

Task 3.26

How would you describe Ron's accident? What were the chain of events which led to it?

Task 3.27

Referring to the case study above, fill in the accident report form for Ron Bush.

If the establishment employs ten or more people and the accident is not serious then an *accident book* should be completed (Figure 3.4).

Fire prevention

In all establishments we will need some means of defence should there be other threats such as a *fire*.

Fire is a chemical reaction called *combustion*. To start and to maintain this reaction you need three ingredients:

1 *Fuel* – something which will burn, either solid, liquid or gas
2 *Oxygen* – the air contains approx 20 per cent oxygen
3 *Heat* – once a fire has started it normally maintains its own heat

ACCIDENT BOOK

1 About the person who had the accident	2 About you, the person filling in this book	3 About the accident
▼ Give full name ▼ Give the home address ▼ Give the occupation	▼ Please sign the book and date it ▼ If you did not have the accident write your address and occupation	▼ When it happened ▼ Where it happened
Name	Your signature Date / /	Date Time / /
Address	Address	In what room or place did the accident happen?
Postcode	Postcode	
Occupation	Occupation	

4 About the accident - what happened

Reporting of Injuries, Diseases and Dangerous Occurrences, RIDDOR 1985

For the Employer only

Please initial the box provided if the accident is reportable under RIDDOR

▼ Say how the accident happened. Give the cause if you can.
▼ If any personal injury say what it is.

How did the accident happen?

Employer's initials

Figure 3.4 An accident book

What are the causes of fire?

There are almost 2000 fires per year in hospitality and catering establishments in the UK. There are many causes of fire, most of them due to carelessness by both customers and staff. The majority are caused by:

- Careless smokers
- Electrical faults
- Open fires
- Stored chemicals
- Incorrect disposal of waste
- Cooking and heating equipment

Task 3.28

Working with a group of others, make a list of the places within hospitality and catering establishments where fires are likely to start. Try a brainstorming session to come up with ideas as to how fires may be prevented in these areas.

Why do we need to be aware of fire safety?

When a fire breaks out there are two main dangers:

1 *Destruction* of human life and of property
2 *Panic* which overcomes people and prevents them from thinking clearly

If we know what to do when a fire breaks out there is no need for any original thought. Our action should be automatic. There is, therefore, a good chance that we will take the correct action and so prevent needless loss of life and damage to property.

What to do in case of fire

Each establishment will set up its own procedures and staff will be trained in their own particular responsibilities. If you hear the fire alarm

- Remain calm
- Walk – do not run
- Alert the customers and make sure they know there is a fire

If you discover a fire

- Raise the alarm by operating the nearest fire alarm
- Call for assistance according to the procedures of the establishment
- Only attack the fire using the equipment provided if it can be done without putting yourself in danger

Before you leave the building

- Switch off all electrical and gas appliances
- Close windows and doors which are not on the escape routes
- Do not collect personal belongings
- Leave the building using the nearest exit.

The law protects us in most public buildings. Under various Acts of Parliament it is unlawful for owners of buildings used by the public to continue with their business unless they possess a *fire certificate* issued by the local authority. This limits the number of people who can be on the premises at any one time. It also covers the provision of:

- Fire warning systems, including notices for staff and guests
- Fire fighting equipment
- Escape routes
- Regular training for staff in firefighting and evacuation procedures

Should a fire start we would trust that there are detectors to locate smoke, flames or heat and that these are connected to an alarm system. We would also expect that the various areas within the establishment are equipped with the most appropriate firefighting equipment.

Task 3.29

Go around your college or school, or another building with which you are familiar, and see where the fire extinguishers have been placed. What type of extinguishers can you identify?

▪ Assignment ▪

Task 1
Working as a group, identify a number of establishments which provide Front Office and Accommodation services. Make a list on a flipchart or a board.

Task 2
Working in groups of two or three, select establishments from the list. Make sure that each group is responsible for a cross-section of establishments and that you include some establishments you can visit easily.

Contact all the establishments by writing to or telephoning at least one of them to request information about the facilities offered.

Task 3
Each small group arranges to visit one of the establishments from their list and investigates the Front Office and Accommodation services offered. Make a presentation of the establishment, explaining the Front Office and Accommodation services, including the arrangments to ensure the safety and security of the customer, to the rest of the group.

▪ PROVIDING FRONT OFFICE SERVICES ▪

In this section we will be examining the way in which establishments provide the many services required of the Front Office. We shall look at systems which may be used to record advance bookings, receive customers and take payment in establishments offering facilities and services for sleeping and eating. We shall also examine the methods of communication which may be relevant to an establishment providing Front Office services.

We will refer to the health and safety procedures which apply particularly to the Front Office. You will also need to consider the health and safety aspects described in the other two sections of this unit as they may also apply.

Many different types of establishment need to use some of the services described in this section. Hotels need to use them all. For this reason the section will refer more frequently to the services offered by hotels.

Front Office services

The Front Office is the central point of many establishments. It is responsible for providing the following services:

1 Selling and marketing the establishment
2 Recording advance bookings
3 Receiving and registering incoming customers
4 Keeping a record of rooms and who is currently staying in each
5 Dealing with incoming and outgoing mail
6 Dealing with the establishment's communication systems such as telephone, telex and fax
7 Providing information in response to a customer's enquiries
8 Dealing with customers who are leaving, including the payment of bills

When we are looking for sleeping accommodation, plan to go out for a meal or to play table tennis or squash the first stage is to decide where to go. If we do not have a hotel, leisure centre or restaurant in mind then we may have to look for one. We may decide to answer an advertisement which interests us or to look up a suitable establishment in the telephone directory. We would then either telephone or write to the establishment to find out more details about the services or the accommodation offered.

When we reply to an advertisement we may be sent a brochure. Some brochures have a booking form attached which we are invited to complete and return. If we do have a favourite hotel, leisure centre or restaurant we may decide to telephone them in order to make the booking.

Advance bookings

Many aspects of the hospitality and catering industry accept bookings in advance. We can reserve rooms and conferences in hotels, tables in restaurants and squash and tennis courts in leisure centres. From the customer's point of view this is a means of making sure that the room, the table or the court will be available when we arrive. At certain busy times of the week or year it guarantees us the accommodation at the time we want it. From the establishment's point of view it gives a guide to expected business and allows us to plan for the future. It also gives us a clear indication to the availability of the facilities if a *chance customer* arrives.

Definition

- *A **chance customer** is one who arrives requesting the use of the facilities without having made a prior booking. In a hotel it is someone who has not previously booked a room and in a restaurant, someone who has not previously booked a table.*

As well as asking whether a room, table or court is available, customers will need to know how much this is likely to cost. In a hotel information about room prices is shown on the tariff:

1. *Room only (European plan)* is the rate for the room with no meals included
2. *Room and breakfast (Continental plan)* is the rate for the room and for breakfast. The breakfast included may be Continental with a supplement for English breakfast
3. *Half board (demi-pension, modified American plan)* includes room, breakfast and one other meal. Customers may not have the choice of which other meal is included in the plan
4. *Full board (en pension, American plan)* includes room, breakfast, lunch and dinner. Some hotels in seaside resorts may also include afternoon tea
5. *All-inclusive terms* are used in hotels with sports and social facilities. The room rate includes all meals and free use of all the facilities
6. *Two for one* is a system where the partner of a guest is offered free accommodation but charges are made for all meals
7. *Children free* is a rate which allows children free accommodation so long as they are sharing the room with one or two adults

All hotels are legally obliged to display details of the room tariff at the reception desk. The law states that the prices quoted must include the service charge and also indicate whether the price quoted includes tax. As members of staff responsible for accepting advance bookings we need a system which will allow us to:

- Check whether there are any vacancies for the period requested
- Record the booking
- Prepare a list of bookings for a particular day just before arrival

Every booking is a legal contract. Although a contract does not need to be in writing for it to be legal, most establishments require certain written records to be kept in case of a dispute. There are three main records which may be used to record advance bookings:

1. Reservation form
2. Bookings diary
3. Booking chart

Reservation form

This is a pre-printed form on which we record the details of one booking or reservation (Figure 3.5). The form is printed in a logical sequence so that all the required information is obtained. It also acts as a prompt when we are taking the booking so that we are sure to give the customer all details about the establishment, such as *release time*.

Definition

- ***Release time** refers to the actual time that a booking will be closed on the expected day of arrival. In busy hotels it may be 6.00 p.m., after which time the room may be sold to another customer. Customers cannot expect that the booking will still be available if they arrive after release time.*

NAME ....
(BLOCK LETTERS)

RESERVED BY ....

ADDRESS ....

.... TEL. ....

REQUIREMENTS ....

ARRIVAL DATE .... LENGTH OF STAY ....

ARRIVAL DATE .... LENGTH OF STAY ....

TERMS ....

REMARKS ....

....

....

DATE .... SIGNATURE ....

Figure 3.5 A pre-printed reservation form

Bookings diary

This is normally a loose-leaf book with one or more pages for each day. The first page is always the current day and new pages are inserted at the back as they are required. Bookings are entered from the reservation form as soon as they are made. In some hotels reservations made by letter may be entered straight into the diary (Figure 3.6). A bookings diary is a method which can also be used to record reservations for a table in a restaurant and for sports accommodation at a leisure club.

It is routine in establishments such as seaside hotels to ask for a non-returnable deposit to be paid at the time of booking. Details of the deposit are noted in the bookings diary and will be credited to the customers' account when they arrive.

Booking charts

There are two types of booking chart:

1 A *conventional chart* shows all the hotel room numbers down the left-hand side and the dates of the month across the top (Figure 3.7). When we record the booking we decide which room to allocate to the customer and then draw a line across the chart from the arrival date to the date of departure. We then write the name of the customer across the top of the line. A conventional chart may be used in small establishments or in those, such as university halls of residence, where the customers stay for more than one or two nights.
2 A *density chart* is used in larger hotels or in hotels where the customers stay only for one or two nights (Figure 3.8). When a reservation is recorded on this chart the customer is not allocated a particular room. The number of single, twin and double rooms are listed down the left-hand side and the days of the week or month across the top. When a booking is accepted we mark off the number of nights required, starting with

11th March 198–

Date of booking	Name(s)	No. of persons	Length of stay	Accommodation required	Terms	Remarks	Room allocated
27-1-8-	JAMES Mr K	1	3N	1 – B	£10·00	arriving late	11
7-2-8-	BROWN Mr/s G	2	1N	1 =	£12·00		23
13-2-8-	SMITH Messrs J&I	2	7N	1 = B	£14·00	garage	18

Figure 3.6 A bookings diary

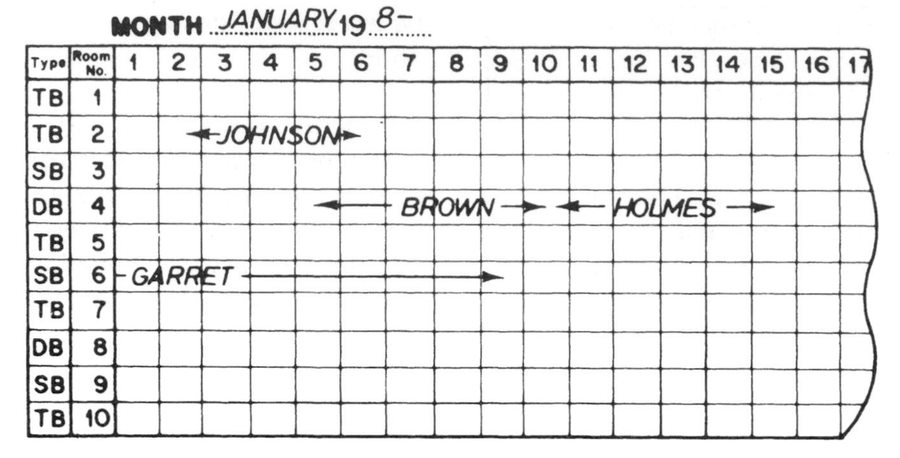

Figure 3.7 A conventional chart

the night of arrival. A *bookings diary* is always used with a density chart. This records all the details of the expected customer such as their name, address and length of stay. The density chart does not show any of these details.

In large hotels it would be very time consuming to refer to the chart every time a request for accommodation was received. These establishments use a *stop-go chart*. This gives a summary of the booking chart and particularly highlights periods when the hotel is full.

Many hotels, restaurants and leisure centres now have a computerized system of recording bookings. When the details of the booking are entered into the program the information is recorded in both the diary and the chart.

Where a booking has been made by telephone the establishment may request that the customer confirms this in writing. Alternatively, many establishments send a letter to the customer confirming the booking. This was originally by letter but the development of more immediate methods of communication has led to confirmation by:

- *Telex*, a system of sending a written message using a telephone line, or
- A *fax* machine which transmits an exact copy of the written information also using a telephone line.

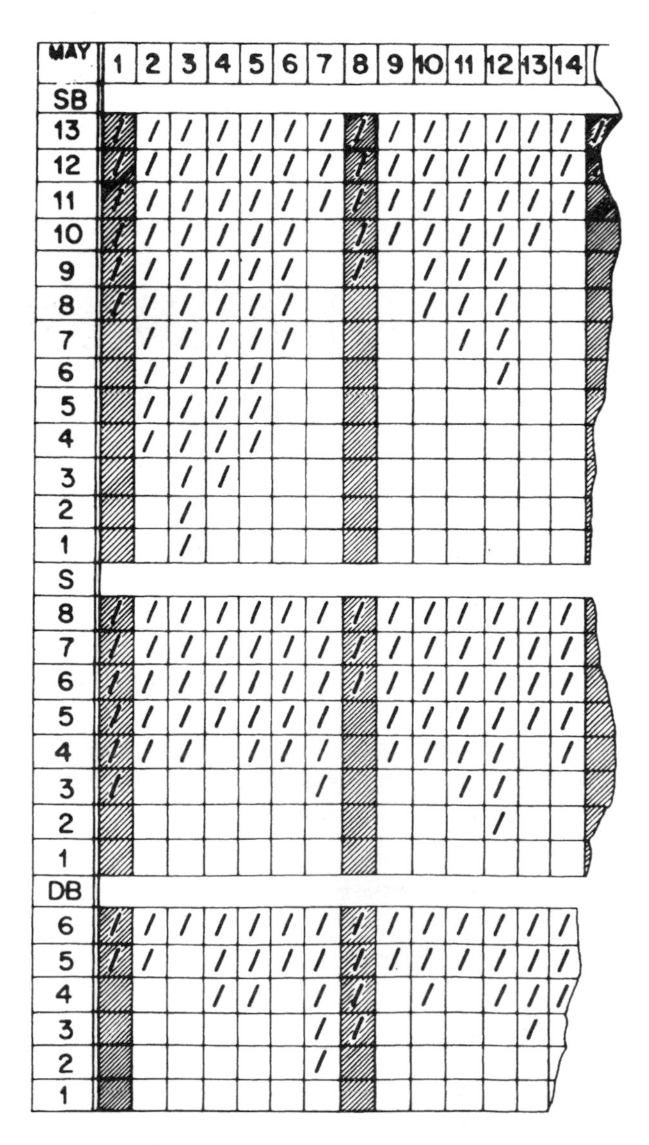

Figure 3.8 A density chart

Some of the computer programs which deal with bookings have the facility to automatically issue a confirmation letter as soon as the reservation is entered.

The section of the Front Office responsible for dealing with bookings is also required to produce an *arrival and departure list*. This is prepared last thing at night and lists all the expected changes in the establishment for the following day. The list shows:

1 The names of all expected arrivals, the number of people included in the booking, the number of nights they are expected to stay and any special requirements (e.g. a baby's cot in the room).
2 The room numbers of all guests who are expected to leave the hotel.
3 The names and room numbers of any guests who are moving from one room to another.

The list is sent to the manager and all the departments of the establishment. The porters then know how much luggage is likely to pass through the lobby, the housekeeping department know which rooms to re-sheet and which require additional items (e.g. baby's cot to put into a room), and the restaurant knows how many customers they are likely to have.

In some hotels a separate list shows the *tour* arrivals.

Definition

- *A **tour** is a number of people, ten, twenty, thirty or more, who are booked into a hotel by a travel agent. They usually have a set itinerary and will, therefore, all arrive and depart at the same time. They will also all probably want to eat in the restaurant at the same time.*

The tour arrival list may be separate from the arrival and departure list. It may be sent out earlier than the latter to allow departments to plan their work and to make sure that they have sufficient staff on duty to deal with the work.

A computerized system of bookings may be able to produce a printout of all arrivals and departures or to allow interested departments to view the list on a monitor in their offices. Alternatively, the list would have to be prepared using information from the bookings diary.

Registration

When a customer arrives at a hotel for sleeping accommodation we are legally obliged to register their arrival in writing. If the customer is a British citizen or from one of the Commonwealth countries we are required to record:

- Their name
- Their nationality

Task 3.30

There are over forty countries in the British Commonwealth. How many of these can you identify?

Customers from other countries, known legally as 'aliens', are also required to provide:

- Their passport number
- The place their passport was issued
- Their next destination

Most hotels provide a pre-printed *registration card* which includes all the details that a hotel requires (Figure 3.9). For example, those with car parking may need details of the customer's car registration. To cut down on costs some

Grand Metropolitan Hotels

Name (Nom)

First Names (Prénoms)

Nationality (Nationalité)

REGISTRATION CARD

Home Address (Adresse du domicile)

OVERSEAS VISITORS

Passport No. (No. du passeport)

Issued at (Délivré à)

Destination Address (Adresse de destination)

Your attention is drawn to the displayed Hotel Proprietors Liability Notice.

Signature

Room No.	No. of Persons	Charge	Date of Arrival	No. of Nights or Departure Date	REMARKS	Rec.

Figure 3.9 A registration card

establishments have the registration details printed on the back of the reservation form.

Hotels which have a computer system are usually able to transfer booking details onto the registration form automatically. All the customer has to do then is to check that the details are correct and sign the form.

The Front Office uses the information about arrivals and departures to keep track of the *room status*.

A room can be:

- Let
- Vacant but not ready for re-letting
- Vacant and ready to be re-let
- Out of service for redecoration or repair

When customers arrive, we need to be able to give them a room as quickly as possible. In small establishments we may have allocated the rooms when we took the booking. In larger ones we may not decide which room to allocate until the customer arrives. In this situation we need to know the status of the rooms. There are a number of methods of doing this.

The *bedroom book* is the simplest system. It is a method which may be used in hotels which have less than twenty rooms. The bedroom book is like a diary with a page for each day. It lists all the room numbers down the left-hand side of the page. When new guests arrive we enter the name against the number of the room they are going to occupy. The name is also written against that room number on the appropriate page for every day of the guest's stay.

Most establishments now have a type of *room status board*. This is a board with a number of slots or a metal rack into which we file a small card with all the customer details written or printed on it. In a large hotel a room status board allows us to register and allocate more than one guest at a time. In busy periods, this prevents large queues from forming at the reception desk.

Some hotels have an *electronic status board* which links the Front Office with the housekeeping department and the cashier's office. It is based on a system of lights:

1. No lights – the room is occupied
2. Red light – the room is vacant but has not been cleaned
3. Red light and white light – the room attendant is working in the room
4. Red light and green light – the room has been cleaned but the standard has not been checked by the housekeeper
5. Green light – the room is ready to re-let

Those hotels which have a computer system can check the room status easily and quickly. When the customer registers, the status of the rooms is immediately updated. It is therefore most unlikely that two customers are allocated the same room.

Keys

When the customers have registered they need to be given a key to get into their room. In large hotels they may also be issued with a *key card*.

Definition

- *A **key card** is a small card or booklet which briefly describes the outlets within the establishment. The customer's name, room number and room rate are written on the card. The customers need to show the card before being issued with a key or charging any meals or drinks to their account.*

The guest room keys are kept at Reception except in large hotels, where they may be held by the concierge, the porter or at the enquiry desk. Keys are usually attached to a large metal or plastic tag in an attempt to prevent customers from taking the key with them when they leave the hotel.

Electronic keys are replacing the traditional metal key. These are flat plastic cards, similar to a credit card, which are programmed with a different combination number for each new arrival. If a customer loses the key it is a relatively simple procedure to reprogram the lock and so maintain high security.

At the same time as we are issuing customers with their key we may also take note of any requests for a morning newspaper or an early-morning alarm call. Many hotels now have either an alarm clock in the room or an automatic system for early-morning calls which is connected to the telephone exchange.

Information and enquiries

While the customers are in the establishment they may need a variety of information. Many customers choose the Front Office as the most appropriate place for this.

All the Front Office staff should be able to deal with customer enquiries and to converse with the customer in a pleasant and friendly manner. In some establishments there may be staff able to communicate in various languages. Customers may require information about:

- Facilities within the establishment
- Events taking place within it
- Facilities in the immediate area of the establishment such as museums, galleries and churches
- Sightseeing tours of the local area
- Shopping facilities
- Visits to the theatre or cinema
- Travel such as bus, train and air timetables and tickets

Task 3.31

In order to answer all the enquiries the Front Office needs to be equipped with a number of reference books. Make a list of the reference books which may be useful to provide the information listed above.

The Front Office may need to provide information about guests in residence. It is the obvious place for a person visiting a guest to make their enquiries. The Front Office will first check to ensure that the customer is staying in the establishment. We would then telephone the guest to inform them of the visitor. If they are not in their room then we may 'page' them using the public address system. If they are out of the hotel then a message will be taken and given to the guest when he or she returns.

It is up to the guest to say whether they wish to receive a visitor. The Front Office should always be aware of security procedures and never send anyone to a room without the guest's permission. A casual visitor should not be told a guest's room number.

Security

Hoteliers have a strict duty to care for the property of their guests. The law defines a guest as a person who has booked a minimum of one night's accommodation. A hotel proprietor is strictly liable, with certain exceptions, for any property of a guest which has been lost, stolen or damaged. Liability may be limited if a disclaimer notice is displayed. The notice must be:

1 On display when goods are brought into the hotel
2 Printed in clear type
3 Displayed at or near the reception desk

NOTICE

LOSS OR DAMAGE TO GUESTS' PROPERTY

Under the Hotel Proprietors Act 1956, a hotel proprietor may in certain circumstances be liable to make good any loss of or damage to a guest's property even though it was not due to any fault of the proprietor or staff of the hotel. This liability, however,

(a) Extends only to the property of guests who have engaged sleeping accommodation at the hotel.
(b) Is limited to £50 for any one article and a total of £100 in the case of any one guest except in the case of property which has been deposited, or offered for deposit, for safe custody.
(c) Does not cover motor cars or other vehicles of any kind or any property left in them, or horses or other live animals.

This notice does not constitute an admission either that the Act applies to this hotel or that liability thereunder attaches to the proprietor of this hotel in any particular case.

This liability is confined to hotels, and that includes areas such as the car park, the swimming pool, the garage and the grounds. It does not include private hotels or restaurants.

The customer may ask that their property is placed in *safe custody*. The establishment may have safety deposit boxes situated in the Front Office area. The customer is given one key and the cashier keeps the other key. The box can be opened only when both keys are used together.

Smaller establishments may place the items in the main safe. The proprietor may ask that it be put into a fastened container or a sealed envelope.

Security alerts

It is an unfortunate sign of the times that establishments such as hotels have been targets for terrorist bombs whether actually placed in the establishment or sent through the post. When this type of security problem arises the Front Office staff must always be alert to suspect packages. If a suspect package is found it should not be touched.

Suspect letter bombs may be discovered by Front Office staff particularly if there are a number of VIPs or dignitaries staying. A letter bomb may be a parcel, package or letter delivered through the post or a courier service that explodes on opening.

If a telephone threat is received the Front Office staff will become most involved as it is usually the telephonist who is the first person to be aware of any potential threat. It is important that every call received must be treated seriously.

As soon as the call is completed or a suspect package is found the manager on duty should be informed. They should then inform the police. The police will advise as to evacuation and will search the building.

Fire precautions

When a fire breaks out the Front Office is the central point of communication. The person discovering the fire will inform the Front Office who are responsible for calling the fire brigade.

The Duty Manager will be informed and will make the decision to evacuate the building. The Front Office staff should make sure that they have a room occupancy list as the fire officer will want to know which rooms were let.

Keeping accounts

Every establishment needs a system to keep a record of the amount to charge the customers. In a number of establishments all that is required is a *cash register* or till and a *cash book* which gives details of the income received. Hotels do not normally expect customers who have booked sleeping accommodation to pay each time they use one of the outlets. Customers who have a prior booking are allowed to charge meals, drinks, newspapers, etc. to their account and to pay for everything just before they leave the hotel. Chance customers may be expected to pay as they go along.

There are three methods we may use to keep a record of customers' accounts.

Tabular ledger

This is a method which is very rarely used nowadays. It is, however, useful to learn how a tabular ledger or 'tab' works as the other two methods are a mechanized and a computerized version of this system (Figure 3.10). The ledger consists of loose-leaf sheets, one for each day. The room numbers are written or printed across the top and the hotel services are listed down the left-hand side.

At the beginning of the day the only entries will be the balance of account owing from the previous day. Whenever the customer uses the outlets of the hotel a bill is written and sent to the Front Office. The amount owing is then copied from the bill to the appropriate column of the ledger. When customers are ready to leave the hotel the ledger is totalled, the charges are transferred from the ledger and presented in the form of a bill, including *value added tax* (VAT).

Definition

- ***VAT** is a government tax which must be added to all bills. If the hotel adds a service charge then this must also be taxed. Records of VAT must be kept and shown to officers of HM Customs and Excise should they request this.*

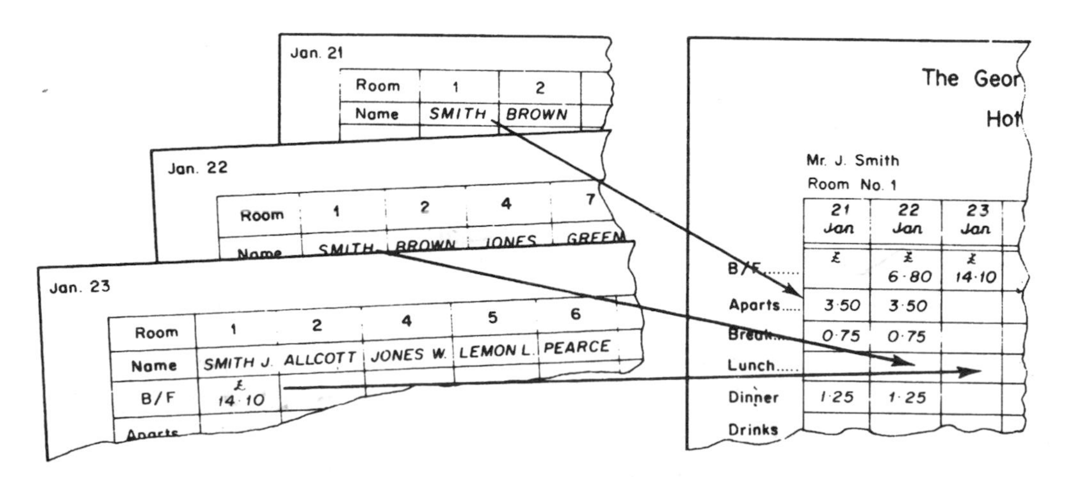

Figure 3.10 A tabular register – this system is now usually computerized

At a set time of the day the room charges will be entered for all accounts. For new arrivals the room charges are entered as soon as the guest has registered and for continuing guests some time in the late afternoon or early evening.

At the end of the late shift, at about 10.30 p.m., the account is balanced. All the vertical columns and all the horizontal columns are totalled. Then all the vertical totals and all the horizontal totals are added together. If both these totals are the same we can close the desk and go off-duty. If they are different then we have made a mistake somewhere and we will have to start checking the columns until we can find it.

Billing machine

This is a machine which, like the tabular ledger, records and stores all the charges for each customer. It will also print the individual bills and produce a daily summary of sales.

Computer billing

Many hotels nowadays have a computer program installed to deal with customers' accounts. Basically the computer is doing the tabular ledger but has eliminated much of the paperwork.

Methods of payment

Cash used to be, and for small transactions still is, the most common method of payment. An establishment may legally insist that a customer pays in cash but most accept other methods of payment as a service to the customer. There are limits to the cash, or legal tender as it is known, which an establishment can accept in coins.

Task 3.32

Go to a bank and find out the limits for payment in 1p, 2p, 5p, 10p, 20p and 50p pieces.

Prices have risen and in some hotels where it is possible to run up a bill of several hundred pounds in a few days cash is not very practical. From the establishment's point of view cash also presents considerable security problems.

Task 3.33

List the types of transaction in the hospitality and catering industry for which cash would be a very suitable method of payment.

Foreign currency is a method of payment most common in areas where there are a number of overseas visitors. Establishments generally accept most well-known currencies such as the French franc or the German mark but not all currencies. A list of those that are acceptable should be kept by the cashier.

In accepting foreign currency the establishment is providing a service to the customer. The establishment will probably charge for this service and so the rate of exchange will be slightly less favourable than that offered by a bank.

Task 3.34

From the finance section of a national newspaper find out the rate of exchange of the common currencies. When you visit a hotel compare the rates offered by the hotel with those quoted in the newspaper.

Cheques are the most common method of payment in many establishments and are a secure method providing the basic rules are followed:

1. The cheque is accompanied by a cheque guarantee card.
2. Only one cheque per transaction is used. Many guarantee cards guarantee payment up to £50. If a bill is more than £50 (say, £70) the bank will not accept two cheques of £35 each in payment.
3. The cheque is signed in the presence of the cashier.
4. The signatures on the cheque and on the card are the same.
5. The bank codes on the cheque and on the guarantee card are the same.
6. The card number is written on the reverse of the cheque.
7. The guarantee card has not expired.

When accepting a cheque the cashier should make sure that:

1. The date is correct. A postdated cheque (i.e. one dated some time in the future), will not be valid until that date. A cheque which is dated more than six months past is 'stale' and is no longer valid.
2. The words and numbers agree. If they are different the cheque will not be paid.
3. Any alterations are signed by the person writing the cheque.

Travellers cheques are a common way for overseas customers to pay their bills. They may be bought in the currency of their own country or in British currency, known as *sterling*. The cheques are bought in advance from a bank or a major travel agent and are issued in *fixed denominations*.

Definition

- ***Fixed denomination*** *means that the cheques are available only in fixed amounts such as £10, £20, £50, etc.*

When travellers cheques are bought they have to be signed in the presence of the issuing cashier, who also takes a note of the numbers of the cheques. This acts as an insurance against theft or loss.

A cashier accepting payment by travellers cheque needs to see the customer sign and date the cheque. If it has been signed already the cashier should ask the customer to sign again on the back of the cheque as a precaution against fraud.

Eurocheques are issued by a bank and are used with a Eurocheque guarantee card. They allow customers to write cheques in the currency of the country they are visiting. The rules for accepting a Eurocheque are the same as those for an ordinary cheque.

Task 3.35

Visit a local bank and ask for information about Eurocheques and travellers cheques.

Debit cards are a common method of payment in establishments which are able to accept them. The card, which has a microchip in the plastic, is 'swiped' through a computerized terminal. This records all details of the transaction and the customer's account is debited immediately.

Task 3.36

During your visit to the bank obtain details of the debit card.

Credit cards are also a very common method of payment. The two main personal credit cards, Access and Barclaycard, are issued through the banks. The customer is charged a small annual fee and interest on any balance outstanding at the end of each month. The establishment has to pay commission to the credit card company.

There are also credit cards issued by companies such as Forte. These cards can be used only in that particular company's establishments and nowhere else.

Charge cards, sometimes called *Travel and Entertainment* or *T and E cards,* are different from credit cards. The customer pays a subscription every year and is required to settle the account in full at the end of every month.

The procedure for accepting credit and charge cards is the same

1 Check that the account is within the establishment's *floor limit.*

Definition

- ***Floor limit*** is the maximum amount of payment by card which the establishment can accept. For an account over the floor limit a cashier would have to telephone the card company for clearance to accept the payment.

2 Prepare a sales voucher.
3 Obtain the card from the customer.
4 Using *an imprinter,* take a print of the card onto the sales voucher.

Definition

- *An **imprinter** is a special machine which embosses information from the plastic credit or charge card onto the sales voucher.*

5 Pass the voucher to the customer to sign – keep the card.
6 Check that the signatures on the voucher and the card are the same.
7 Give the card and the top copy of the sales voucher to the customer.

Credit card sales vouchers are paid into the bank along with the cash, cheques, etc. Charge card sales vouchers are sent to the card company at regular intervals and a cheque is sent in return.

In establishments where there is a computer terminal at the paying point it may be possible to 'swipe' the card. This will record all the transactions and print out a slip for the customer to sign.

Task 3.37

Many garages and large supermarkets have a 'swipe' system for accepting card payments. If you have not seen one in operation try to accompany someone who is going for petrol and paying by card so that you can watch the transaction.

Ledger accounts are offered by the management to customers who use the establishment frequently. This allows the customer to sign the bill on leaving and the establishment will then send an account at the end of the month. They may be offered to companies or to individuals. Both will need to have proved that they are creditworthy by providing bank references. For a company there may be a list of people who are authorized to sign their bills and also a limit as to what they can sign for. For example, they may be able to sign for accommodation and meals but not for telephone calls or drinks in the bar.

Lien

Lien gives the proprietor the legal right to keep a guest's property in the event of an unpaid bill. It can only be used to offset bills for food and accommodation. The proprietor may keep a guest's property, except for a car, until such time as the bill is paid.

If the bill remains unpaid for six weeks the goods may be sold. This must be at a public auction which is advertised at least one month before the sale in a London and a local newspaper. After the sale the proprietor may keep:

- The amount of unpaid bill
- Any necessary costs
- The expenses of the sale

Any surplus must be returned to the guest.

Customers who fail to pay for food, drink or accommodation before departure may be charged under the Theft Act 1978 which provides power of arrest for anyone who has reasonable cause to suspect that a guest is intending to leave without payment. If that guest is subsequently convicted the maximum penalty is 5 years' imprisonment.

▪ PROVIDING ACCOMMODATION SERVICES ▪

In the first section of this unit we identified that customers staying away from home require accommodation for eating, drinking, sleeping and personal hygiene. In this section we will be looking at how establishments provide the accommodation services that their customers require.

One of the most important services is that of keeping the building clean. In order to do this it is necessary to know which chemicals and equipment are used to maintain the appropriate standards for a clean and safe environment. We shall also examine some of the skills required to carry out the basic services and identify the need for the operation of safe working practices.

The importance of hygiene

The type of accommodation that the customers select may well depend on their first impressions of the establishment.

- Is it clean?
- Is it attractive to look at?
- Are the furniture and furnishings in good repair?

If we describe something as 'clean' we usually mean that it is free from dust, dirt, grease, stains or litter. A large amount of the work involved in providing accommodation services is that of keeping the building clean. We clean so that:

1 All areas of the building look attractive
2 The health of the people who use the building is not damaged
3 The required areas within a building are hygienic
4 The furniture and decoration will last longer

Task 3.38

Which of the above reasons is the most important to customers using a:

- Restaurant?
- Kitchen?
- Bathroom?

Place these reasons in order of importance for

- A hotel
- A hospital

Cleaning standards

We all expect to stay in accommodation which is clean but often we have different expectations from each type of establishment.

Task 3.39

Look back at your answers to the previous task. Did you identify different reasons for cleaning in the various areas? Did you have a different order of priorities for a hospital and a hotel?

A guest in a hotel will expect cleanliness which is different from that expected by a patient in a hospital or a student in a hall of residence. There are basically three standards of cleanliness:

1 *Normal or basic standard* is the standard which we will find in most colleges and schools. It is a level of cleanliness where all litter and obvious dirt is removed daily. University halls of residence and staff accommodation in hotels and hospitals are usually cleaned to this standard.
2 *Clinical standard* is a level of cleanliness which must be very high. Surfaces are frequently tested to see that harmful bacteria are not present. Operating theatres and high-risk areas of a hospital such as a burns unit need to be kept at this standard.
3 *Prestige standard* is where the level of cleanliness is high but emphasis is placed on the appearance of the surfaces rather than on the level of bacteria. Surfaces are kept shiny and dust free. If necessary, areas will be cleaned more than once per day. It is a standard at which many hotels aim.

Task 3.40

Identify areas, other than those given, within the various sectors of the hospitality and catering industry which should be cleaned to each of these standards.

We are cleaning away

- *Dust* which is made up of minute particles of skin, hair, leaves, ash, textile fibres, salt
- *Dirt* which is dust mixed with grease or water
- *Stains* which are marks that cannot be removed by normal washing
- *Litter* which is identifiable pieces of paper, metal or plastic

Routine cleaning is the type of cleaning which we carry out on a regular basis, every day, every night or every week. It includes daily (or nightly) tasks such as low dusting, sweeping, suction cleaning, damp mopping, cleaning glass, cleaning sanitary fittings, emptying ashtrays and wastepaper bins. It also includes weekly or monthly tasks such as buffing or spray cleaning hard floors and high dusting.

Periodic cleaning is carried out at specific times during the year. It is sometimes known as 'spring cleaning'. It includes tasks such as carpet shampooing, wall washing, floor stripping and repolishing.

Routine cleaning methods

Low dusting

Low dusting is the control of dust from areas which are within arm's reach when you are standing on the floor.

Task 3.41

Make a list of all the surfaces and items in a room which are within arm's reach.

It is not possible to remove dust completely and so you need to select the method which is the most suitable for the surface. The following equipment can be used:

Low dusting

- *Dusters* – cotton check or pieces of brushed cotton cloth suitable for dusting or polishing wood, glass or metal surfaces. When using dusters they should be folded several times to provide a number of clean surfaces. They should be laundered frequently
- *Carpet brush* – a stiff hand brush for cleaning carpeted stairs and for the edges of the carpet near the skirting
- *Radiator brush* – a stiff round brush for cleaning behind a radiator

Sweeping

Sweeping is the control of dust from a hard floor. You can use:

- *Brooms* – long-handled brushes for sweeping hard floors
- *Dust control mops* – a more efficient method of controlling dust on hard floors than sweeping with a broom. They are made from a wooden, metal or plastic frame attached to a long handle. You have to stretch the mop head over the frame before you can use it. When using a dust control mop you should use straight or 'figure-of-eight' strokes, keep the mop in contact with the floor surface all the time and launder the mop head frequently
- *V sweepers or scissor mops* – two large dust control mops which are joined together like a pair of scissors. These are very suitable for large areas of floor such as a ballroom or a wide corridor
- *Hand brushes* – soft brushes with a short handle used for collecting sweepings after using a broom or a dust control mop. Used together with a dustpan
- *Box sweepers* – manually operated, sometimes called carpet sweepers, are used for light cleaning of carpeted floors

High dusting

High dusting is the control of dust from areas which are beyond arm's reach. What happens is that the dust is moved from the high surface. It falls to a lower level where it can be collected with either a dust control mop or a suction cleaner, and then disposed of.

Task 3.42

Make a list of all the areas in a room which are beyond arm's reach.

The following equipment can be used:

- *Cornice brush* – an oval-shaped brush used for dusting ceilings and tops of walls
- *Feather duster* – a bamboo handle with feathers attached for 'flicking' dust from walls, light fittings and the tops of pictures
- *High dusting mop* – a long-handled mop, which can be extended, with a cotton mop head used for dusting walls and ceilings

Task 3.43

Collect a range of equipment suitable for controlling dust. Use each one for its intended purpose. Make notes on each item of equipment – does it do the job well, is it heavy to use, are there any other points you notice?

Suction cleaning

Suction cleaning is the control of dust using an electric suction cleaner with a variety of attachments. You can use:

- *Upright cleaners* are primarily designed for cleaning soft floor coverings such as carpets. Some models have attachments which may be used to control dust from other surfaces (Figure 3.11)

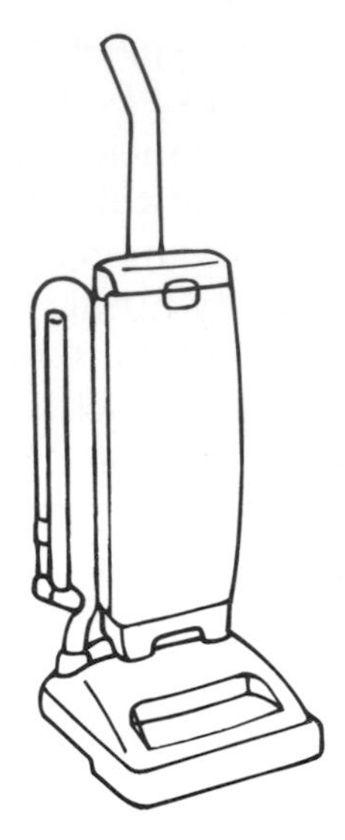

Figure 3.11 An upright cleaner

- *Cylinder cleaners* are suitable for light suction cleaning of surfaces such as hard floors, stairs, furniture and upholstery. They must be used with the appropriate attachment
- *'Back vacs'* are cylinder cleaners which are designed so that you can carry them on your back like a rucksack and use them with one of the attachments. They are best for areas which are not easy to reach with the other types of suction cleaner
- *Canister or tub cleaners* are suitable for light suction cleaning from surfaces similar to cylinder cleaners using the appropriate attachment (Figure 3.12). Because the air flow passing through the machine does not pass the electric motor, they can be adapted by the manufacturer so that you can use them to pick up dust or water.

Definition

- ***Centralized vacuuming*** *is based on a central dust collection area. The building is linked with pipes and there are vacuum points around the building. Hoses are fitted to the vacuum points and the dirt is sucked along the pipes to the central collection area.*

Figure 3.12 A canister cleaner

If we are using a wet suction cleaner we should:

5 Make sure the *float valve* works properly

Definition

- *A **float valve** is fitted to a wet suction machine between the water tank and the electric motor. As the water level rises the valve floats on the surface. When the water reaches a predetermined level the valve closes a small hole, cutting off the air supply to the motor. This prevents any water reaching the electric motor and the operator receiving an electric shock.*

Task 3.44

Collect a range of suction cleaners. Use each for its intended purpose. Make notes on each item of equipment – does it do the job well, is it heavy to use, are there any other points you notice? Compare your notes with those you made for dust control.

Task 3.45

Suction cleaners used to remove dust are often known as 'Hoovers'. This is not a correct description as there are other manufacturers who make suction cleaners. Look in a variety of catering or cleaning industry magazines. How many different manufacturers of suction cleaners can you identify?

Before using a suction cleaner we should:

1 Use the most appropriate machine and the correct attachments
2 Make sure that the cable and the plug are in good order
3 Check that the dust bag is not full
4 Check that the filter is clean

After using a suction cleaner we should:

1 Empty bags and containers
2 Remove and clean all attachments
3 Clean the machine and cable
4 Change the filter regularly

Damp wiping

Damp wiping is when we use a cloth dampened with water and a cleaning chemical to remove dirt from surfaces which are within arm's reach. Dirt is a mixture of grease or water and dust. It often gets embedded into a fabric or surface and can be difficult to remove. The following equipment can be used:

- *Dishcloth* – knitted cotton cloth used for washing or wiping dirt from a wide variety of surfaces
- *Disposable cloths* – paper or reprocessed cotton cloths for general cleaning designed

to be thrown away after they are no longer fit for use

- *Sponge* – synthetic cellular cloths which can hold a lot of water
- *Wipes* – non-woven cotton cloths for general cleaning available for a range of tasks, from wiping surfaces to cleaning cookers

After using equipment for damp wiping we should:

- Wash them and leave them to dry
- Alternatively, we could send them to be laundered
- If they are disposable throw them away
- *Not* leave them standing in cleaning solution

Cleaning chemicals for damp wiping

Water is cheap and easy to obtain but used on its own it has poor cleaning powers. In order to successfully remove dirt it is necessary to add a cleaning chemical to the water to improve its cleaning power.

Detergents are the chemicals most often used with water for cleaning. They contain a wetting agent which helps the water to soak into the surface more quickly. There are a number of detergents from which to choose:

1. *Soap*, which is not regularly used in the hospitality and catering industry for cleaning surfaces as it is not effective in hard or cold water. It is, however, used for personal hygiene.
2. *Synthetic or soapless detergents*, which are widely used for cleaning surfaces of all types.
3. *Neutral detergents* are those used for washing up and general cleaning. The majority of neutral detergents for general cleaning are supplied as liquids and usually require further dilution before use. They are also available in powder form, mainly for laundrywork.
4. *Alkaline detergents* are used to remove grease and heavily embedded dirt particularly from cookers and stoves. These are available in liquid or powder form and usually require dilution before use. When using this type of detergent it is important to remember to wear rubber gloves.
5. *Germicidal detergents* are a mixture of detergent and disinfectant and are designed for use in food hygiene areas. It is not advisable to try to mix these yourself as many types of disinfectant become ineffective when mixed with a detergent.

Control of Substances Hazardous to Health (COSHH) Regulations

These came into force on 1 January 1990. They were introduced to protect people from most hazardous substances at work including cleaning chemicals. The Regulations require an employer to:

- Conduct an assessment of substances used or produced in the workplace by relating to all situations in which they are used and the employees who use them
- Control the exposure of employees to those substances by means ranging from the prevention of their use to providing satisfactory ventilation and personal protection
- Monitor the workplace atmosphere and conduct health checks on employees where appropriate
- Inform, instruct and train employees on the risks created by exposure and precautions to be taken when using hazardous substances

Knowledge of hazardous substances bought in, such as cleaning chemicals, is readily available from reputable suppliers.

Glass cleaning

Glass is a surface which is used extensively within the hospitality and catering industry.

Task 3.46

Make a list of all the different ways that glass may be used as a surface cover within the hospitality and catering industry.

Task 3.47

Collect a range of chemicals and equipment suitable for cleaning glass. Make notes on each item of equipment and each chemical. Does it do the job well, is it heavy to use, are there any other points you notice?

Some equipment is specially designed for glass cleaning:

- *Chamois leathers* – originally these were made from the skins of the chamois, a type of wild antelope, but are now either split sheepskin or a synthetic alternative. You should use a chamois leather with water by itself or water and vinegar. It should never be used with a synthetic detergent
- *Scrim* – is an unbleached linen cloth which does not leave bits of fibre on the surface after cleaning. This makes it especially suitable for glass
- *Squeegee* – is a blade, rather like a windscreen wiper, fixed to a handle. It is used to wipe the water from the glass leaving it clear and with no streaks

Chemicals used for cleaning glass surfaces include:

- *Synthetic neutral detergent* diluted with water
- A solution of *vinegar* and *water*
- *Manufactured glass cleaners* are made from water, a solvent and a synthetic detergent or alkali. Some have also a fine abrasive added to improve the cleaning effect

Cleaning of sanitary fittings

All hospitality and catering units will have sanitary fittings which will require cleaning regularly. Sanitary fittings are fitted to the drainage system and are for the disposal of waste.

There are two types:

1. *Waste appliances* such as sinks, slop sinks, baths, wash basins, bidets and showers collect and dispose of dirty water
2. *Soil appliances* such as toilets, urinals, sluices and bedpan washers collect and dispose of human waste matter

Task 3.48

Walk around your college or school and identify as many of the above appliances as you can. Compare the type and design with those at home or in places such as hospitals, hotels, restaurants.

All the equipment suitable for damp wiping hard surfaces may be used to clean sanitary fittings. In addition the following pieces of equipment may be used:

- *Bottle brush* – a small, round brush for cleaning taps, sink and wash-basin overflows
- *Toilet brush* – a stiff, round or angled brush for cleaning inside a toilet bowl
- *Abrasive pads* – non-woven nylon pads used for the removal of small patches of heavily ingrained dirt. They are sometimes fixed to one side of a sponge

Chemicals suitable for cleaning sanitary fittings include:

- *Synthetic neutral* and *alkaline detergents* as well as
- *Abrasive cleaners* which 'scratch' the dirt from a surface. The most commonly used abrasive cleaners are designed for cleaning enamel or ceramic sanitary fittings such as wash basins, baths and showers and are available as liquids, creams, pastes or powders. They should not be used on plastic or painted surfaces
- *Acid cleaners* are used for cleaning toilets and urinals and for removing stains in baths and wash-basins caused by dripping taps. They are harmful to the skin and, if mixed with household bleach, will produce a toxic chlorine gas.

Task 3.49

Collect a range of chemicals and equipment suitable for cleaning sanitary fittings. Use each item/chemical for its intended purpose. Make notes on each item of equipment and each chemical. Do they do the job well, are they difficult to use, is there an unpleasant smell with any of the chemicals?

Damp mopping

Damp mopping is when you use a damp mop and a bucket containing water and a detergent to remove dirt from hard floor surfaces. Equipment used for damp or wet mopping includes:

- The *socket or do-all mop* – a round mop consisting of strands of cotton attached to a metal socket. The socket is fixed to a long wooden handle. It should be used with a *strainer bucket* which has a cone-shaped strainer to one side designed for squeezing the water from the mop
- The *Kentucky mop* – a flat mop made from cotton strands which is clipped to a specially designed quick-release fitting on a long handle (Figure 3.13). The Kentucky mop should be used with either a roller bucket or a lever bucket

Figure 3.13 A Kentucky mop

- The *Foss mop* – a dense cotton fringe attached to a weighted base. It is used with a specially designed bucket
- The *sponge mop* – a piece of synthetic sponge attached to a handle and fitted with a self-wringing device. Oblong or oval buckets may be supplied with this type of mop

- A *roller bucket* which has two rollers across the top which are operated by a foot press to squeeze the water out of the mop
- *Lever buckets* – single, double or triple bucket systems either fitted with castors or mounted on a trolley. They have one or more detachable presses which squeeze the water from the mop

Buckets are made from either galvanized steel or reinforced plastic.

When using wet mopping equipment we should:

1 Allow the mop to do the work – do not press down onto the surface
2 Work in a side-to-side or 'figure-of-eight' action
3 Keep a straight back and do not overstretch
4 Change the cleaning and rinsing water frequently

After using wet mopping equipment we should:

1 Wash the mop head and leave it to dry
2 Rinse out the bucket and store upside down – this stops pools of water remaining

Remember – bacteria grow and multiply in dirty water and wet mops.

Task 3.50

Collect a range of equipment and chemicals suitable for damp mopping. Use each for its intended purpose. Make notes on each item of equipment – does it do the job well, is it heavy to use, are there any other points you notice?

Rotary floor machines

Cleaning floors is made easier by using a rotary floor machine. The base of the machine is fitted with either a drive disk with an abrasive pad or a brush and this rotates at high speed. These machines are powerful and can be very dangerous if used by people who have not been trained to use them properly.

Methods used to clean and maintain hard floor surfaces using a rotary floor machine

- *Dry buffing* – using a tan or white polyester pad fixed to a drive disk to make a floor shine
- *Spray cleaning* – with a detergent solution in a hand spray and a blue or red polyester pad fixed to a drive disk to clean and shine in one operation
- *Spray polishing* – with a specially designed floor polish in a hand spray and a blue or red polyester pad fixed to a drive disk to clean and shine in one operation. This method leaves a film of polish on the surface to achieve a deeper shine
- *Spin mopping* – with water and a detergent and a specially designed bonnet fixed to a drive disk to damp mop more quickly than with a mop and bucket
- *Bonnet buffing* – with carpet shampoo in a hand spray and a specially designed bonnet to remove surface greasy dirt from a carpet
- *Carpet skimming* – with carpet shampoo in a hand spray and a thin white polyester pad to remove greasy surface dirt from a carpet
- *Scrubbing* – with water and a detergent and either a green nylon pad or a brush to remove ingrained dirt and grease from a floor surface
- *Stripping* – with water and an alkaline detergent and a coarse brown or black polyester pad to remove old polish from a floor surface before putting down a new layer
- *Carpet shampooing* – with carpet shampoo and a shampoo brush to remove dirt from a carpet

Before using a rotary floor machine we should:

1 Always check that the plug and the flex are in good order
2 Fit the pads or brushes with the machine switched off
3 Do not switch on at the mains until ready to operate

When using a rotary floor machine we should:

1 Work backwards towards the socket point
2 Keep the cable tidy and away from the rotating machine

After using a rotary floor machine we should:

1 Remove the disk and pad or the brushes – never store a machine resting on the disk or on the brushes
2 Make sure the pads and brushes are cleaned
3 Make sure the machine and cable are cleaned

Hot water extraction is an alternative method of cleaning carpets using a specially designed carpet-cleaning machine and a low-foam detergent in hot water. *Carpet and upholstery cleaners* are neutral detergents designed for use with carpet- and upholstery-cleaning machines. Some machines require a high-foam detergent whereas others must be used with a low-foam detergent. It is important that you use the correct type.

Polishes are used to protect and to improve the appearance of floors, furniture and metals. Floor polishes fall into two categories. *Solvent-based* wax is designed for use on wood, cork and linoleum floors and *water-based* wax, which is an emulsion of wax and water. Furniture polishes are a blend of wax, spirit solvent and silicone available as a solid wax, as a liquid or cream or as an aerosol spray. Metal polishes are manufactured from a fine abrasive powder and a solvent, an acid or an alkali depending on the type of metal for which they are designed. They are available as an impregnated cloth, sponge or wadding or as a liquid.

Miscellaneous

There are a number of chemicals which do not fit neatly into the above categories. There is a carbon dioxide aerosol spray specifically designed for assisting in the removal of chewing gum. The carbon dioxide freezes the chewing gum, making it easier to 'chip' off the surface.

Bleaches are chemicals which remove the colour from fabrics and surfaces. They are used in cleaning to remove stains from white surfaces and may also be used as a disinfectant.

Organic solvents are a group of chemicals which dissolve fats, oils, grease and a variety of other substances including plastic. They include methylated spirit, white spirit and acetone. Some are flammable and others are dangerous if inhaled.

Disinfectants cannot clean surfaces and should therefore only be used after cleaning has taken place. There are a number of different types of disinfectant available and for each of these to be fully effective it is essential that you follow the manufacturer's instructions.

1 Most cleaning chemicals are designed for specific tasks and these are indicated on the label.
2 You should always use the correct chemical to prevent wastage and to avoid any danger.
3 Use the correct quantities as specified on the label. Using more than the recommended amount will not make the surface any cleaner. In some cases, such as adding too much foamy detergent to a bucket of water for damp mopping, it will make the task longer to carry out.
4 Do not mix chemicals as this may injure skin or eyes or create toxic fumes.
5 It is important to know that:
Strong acids and alkalis are corrosive and will damage human skin and many surfaces
All alkalis, even mild ones, can cause skin irritation

The colour dyes used in carpets and in furnishing fabrics may be destroyed by alkaline detergents

Task 3.51

Under supervision and wearing protective gloves as you will not know which chemicals might irritate your skin, mix some solutions of common cleaning chemicals. Use samples of washing-up liquid, glass cleaner, toilet cleaner, toilet soap, washing soda, household bleach. Dilute according to the manufacturer's instructions. Use Universal Indicator Paper to find out which are acid, which are alkali and which are neutral.

Trolleys

When cleaning we usually have to carry around a variety of cleaning chemicals, equipment and supplies which are awkward to transport. Trolleys are useful for:

- Carrying cleaning agents and small equipment
- Holding rubbish
- Holding soiled linen
- Carrying supplies of clean linen
- Carrying guest supplies such as soap and toilet paper

If only a small amount of items are to be carried or a trolley would create a nuisance, then a *housemaid's box* may be used.

Cleaning methods

Choosing the most suitable method of cleaning depends on:

1 The surface finish: is it hard or soft? Will it be damaged by water? Are there any chemicals which damage it?
2 The level of soiling: how dirty is it?
3 The place which needs cleaning: is it completely free of people or is access required?

Task 3.52

The most common cleaning methods have all been described earlier in this section. Without looking them up *see how many you can remember.*

Cleaning is like any other type of work. You get the best results if you follow the rules.

General guidelines

- Dust, suction clean or damp wipe hard surfaces
- Suction clean or shampoo soft surfaces
- Use polish sparingly
- Do not wet the backs of mirrors
- Dust, suction clean or damp wipe picture frames
- Wipe telephone mouthpieces with germicidal detergent
- Synthetic, neutral detergent is sufficient for most routine cleaning
- Disinfectants, including bleach, are unnecessary if cleaning is carried out correctly
- Always work safely
- Use safety warning signs in public areas
- Empty ashtrays into fireproof containers (old catering size instant coffee tins are ideal)
- Do not stretch cables across walkways
- Leave a dry path when damp mopping
- Open windows and remove litter and obstructions first
- Carry out jobs which produce dust, such as bed making, before dusting
- Start from the point which is the furthest from the exit and work towards the exit

- Finish wet work, except for floors, before dusting and polishing
- When cleaning sanitary areas work from clean surfaces to dirty surfaces
- Close the windows before dusting
- Use the method which will not disturb the customer – do not vacuum early in the morning, always damp wipe in patient areas of a hospital
- Dust from high to low – work from the top down
- Mop sweep before damp mopping or using a floor machine
- Always clean the floor last

One way to show cleaning methods in a way which everyone can understand is to use a *work card.*

Definition

- *A **work card** lists all the equipment and chemicals which are required to do a particular task. It also gives the method to follow in order to complete the task.*

Example: Routine cleaning of a wash basin

Equipment	*Chemicals*
Damp dishcloth	Synthetic detergent
Dry cloth	
Nylon web pad	

1. Remove soap and personal property to one side
2. Remove any waste from the overflow and the plug hole
3. Half-fill the basin with hot water
4. Apply a little synthetic detergent to the damp dishcloth
5. Clean outside the basin, the pipes, the splashback, the taps and the area behind the basin
6. Empty the basin and refill with clean water
7. Rinse all the areas
8. Empty the basin
9. Apply detergent to the damp cloth and clean the remainder of the basin, the plug and the chain
10. Rinse well
11. Dry the taps, plug, chain and inside the basin with the dry cloth
12. Replace personal possessions and soap

This method may also be followed when cleaning a bath, a shower or a bidet

Task 3.53

Using the above guidelines, write out orders of work for cleaning areas such as a lounge area in a hotel or a waiting room in a hospital. Use areas of your college or school, such as the restaurant, and work out the procedures for cleaning them.

Methods of organizing cleaning

- *Conventional cleaning* – where one person completes all the tasks required in one room before moving on to the next. For example, a room attendant in a hotel cleans 16 rooms. When conventional cleaning, all the tasks in one room will be completed before moving on to the next room.
- *Block cleaning* – where one person completes one task in all rooms before moving to the next task. (For example, a room attendant in a hotel cleans 16 rooms. When block cleaning, one task (e.g. bed making) will be completed in all 16 rooms before moving on to the next task.)
- *Team cleaning* – where a group of three or four people work together each having their own task to complete in an area before the whole team moves on to the next area. (For example, room attendants work in a group of three responsible for 48 rooms. They will go

into each room, one will clean the bathroom while the other two make the beds. One of these two will then dust and clean the bedroom while the other will suction clean the carpet.)

Task 3.54

Identify situations in the hospitality and catering industry where each of the above methods of organization would be appropriate

Linen and laundry services

The result of many of the operations in the hotel and catering industry is a very large pile of dirty washing! Customers to any establishment providing sleeping accommodation will expect to be supplied with bed and bathroom linen and it is these residential establishments which have the largest amount of what is generally referred to as *linen*.

Definition

- ***Linen*** *refers to those items which are launderable (i.e. they can be washed). It includes sheets, pillow slips, towels, bath mats, tablecloths, napkins, tea towels, bar cloths and kitchen cloths.*

Bedrooms in hotels are either:

1 *Departures* – the current guest is leaving and the room must be prepared for a new guest. This means that the bed linen and bathroom linen must all be changed and additional guest supplies placed in the room. The room must be checked thoroughly for any lost property left behind by the departing guest.
2 *Stayovers* – the current guest is staying in the room for a further night or nights. The bed linen is not changed daily, except in luxury hotels, but may be changed every two to three days. Guest supplies will only be replenished where they have been used and the guest's personal possessions should not be disturbed.

Rooms in halls of residence are thoroughly cleaned weekly. They may be checked and rubbish removed daily. In most halls students are expected to make their own beds. Linen is usually changed once every two weeks.

In a hospital ward the cleaning staff may not be responsible for making beds particularly if the patients are not able to get up. Linen is renewed when necessary. If someone is spending all their time in bed this may be every day. Patients who can get up and walk about will need to have their bed linen changed less often.

Domestic staff in hospitals do need to replenish water jugs and rubbish bags fixed to each patient's locker.

Health and safety

The main legal obligations towards health and safety at work in Great Britain and Northern Ireland are contained in the Health and Safety at Work Act 1974 (sometimes referred to as HASAWA). The two most important aspects of this Act are:

1 That *everyone* at work such as employers, employees, self-employed people, trainees, contractors *and* anyone else who may be affected by the work such as guests, customers, clients, visitors, members of the general public are protected by the Act.
2 That *everyone* at work has a legal duty to look after the health and safety of colleagues and

anyone else, including people who are not employees, who may be affected by their work.

Task 3.55

Identify procedures which may be followed by staff in accommodation services departments of the hospitality and catering industry to look after the health and safety of their colleagues and customers

Employees at work have a legal duty to

- Take reasonable care for their own health and safety
- Make sure that colleagues and other people are not harmed by their acts or omissions
- Cooperate with the employer to meet health and safety requirements
- Make sure that they do not interfere with anything or misuse anything provided in the interests of health and safety

Task 3.56

Identify ways in which cleaning staff can ensure the health and safety of customers, visitors and staff using the building.

The people responsible for enforcing the Health and Safety at Work Act in most of the hospitality and catering industry are the *Environmental Health Officers* (EHOs). They work from environmental health departments run by local authorities.

EHOs may enter our premises at any reasonable time and carry out an inspection. They do not have to give us any prior warning and they do not require the permission of the owner, occupier or person in control of the premises. If the EHOs have reasonable grounds for expecting any trouble they may take a police officer with them.

If the EHOs discover a breach of the law they may

1. Advise you of the problem and ask you to correct it within a stated period of time
2. Issue a prohibition notice forbidding the use of a piece of machinery or equipment
3. Issue an Improvement Notice stating that equipment or machinery should be repaired or renovated within a stated time span
4. Prosecute the proprietor of an establishment where unsafe equipment is being used
5. Seize, render harmless or destroy items equipment which they consider to be unsafe

If you are found to be guilty in the criminal court you could end up with a fine of up to £2000, imprisonment of up to 2 years or both.

Case study

A cleaning supervisor was electrocuted when using badly maintained equipment. Mrs Mary Smith had hospital treatment for several days and had to take several weeks off work after she received an electric shock from a vacuum cleaner. Her employers were fined a total of £5000 by the county magistrates after pleading guilty to eight offences under the Health and Safety at Work Act. The court heard that the firm had not properly maintained five items of electrical equipment provided for use by the staff. It was also revealed that the firm has failed to provide health and safety training and information for its employees and had not produced a written health and safety statement. The company was fined £1000 for not having a written policy, £1000 for the unsafe vacuum cleaner and £500 for each other item of faulty equipment. They were also ordered to pay costs of £348 to the Borough Council.

The Health and Safety at Work Act states that employers must provide instruction, training and supervision of health and safety. The Act also states that employees have a legal duty to cooperate with employers to meet health and safety requirements and, therefore, must attend any training session offered.

Security

Customers to hospitality establishments such as hotels, hospitals, restaurants and leisure centres expect to feel secure. Staff working in establishments which provide accommodation services must be aware of the particular threats and

- Never open doors for guests who have 'lost' their key
- Never unlock doors for workmen without authorization
- Apply for a package pass if they have received a gift from a guest
- Keep keys on their person at all times – never leave them around
- Place a trolley across the door when working in rooms
- Keep an eye out for suspicious persons and report them (i.e. guests with little or no luggage or guests who do not sleep in their rooms)

▪ WORKBOOK ▪

Accident reporting

University of Rutland

The halls of residence at the University of Rutland change bed linen on a Tuesday, Wednesday or Thursday. In the past, the students were expected to change their own beds but, as a number of them did not do so, the Halls Manager decided to organize the domestic staff to change the linen.

Whissendine Hall is an eight-storey tower block. At 10.30 a.m. on Tuesday 12 April Mary Harper waited for the service lift at the sixth floor so that she could take her soiled linen to the Linen Room and exchange it for clean linen.

After waiting for about 20 minutes she began to get impatient. If she did not get her clean linen soon she would not finish her work on time. Mary decided not to wait for the lift any longer and so she bundled all the soiled linen together and proceeded to roll it down the stairs. When she reached the top of the stairs at the second floor she gave the bundle a strong push and, as it gathered speed, she raced after it. She did not see Jane Vincent, a Domestic Assistant on the first floor, who walked onto the landing just as the bundle of linen fell down the stairs. The bundle knocked Jane over causing severe bruising to her left shoulder, arm and hip.

Complete the accident report from.

Practical exercises

1 Dust control

Aim

- To understand the simple terminology of dust control
- To understand and demonstrate the safe use of basic cleaning equipment

Working in groups:

1 List all the surfaces where dust is likely to gather in:
   (a) A bedroom
   (b) A restaurant
   (c) A lounge
   (d) The reception area
   If possible, find areas in the college or school which are similar to these.
2 Identify all the item(s) of *manual* equipment which could be used to control dust on each of the surfaces you have listed above.

3 Collect as many of the items of equipment as are available which you have listed in 2 above.
4 In your groups, use each item of equipment to control dust from surfaces which are similar to the ones you have identified in 1. Take note of any items of equipment which are suitable for more than one type of surface.
5 Prepare a chart to show which pieces of equipment are suitable for which surfaces. (Each member of the group should have a copy of the chart – either copy from each other or photocopy it.)

2 Suction cleaning

Aim

- To understand the simple terminology of suction cleaning
- To understand and demonstrate the safe use of suction cleaning equipment

Working in groups:

1 Prepare a list of different makes of suction/vacuum cleaners:
   (a) Classify the cleaners into those which are upright and those which are canister/cylinder.
   (b) List, where applicable, the attachments for each model.
2 Collect all the suction cleaners available and the attachments for each.
3 Using each type of suction/vacuum cleaner, practise mechanical methods of controlling dust from the surfaces which you listed in Exercise 1.
4 Compare the mechanical method with the manual methods which you tested.
5 Check each suction/vacuum cleaner and find out, where appropriate, the correct method of
   (a) Changing/emptying the dustbag
   (b) Fitting the drive belt
   (c) Changing the filter
   (d) Unblocking the hose

3 Damp mopping

Aim

- To demonstrate the safe use of equipment and the safe methods of damp mopping hard floor surfaces

1 List the various types of mop available and indicate the correct types of bucket which should be used with each mop.
2 Collect the items of mopping equipment which are available from the ones you have listed above.
3 Use the equipment and three different brands of synthetic detergent to damp mop a range of hard floor surfaces – corridor, stairs, kitchen, etc.
4 In your group decide which you consider to be the most appropriate mop and bucket system for use in
   (a) A kitchen during working hours
   (b) A kitchen after working hours
   (c) A hospital corridor
   (d) A hospital ward area
   (e) An entrance hall in a hotel
   (f) A bathroom in a hotel
   (g) A hall of residence utility room
   (h) A hall of residence dining room

4 Care and maintenance of glass and mirrors

Aim

- To identify the range of glass surfaces which need to be cleaned
- To identify the most effective method of cleaning the different glass surfaces

Working in groups:

1 Make a list of the glass surfaces that would need to be cleaned in any catering establishment.
2 Collect a variety of equipment and cleaning agents suitable for cleaning glass surfaces.

3 Use the different pieces of equipment and the agents to clean a variety of glass surfaces similar to those you identified in 2.
4 Decide which pieces of equipment and which agents are the best ones for each of the surfaces you identified.
5 Write a report stating which of the methods tested you would recommend to clean each of the surfaces you listed in 1.

5 Floor maintenance

Aim

- To identify the range of floor surfaces
- To identify and practise the methods of maintaining the range of floor surfaces.

Go round the school or college and any nearby buildings taking note of the floor coverings and finishes.

1 Classify the areas into those which are carpeted and those which have hard floor surfaces.
2 Describe each type of floor surface and each type of carpet noting the differences and similarities between the various types of carpet and the various types of hard surface.
3 Estimate the amount and type of *traffic* in each area.

Definition

- ***Traffic*** *is the number of people and equipment such as trolleys which travel across the floor surface.*

4 Consider the standard of cleaning – is it appropriate for the area? If not, what standard should it be?
5 List and describe the method(s) you would use to clean the carpets and the hard floor surfaces.

6 Sanitary facilities investigation

Working in pairs, investigate the sanitary facilities found in your school or college to include cloakrooms, classrooms, workshops and kitchens. For all areas note:

1 The type(s) of facilities available and how many of each.
2 What other facilities are there?
3 Is the standard of cleanliness acceptable for a building such as this?
If not, why not?

For the cloakrooms note:

1 Whether they are ladies or gentlemen's – whether they are staff or students.
2 Is there any evidence that the area is used for smoking or as a student common room?
3 Find out if there are any facilities for disabled people within the college. How are these facilities different from the standard ones?
4 If necessary, is there an existing cloakroom that could be adapted to allow easy access for disabled people?

Test questions

1 The correct extinguisher to use on a paper fire is
(a) BCF
(b) Foam
(c) Water
(d) Dry powder
2 A density chart is most likely to be used to record advance reservations in a
(a) Hotel
(b) Restaurant
(c) Hall of residence
(d) Leisure centre
3 The electronic room status board links the Reception office with
(a) The housekeeper and the restaurant
(b) The telephonist and the restaurant
(c) The housekeeper and the cashier
(d) The telephonist and the cashier

4 The method of payment which requires two corresponding signatures, one of which must be signed at the time of payment, is a
   (a) Charge card
   (b) Credit card
   (c) Crossed cheque
   (d) Travellers cheque

5 The correct order of work to follow when cleaning and servicing a bedroom is
   (1) Strip and make bed
   (2) Low dust surfaces
   (3) Open windows, remove waste and any dirty crockery
   (4) Suction clean carpet
   (5) Check and replenish guest supplies

   (a) 3 4 5 2 1
   (b) 3 1 2 5 4
   (c) 3 2 5 1 4
   (d) 1 3 2 4 5

6 The prime cause of damage to carpets is
   (a) Grit
   (b) Dust
   (c) Cigarette ash
   (d) Spilled drinks

7 A patterned carpet in the entrance lobby of an hotel would need to be suction cleaned
   (a) Three times per week
   (b) Five times per week
   (c) Once per day
   (d) Twice per day

8 A bed board is
   (a) Attached to the bed at the head end
   (b) Attached to the bed at the foot end
   (c) Placed between the mattress and the bed base
   (d) Placed on top of the mattress

9 The simplest cleaning chemical is
   (a) Soap
   (b) Soda
   (c) Water
   (d) Vinegar

10 An international company wishing to confirm a booking for tonight would use
   (a) A fax
   (b) A courier
   (c) An air-mail letter
   (d) A telegram

Which of the following statements is *true* or *false*?

11 Both employees and employers are responsible for health and safety in an establishment.

12 On hearing a fire alarm sound a receptionist should telephone the fire brigade.

13 Hotel management are not responsible for items of value left in guests' bedrooms.

14 A regular guest in a hotel should be asked to pay for a room in advance.

15 A Michelin star would be awarded to an establishment which has a large garage.

Match the chemical with the surface

16 Acid cleanser	(a) Hard floor
17 Low-foam shampoo	(b) Glass
18 Neutral detergent	(c) Toilet bowl
19 Alkaline detergent	(d) Carpet
20 Vinegar	(e) Wash basin

PROVIDE FOOD AND DRINK

UNIT 4

This unit introduces you to the provision of food and drink in a wide variety of outlets. The text explains the differences between the methods of preparation and cooking and the variety of ways food can be served according to circumstances. The underpining knowledge provided enables you to practise practical skills with more confidence. The unit also introduces you to the use of numbers and basic costing and provides in the tasks and assignments for the integration of core skills. The unit covers:

- Methods of preparing and cooking food
- Methods of food and drink service
- Factors which influence cost and selling price
- Commodities
- Preparation and knife skills
- Processes of cooking foods
- Health, safety and hygiene
- Legal requirements associated with food and drink service

▪ METHODS OF PROVIDING A FOOD AND DRINK SERVICE ▪

In this section we will be taking a look at the main hygiene, and health and safety practices, which must be followed by the hospitality and catering industry. All the procedures which you will have to follow when you are at work are based on laws passed by Parliament. To help you understand how the law works, there is a varied range of codes of practice available. Some employers also produce their own, to ensure that you are fully aware of your responsibilities. You will find that both hygiene and health and safety have a high profile in the industry, with time and money being invested to ensure high standards.

Good practices for hygiene

We have become very concerned about food hygiene in the last few years because the number of cases of food poisoning each year is too high to be acceptable. It is now one of the most common diseases affecting people in the UK. Some groups, especially the young, elderly or sick, are particularly vulnerable to food poisoning. This means that you must be especially careful if you are providing catering services in hospitals or residential care homes.

People becoming ill is only one of the consequences of poor standards of food hygiene. A business may soon lose its reputation, which could cost you your job. You may also be prosecuted if you do not comply with food legislation. Customers who become ill may claim damages, costing a lot of money in compensation payments.

What is food hygiene?

Food hygiene means that you must:

- Keep yourself clean
- Wear clean workwear
- Protect food from contamination by micro-organisms
- Store food at the correct temperature
- Cook food thoroughly to kill harmful bacteria

What is food poisoning?

Definition

- ***Food poisoning*** *is an illness caused by eating contaminated food.*

The most common kind of contamination is due to certain types of bacteria. Although you may think that the symptoms sound fairly ordinary, food poisoning makes you feel very ill indeed, with young, elderly or sick people most likely to die from the disease. The main symptoms of food poisoning are:

- Vomiting
- Diarrhoea
- Nausea
- Stomach pains

It may take as little as two hours for the symptoms to show after eating infected food. Some types of food poisoning take longer to cause illness, up to two days in some cases. The symptoms usually start very suddenly and may last for one to two days, although you may be ill for a week or more.

Task 4.1

Make a list of the types of catering operations in which serious problems could be caused for both staff and customers, if food poisoning developed within two hours of eating a meal.

Why has food poisoning become so common?

Some of the reasons you will find given to explain the increase in food poisoning which has taken place over recent years are:

1. Eating out has become very popular
2. A wider variety of eating establishments is available
3. Different types of foods from all over the world are eaten
4. New catering systems, like cook–chill, have been developed
5. Microwave ovens may not reheat food adequately
6. Bulk buying of perishable foods
7. Few restrictions on the setting up of food businesses

How the incidence of food poisoning may be reduced

One of the main ways of tackling the food-poisoning problem is to ensure that all food handlers are better educated in food hygiene. This means that you will have the knowledge and skills to carry out good practices, while you are at work.

New legislation has brought in stricter hygiene standards, which have meant that the hospitality and catering industry has had to make significant changes to catering practice. The Food Safety Act 1990 is the first major review of the food safety laws since 1955. The new law has taken into account the changes in our society, which you have just read about in the list above, in its attempt to reduce food poisoning. Since the food production chain has become longer and new methods of preservation have been introduced, the Food Safety Act has put responsibility for food safety on each link of that chain. Remember that you are one of the links of the *food production chain*.

Definition

- ***Food production chain:*** *growing, processing and selling our food.*

How food poisoning is caused

We have already said that the most common cause of food poisoning is bacterial, so we will concentrate on this type.

Bacteria

The problem with bacteria is that as they are single-celled micro-organisms, they are far too small to see unless we have a powerful microscope. So we must always be reminding ourselves of their presence in our environment.

Although most bacteria are harmless we must take precautions to protect ourselves from those which cause us to become ill. Bacteria belonging to this last category are called *pathogens*.

Definition

- ***Pathogens*** *are bacteria which cause disease.*

Types of bacteria causing food poisoning

There are several different types of bacteria which may contaminate our food. In this section we shall concentrate on those which are most commonly found (Table 4.1).

Table 4.1

Bacteria	*Source*
Salmonella	Animal/human intestines
Clostridium perfringens	Animal/human intestines
Staphylococcus aureus	Human skin, hair, mouth, nose and throat, cuts, septic infections
Bacillus cereus	Soil

How food becomes contaminated with bacteria

The way in which food becomes contaminated depends on the source of the bacteria. Those which originate in the animal's gut may be transferred to the meat when the animal is slaughtered. Alternatively, animal and human sewage pollutes our water, causing contamination of seafood such as shellfish. If humans carry bacteria such as *Salmonella*, then they might transfer these to food if they visit the toilet and then handle food, without first washing their hands. Flies feed on animal excreta, transferring both *Salmonella* and *Clostridium perfringens* to the food. Pests also carry *Salmonella* in their intestines, making them a danger in food premises.

The most likely way of food becoming contaminated with *Staphylococcus aureus* is

Table 4.2

Bacteria	*Type of food likely to be infected*
Salmonella	Meat, especially pork and poultry Eggs Shellfish
Clostridium perfringens	Meat
Staphylococcus aureus	Cooked meats: e.g. ham, tongue, poultry, Desserts: e.g. custards, trifles and creams
Bacillus cereus	Rice

through the food handler, usually because of poor personal hygiene. We shall see in a later section that many food hygiene practices are designed to stop this type of contamination. *Bacillus cereus* passes from soil to crops such as cereals. Although it has been found to contaminate a wide variety of foods, you are most likely to find it in boiled or fried rice in Britain (Table 4.2).

We must always assume that raw food is contaminated with food poisoning bacteria. For this reason, we must think of it as 'dirty'.

Task 4.2

Answer these questions to complete the grid.

Down

1 *Insects which spread food poisoning*
2 *Bacteria found on skin*
4 *A symptom of food poisoning*
10 *Animal which spreads disease*
12 *The number of cells in bacteria*

Across

3 *Food which often causes* Clostridium perfringens *food poisoning*
5 *Bacteria which cause disease*
6 *Birds often infected with* Salmonella
7 *Food often infected with* Bacillus cereus
8 Bacillus cereus *is found in this*
9 Salmonella *are found in here*
10 *Meat which may be contaminated with* Salmonella
11 *You need this to see bacteria*
13 *Desserts which may cause food poisoning*

How bacteria multiply in food

Bacteria cause food poisoning when they build up to sufficiently high numbers in your food. Most people would become ill after eating food with one million food poisoning organisms per gram.

We give bacteria the opportunity to grow and multiply in our food by poor food-handling techniques. Recent legislation has concentrated particularly on how we control the temperature of our food, as we shall see in a later section.

Multiplication of bacteria is a simple process, the bacterial cell splits into two once every 10–20 minutes, provided it has suitable conditions. If you work this out, using 10-minute intervals, you will find that one bacterium can become over one million in 3 hours and 20 minutes. Since our food may be already contaminated with thousands of food-poisoning bacteria per gram, before we even start to handle and prepare it, you can see the potential bacteria have for making us sick.

We have just said that bacteria need the right conditions in which to grow and multiply. They require:

- Food
- Moisture
- Warmth
- Time

Each of these is explained below.

Food

Protein foods such as meat, poultry and dairy produce provide an ideal mixture of nutrients, in which bacteria grow especially well. *High-risk foods* are those that encourage bacterial growth. The main groups are:

1 Meat and poultry
2 Cooked meat, gravy, soup and stocks
3 Shellfish and seafood
4 Milk, cream and eggs
5 Cooked rice

Low-risk foods are unsuitable for bacteria to grow in. They have often been preserved with sugar, salt or vinegar. Chemical preservatives may also have been used. Dry foods such as bread or biscuits are not prone to bacterial growth. You must remember that when dried foods are reconstituted with water or milk, then bacteria will be able to grow.

Water

The amount of water which is needed by bacteria to grow is relatively high. Foods which have a water content of 70 per cent or more provide ideal conditions for growth. High-risk foods come into this category. You must remember that some bacteria remain dormant in dry foods, only to grow again when water is added.

Temperature

Food-poisoning bacteria grow best at a temperature of 37°C. They will multiply rapidly between 30°C and 50°C, but are able to grow from as low as 5°C to as high as 63°C. The *danger zone* is from 5°C to 63°C. Temperature control keeps food out of the danger zone.

Most food-poisoning bacteria do not grow at refrigerator temperature, which is usually 1–4°C. In frozen storage (–18°C) some will die, but a proportion will survive and grow again in warm conditions.

On the other hand, high temperatures will kill bacteria. If food is cooked for 10–30 minutes, then you will have destroyed any bacteria present provided the temperature inside the food has reached 75°C. The temperature at the centre is called the *core temperature*.

Time

You saw earlier that bacteria grow and multiply rapidly provided they have suitable conditions for growth. Food kept in these conditions may become a serious risk of food poisoning in as little as 2 hours. When you are cooling food you should do it as quickly as possible and in no longer than *1½ hours*.

As a food handler, the two factors you have control over are *temperature* and *time*. You are the last vital link between the consumer and food poisoning.

Task 4.3

When you have your next kitchen session, keep a record of the foods you use and prepare for service. Track their progress from start to finish, noting where in the kitchen they are prepared and kept. Note any temperature controls which are used.

More problems for the food handler

Some bacteria still hold a few surprises for you, which make them particularly difficult for the food handler to deal with. This section looks at *spores* and *toxins*.

Clostridium perfringens and *Bacillus cereus* are both types of bacteria which form spores inside their cells. If the bacteria die, the spores will contaminate the environment or your food.

- Using bain-maries to keep food hot
- Leaving food at room temperature only during preparation or service
- Throwing away left-over food

You can destroy bacteria in food by cooking food thoroughly to a core temperature of 75°C.

The best way you have of preventing bacteria multiplying in your customers' food is correct temperature control. You must always remember to:

1 Keep food hot
2 Keep food cold
3 Keep prepared food out of the danger zone

Personal hygiene

In the section dealing with how food becomes contaminated with bacteria we saw that the food handler is a source of contamination. It is not just the body, but also clothing and jewellery that harbour bacteria and put your food at risk. Your *hands* are most likely to cross-contaminate from one food to another.

Hands

You must thoroughly wash your hands and scrub your finger nails using hot water and liquid soap (Figure 4.1). It is best to fill the wash basin with water if you have ordinary hand-operated taps. Your nail brush should be clean and made of plastic with nylon bristles.

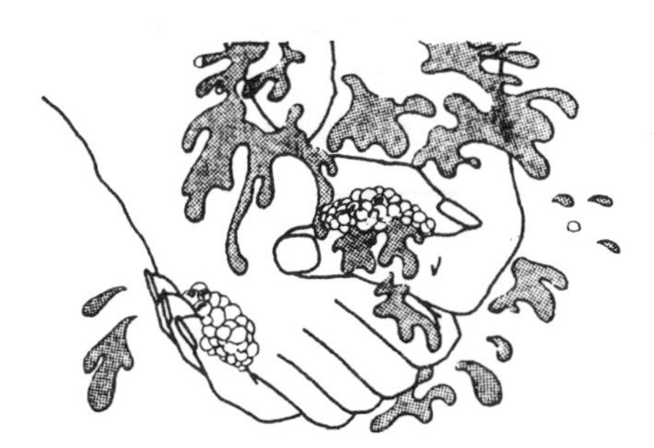

Figure 4.1 Hands must be washed thoroughly and frequently

Then dry your hands using either a disposable paper towel or a hot air dryer. Make sure they are thoroughly dried, especially if you are using a hot air dryer. Correct hand-washing routines ensure that you do not contaminate your hands during washing and drying. As a food handler you must wash your hands:

- When you go into the kitchen, before touching food
- After handling raw food
- In between touching raw and cooked food
- After handling waste food
- After eating or smoking
- After coughing, sneezing or nose blowing
- After touching your face, ears or hair
- After using the lavatory
- After cleaning up

Personal cleanliness

Self-respect is an important quality for any food handler, pride in your appearance enables you to have a high standard of cleanliness and personal fitness. People who suffer from ill-health or who are not clean should not handle food, as they may contaminate it with bacteria such as *Staphylococci* or *Salmonella*.

You should take several baths each week, a daily bath or shower is ideal, but if this is not possible a thorough wash is satisfactory. Your hair should also be washed regularly and either kept short or tied back (Figure 4.2). Hair which is not cared for may come out or shed dandruff onto food.

Your finger nails should be kept short so that they do not collect dirt and bacteria (Figure 4.3). You should not wear nail varnish when handling food, as it may chip into food. If you bite your finger nails, your fingers are frequently in your mouth so you may find it more difficult to get a job working with food.

Your mouth and teeth are a source of bacteria. You should keep your teeth clean and visit the

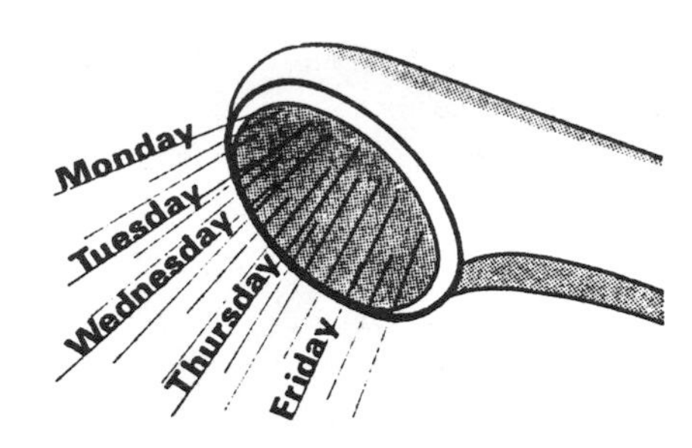

Figure 4.2 Regular bathing and washing the hair is essential

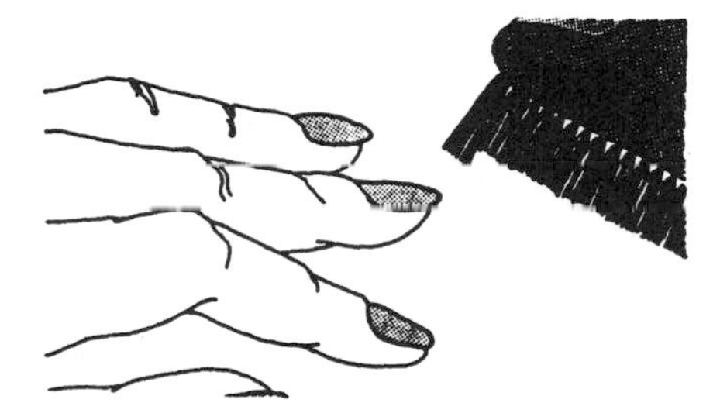

Figure 4.3 Finger nails must always be kept clean

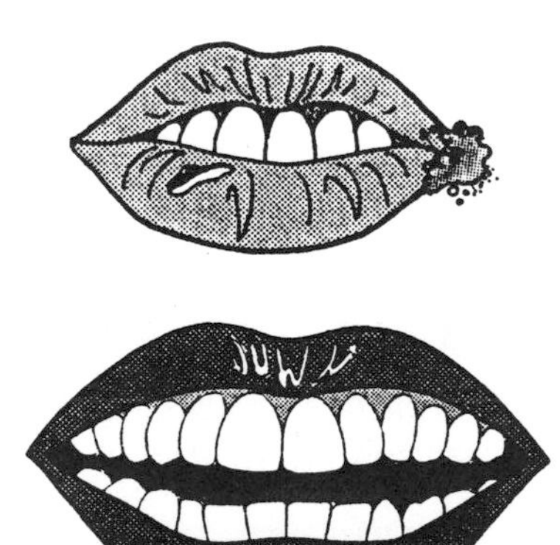

Figure 4.4 A healthy mouth and sound teeth are essential

Figure 4.5 As food handlers are standing for many hours, care of the feet is important

dentist regularly. Sound teeth are essential to good health (Figure 4.4).

Caring for your feet is equally important, as you will be on your feet for many hours (Figure 4.5). As well as washing them regularly, you should keep your toe nails short and clean. Tired feet make you feel tired, which means that you become careless and also lower your standards of hygiene.

You should not wear rings, watches and jewellery when you are handling food. Food may be caught in rings, encouraging bacteria to multiply. Watches prevent you washing food and equipment thoroughly, as you do not want to get them wet. Jewellery may also fall off into food or contaminate it with stones or pieces of metal. Your customers are then likely to complain about the food you have prepared for them.

Personal habits

You should only use cosmetics in moderation, making sure you do not apply them in the kitchen. Wash your hands well afterwards, so you do not transfer *Staphylococci* to food. Cosmetics should be put on a clean skin, you should not use them to cover up dirt (Figure 4.6).

Strong-smelling perfume/after-shave is not suitable for food handlers, as it may transfer its smell to food, especially fatty food. It also spoils the nice aroma of food when it is being served. Other cosmetics that you should use regularly,

Figure 4.6 Cosmetics should be used in moderation

Figure 4.8 Smoking must never take place where there is food

like deodorants, should also be neutral rather than heavily perfumed.

You should not touch your nose, mouth or ears while you are handling food (Figure 4.7). It is best to use paper handkerchiefs, which you can throw away after use. You should avoid coughing or sneezing over food, people and working surfaces. Try to cough or sneeze into your handkerchief. Never spit, as this also spreads bacteria. You must never smoke in food rooms or while you are handling food. This is because when you take a cigarette from your mouth you may transfer *Staphylococci* onto your fingers and from them onto food. When cigarettes are put down, the end which has

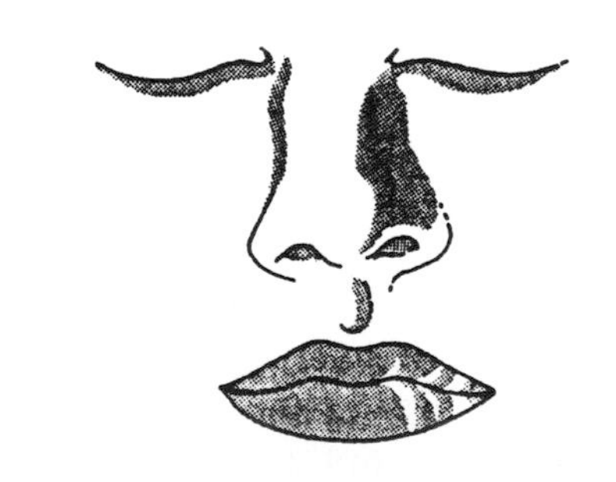

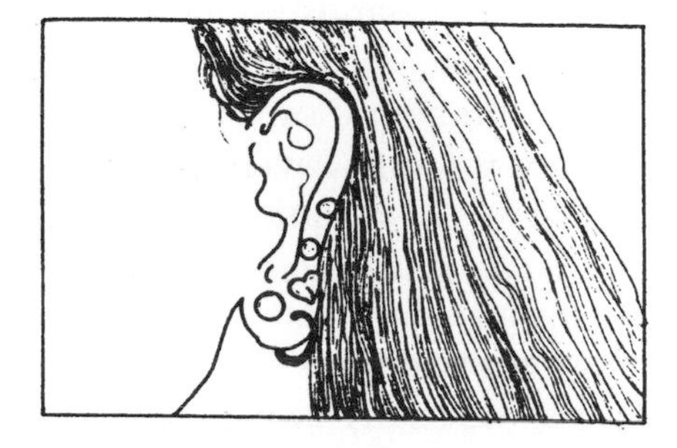

Figure 4.7 The nose or ears should not be touched when food is being handled

been in the mouth can contaminate work surfaces. It is also possible for cigarette ends and ash to find their way into food.

Another point is that smoking in food rooms or where there is food is illegal, and may result in an offender being prosecuted (Figure 4.8).

Personal injuries and illness

Cuts, burns, scratches and open sores are ideal places for *Staphylococci* to multiply. To prevent these from contaminating food, you should cover them completely with a blue or green waterproof dressing. These show up if they fall off into food. You can give cuts on fingers extra protection by using a waterproof fingerstall. If an infection is septic, as with certain cuts, boils or carbuncles, then you should not handle food.

Any discharges from ears, eyes and nose can easily contaminate food. You must report these to your supervisor, who will not let you work until you have been given permission by a doctor.

You should also report any symptoms, such as vomiting and diarrhoea, to your supervisor. Again you will not be permitted to work until a doctor says that you are fit to handle food.

Protective clothing

When you handling food, you should wear clean, washable protective clothing. Kitchen clothing is often white, to show when it is soiled and requires changing. Protective clothing prevents your own clothing from contaminating food with bacteria, dust, pet hairs and fibres.

You should change your protective clothing each day and only wear it at work. If you get your apron dirty in the course of a job, then you should change into a clean one as soon as you finish, before moving on to do something else. Disposable plastic aprons are available to protect you if you are doing a dirty job such as preparing raw meat.

Your outdoor clothes must be left in the staff changing room. They cannot be taken into a food room unless you are provided with a locker to keep them in.

You must also cover your hair with a hat which has been specially designed for the purpose. There is quite a selection of styles, some which are particularly suitable for long hair. Sometimes a hairnet has to be worn beneath the hat to ensure that hair does not fall into food.

Practising clean habits in the kitchen is the only way to make sure that your hygiene is of a satisfactory standard. The following list will remind you of the main points:

1 *Hands* must be washed frequently and always after using the lavatory. Food should be handled as little as possible.
2 *Bathing* must be frequent.
3 *Hair* must be kept clean and covered in the kitchen. It should not be combed or handled near food.
4 *Nose and mouth* should not be touched with the hands.
5 *Cough and sneeze* into a handkerchief, not over food.
6 *Jewellery, rings and watches* should not be worn.
7 *Smoking, spitting and snuff taking* are forbidden where there is food.
8 *Cuts and burns* should be covered with a waterproof dressing.
9 *Clean clothing* should be worn and only clean cloths used.
10 *Food* should be tested with a clean teaspoon.

Task 4.6

Answer the following questions on food hygiene. Food handlers are not allowed to smoke while handling food. The main reason for this is:

- *Ash may contaminate food*
- *Non-smokers may object*
- *Bacteria from the mouth may contaminate food*
- *Cigarette smoke may taint food*

Which of the following temperatures is most likely to cause growth of bacteria in food?

- *27°C*
- *37°C*
- *47°C*
- *57°C*

Staphylococci *infect food from:*

- *Mouse droppings*
- *Animal intestines*
- *Flies*
- *Pus from infections*

The safest way of thawing food is in:

- *A microwave cooker*
- *A refrigerator*
- *Cold water*
- *A hot cupboard*

During the defrosting of a refrigerator, the core temperature of the food in the refrigerator has risen to 12°C. What would you do with this food?

- *Place the food in a freezer*
- *Use the food for service as usual*
- *Throw the food away*
- *Use the food for staff meals*

The equipment found in a kitchen includes:

- *Colour-coded chopping boards*
- *Waste disposal unit*
- *Microwave oven*
- *Refrigerator*

Which piece of equipment will reduce the risk of

- *Food poisoning?*
- *Pests?*
- *Cross-contamination?*

Each of the following foods is associated with a particular type of food poisoning:

- *Beef casserole*
- *Chicken in mushroom sauce*
- *Sherry trifle*
- *Egg fried rice*

Which food is the most likely cause of:

- Salmonella?
- Staphylococcus aureus?
- Clostridium perfringens?

Your are able to reduce the risk of food poisoning by protecting food from contamination with bacteria. How can you best prevent cross-contamination?

- *Keeping food in the refrigerator*
- *Washing your hands regularly*
- *Using a sanitizer*
- *Cooking food thoroughly*

Work flow

Food premises must be planned in such a way that the risk of cross-contamination is reduced to a minimum. You will find that catering operations follow a sequence, which is called work flow. This means that the building itself must conform to this chain of events.

First of all, food comes into the delivery room area. The storage area is sited next, so that food can be stored, without having to pass through the kitchen. The food-preparation areas follow, after which is the service area. The potwash is usually situated near the service area, so dirty dishes do not have to be carried through the kitchen.

Work flow is:

Delivery → storage → preparation → service

Task 4.7

Draw a plan of your school/college catering facilities, marking the delivery, storage, preparation and service areas. Show on the plan the route the food takes from delivery to service. Is the work flow sequence correctly followed?

Workplace hygiene

Hygiene in food premises is another factor in the fight against food poisoning. It begins when the workplace is designed and planned, when materials are chosen to construct the building and when equipment is selected. Unless this is done correctly, the food handler's job of preventing contamination will be very difficult.

Kitchen layout

Kitchens should be planned so that vegetables and fruit can be prepared near to their storage area, away from other preparation areas. This reduces the possibility of soil spreading bacteria onto other foods. Raw meat and poultry should also be prepared in an area set aside for this purpose. The best place for preparation sites is around the sides of the kitchen. This leaves the

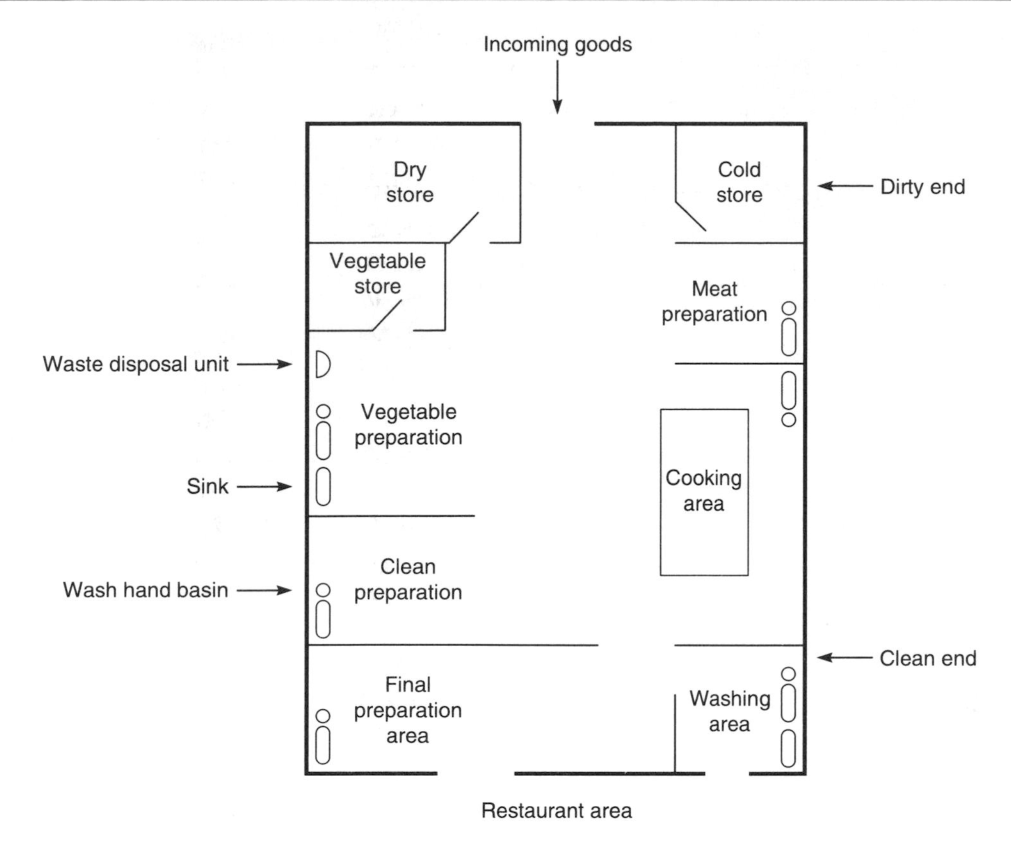

Figure 4.9 A kitchen plan

centre for islands of cooking equipment. By designing kitchens in this way, raw food is separated from cooked, also waste is kept away from food-preparation areas (Figure 4.9).

Choosing materials

When materials are chosen for floors, walls, ceilings and work surfaces, they should be:

- Non-porous
- Easy to clean
- Hard wearing

Materials which chip or crack easily, which rust or tarnish, or are likely to react with food are unsuitable for use in food premises. The types of materials which conform to these requirements are:

- Stainless steel
- Plastic laminate
- Quarry tiles
- Ceramic tiles
- Non-slip vinyl sheet

In most kitchens (Figure 4.10) you will find that:

1 *Work surfaces* are made from stainless steel. They should be on legs and placed eighteen inches from the walls so that you are able to clean underneath and behind quite easily. Stainless steel tables on legs are also a good idea. They are usually on castors so that they can be moved for easy cleaning of the floor.
2 *Floors* are covered with thick non-slip vinyl sheet or quarry tiles. Waterproof grouting should be used to fill the gaps between the tiles. Quarry tiles may have ridged surfaces to reduce the risk of slipping, but crevices can develop between the tiles. The amount of traffic in the kitchen is one of the factors which decides the type of flooring material

Figure 4.10 A typical kitchen

chosen. There may be several different types used even in one kitchen. Crevices must be avoided between the floor and the walls, otherwise food and bacteria may accumulate and pests may find a home. This is done by curving the flooring material up the bottom of the wall to form a *coving*.

3 *Walls* are frequently covered with ceramic tiles, with edges protected from chipping and cracking by metal strips. Sometimes plaster walls covered with emulsion paint are found, with tiles being used behind sinks and work surfaces, where splashing is likely.
4 *Ceilings* are often smooth plaster, covered with a washable emulsion paint. There should also be a coving where the ceiling joins the wall. Like walls, they should be painted a light colour, to show up dirt and grease easily.

Lighting the kitchen

Kitchens should be well lit to ensure that cleaning has been done thoroughly and to prevent accidents. Fluorescent strip lights fitted flush with the ceiling give the best light. Too many windows allow the kitchen to become too hot in sunny weather.

Ventilating the kitchen

Hot, humid conditions encourage the growth of bacteria and also make it unpleasant for staff to work. Good ventilation is required to remove heat, steam and cooking fumes. Extractor fans are best placed in hoods, directly over cooking equipment. Ventilation systems may also be found in ceilings. More sophisticated systems extract foul air and replace it with fresh. If windows are kept open, they should be fitted with a wire mesh screen to keep out dirt, birds and insects like flies.

Personal washing facilities

The wash hand basin should be situated just inside the entrance to the kitchen, well away from food-preparation areas. You should find hot and cold running water, liquid soap, nail brush, paper towels or hot air dryer. There should also be a 'now wash your hands' notice nearby.

Disposing of waste

Waste food is a breeding ground for bacteria, as well as attracting rodents and insects. It must be disposed of regularly and never allowed to build up in a food room. Often, food is put down waste disposal units, which chop up the food and rinse it away into the drains. This means that you can get rid of waste as soon as you make it.

Disposable polythene sacks, held in a ring, fitted with a lid and foot pedal, or plastic bins with tight-fitting lids may also be used. They should be kept away from food-preparation areas, preferably outside the kitchen, in a special storage area. You should empty them as soon as they are full at the end of the day. When you have emptied a plastic bin, it must be washed before being used again.

Task 4.8

Draw a plan of your school/ college kitchen showing where the following foods are prepared:

- *Fruit and vegetables*
- *Raw meat and poultry*
- *Pastry*
- *Desserts*

Show the position of:

- *Cooking equipment*
- *Refrigerators*
- *Freezers*
- *Wash hand basin*
- *Sinks*
- *Waste disposal equipment*

Label the materials used for:

- *Work surfaces*
- *Walls*
- *Floor*
- *Ceiling*

Equipment

Your job as a food handler is also made much easier if equipment is designed with hygiene in mind. Grooves and ridges may look attractive, but harbour food and bacteria. Smooth, clean lines are required, so that you can clean equipment thoroughly. It also helps if equipment can be taken to pieces, to avoid awkward corners and spots which are difficult to reach. Most equipment is made from stainless steel which is resistant to damage by food or corrosion.

Equipment should be on legs, so that you can clean underneath more easily, or on wheels, so that it can be moved when you want to clean. Preferably, it should be placed 18 inches from walls, to enable you to clean behind.

Chopping boards, knife and brush handles are made from polypropylene, because it does not absorb food and bacteria. It may also be colour coded.

Another very important point is that separate equipment should be used for raw food, to avoid cross-contamination. This equipment must also be colour coded or labelled. It is essential that you know how to use equipment, so that you maintain hygiene standards and also do not injure yourself.

Refrigerators are essential pieces of equipment, since temperature control is the most important factor in preventing food poisoning. Provided the temperature in the refrigerator is below 5°C, most food-poisoning bacteria will not grow. Food spoilage due to bacteria and mould is also slowed, but still food will only keep for a few days.

The temperature of your refrigerators must be checked and logged, at least once a day. Refrigerators usually have a dial thermometer or digital readout on the front. Some refrigerator temperatures are monitored by computer, which produces a printout every two hours recording the temperature. It should be between 1°C and 4°C.

Checking the core temperature of food is done by keeping pots of jelly in the refrigerators. The jelly is called a food simulant. It avoids having to destroy pre-packaged food during temperature probing. Synthetic materials are now available, instead of using jelly.

Temperature probes are used to take core temperature readings of the jelly (Figure 4.11). You need to change the jellies every four days. They should not be eaten. This saves you having to test the food itself, unless you suspect something is wrong. You must also clean the probe with a sanitizing wipe after each temperature check.

If the temperature rises above the permitted level, then the food must be thrown away. The exact temperatures and times are explained in the section on the Food Hygiene (Amendment) Regulations 1990 and 1991.

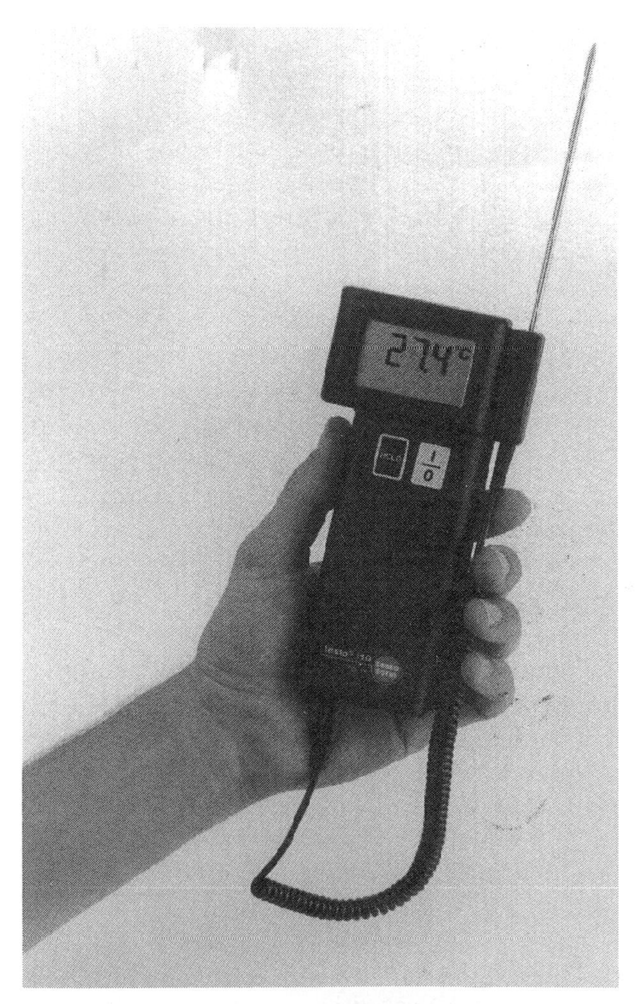

Figure 4.11 A temperature probe

Task 4.9

Using a chart like the one shown in Figure 4.12, check the temperatures of the refrigerator in your school/college kitchen. Fill in the time, air temperature in the refrigerator and core temperature of the jelly kept in the refrigerator for this purpose. This is your temperature log. Do two checks, one in the morning and one in the afternoon, for one day of the week.

Foods that you must refrigerate for short storage are:

- Raw meat and poultry
- Fresh fish
- Milk
- Cream
- Cheese
- Eggs
- Cooked meat
- Prepared foods
- Foods made with milk, cream, cheese or eggs

Cross-contamination

You must also take care to prevent cross-contamination in refrigerators. Separate refrigerators should be used for raw meat, fresh fish and prepared foods. If you have to put raw meat and cooked food in the same refrigerator, then put the raw meat at the bottom, where it cannot drip juices onto other food. You should also cover food, to prevent cross-contamination and drying out. A well arranged, neat, orderly refrigerator, which is not packed to capacity, shows that you have followed the hygiene rules (Figure 4.13). You need to make sure that you do not put hot food into the refrigerator. This will increase the temperature of the food in it. Leaving the refrigerator door open will also

Room Number ______________________

Refrigeration Unit: ______________________
Deep Freeze/Refrigerator (delete one)

Week Commencing: ______________________

	First check AM				Second check PM			
DAY	TIME	AIR TEMP	CORE TEMP	SIGNATURE	TIME	AIR TEMP	CORE TEMP	SIGNATURE
Mon								
Tues								
Wed								
Thurs								
Fri								
Sat								
Sun								

Figure 4.12 A temperature record for a deep-freeze and refrigerated unit

raise the temperature inside the fridge. You must close it as soon as possible, and open it as little as possible.

When frozen food has to be thawed, then the best place to do this is in a separate refrigerator, set aside for this purpose, or a rapid-defrost cabinet. Food takes a long time to thaw under these conditions. It must have defrosted right through to the centre. You should take particular care with raw, frozen meat, especially poultry. If it is cooked while the centre is still frozen, then the core temperature will not get hot enough to kill bacteria. Remember also that *most* poultry is contaminated inside with *Salmonella*.

Keeping the workplace clean

By keeping the workplace clean you avoid exposing food to the risk of contamination.

Figure 4.13 A well-organized refrigerator (adapted from *Basic Food Hygiene Certificate Coursebook*, Chartered Institute of Environmental Health)

Bacteria grow on waste food, which also attracts pests. You make your working environment safer and more pleasant. Your customers will be favourably impressed by clean, well-organized conditions.

You are responsible for keeping your own work area clean. The golden rule is *clean as you go*. This includes dish washing. By doing so, you will reduce the risk of bacteria spreading around the kitchen and contaminating food.

Cleaning schedules

Your supervisor will plan your cleaning routine by producing a cleaning schedule (Figure 4.14). This will tell you what to clean, how often you must do it, the cleaning method you must use, and the equipment and cleaning agents to use. You must also know of the safety precautions required. You may have to wear protective clothing, such as rubber gloves or goggles (Figure 4.15). You should also read and follow the manufacturer's instructions on how to use the cleaning chemicals. When you have finished with them, they must be returned to a locked cupboard, which is not in the kitchen.

Cleaning equipment

Cleaning equipment and cleaning cloths are often colour coded. Hospitals use blue for

(HYGMNSEV) .Main Servery 1......... DAILY / WEEKLY CHECKLIST

WEEK ENDING.. INITIAL ON THE COMPLETION OF TASK.

1.Sanitise solution must be made up fresh. Use **HOT** water, wear rubber gloves.
1ounce per 4 pints of water. USE THE CORRECT MEASURE
2.Report any faults **at once** to a Supervisor.

ITEM	TASK	NOTES	HOW OFTEN	MON	TUE	WED	THU	FRI	SAT	SUN
Bain Marie (interior)	Empty, hot water wash, Empty, cold water sanitise, rinse and dry abrasive pad where necessary		AFTER EACH MEAL SERVICE							
Bain Marie (exterior) Including filling tap	Hot water wash, damp dry Abrasive pad where necessary		AFTER EACH MEAL SERVICE							
Bain marie cupboard	Wash, Damp dry	Plate cupboard	DAILY							
	Sanitise Wash, Rinse, Dry	Completely empty, Use abrasive pad where necessary	MONTHLY							
Hot cupboard doors and runners	Wash, Damp dry	Abrasive pad where necessary	DAILY							
Refrigerated Display Units	Remove food - Sanitise wash, rinse and dry. Interior and exterior		DAILY							
Shelving	Damp dry Tidy		WEEKLY DAILY							

Figure 4.14 A cleaning schedule

Figure 4.15 A chef in rubber gloves and goggles

kitchens. In some cook–chill units, each preparation area has its own colour code, like the one used for chopping boards. Disposable cleaning cloths are the best type to use.

Cleaning equipment must be kept clean. If mops, brushes and cloths are to be re-used, they should be washed after use. The laundry cycle should include a wash or rinse which is at least 65°C to prevent bacterial growth.

You must avoid spreading bacteria by using dirty cleaning equipment. Drying cleaning equipment after washing prevents the multiplication of bacteria.

How to clean

Cleaning is the most useful method of removing bacteria from food-preparation areas and equipment. The two most important factors in cleaning effectively are care and effort. The best way of doing it is by using clean hot water and detergent. Some kitchens are designed so that they may be cleaned with high-pressure hot water sprays or steam. Generally, you will find gulleys in the kitchen floor, to take away surplus water from cleaning either the kitchen itself or equipment.

After cleaning and rinsing, a *sanitizer* is used to kill bacteria. Work surfaces and refrigerators are examples of places where you would use a sanitizer. They are available in powder or liquid form and are often applied using a plastic spray bottle. When you are mixing sanitizer powder with water, you need to follow the quantities given by the manufacturer. Too little will not do the job, too much is a waste of money.

Definition

- ***Sanitizer:*** *a chemical which cleans and disinfects surfaces and equipment.*

There are six stages to good cleaning:

1. *Pre-clean:* by sweeping, wiping or pre-rinsing.
2. *Main clean:* removes dirt and grease using clean, hot water and detergent.
3. *Rinse:* removes dirt and detergent with clean water.
4. *Sanitize:* kill bacteria by spraying on sanitizer and wiping surfaces with a disposable paper cloth.
5. *Final rinse:* removes sanitizer with clean water.
6. *Dry:* air dry if possible or use disposable paper cloths.

Dish-washing machines are useful for cleaning crockery, cutlery and parts dismantled from equipment. The wash cycle is maintained at 60°C. A rinse at 82°C for 30 seconds kills bacteria. The dishes emerge hot enough to air dry. If you have to polish cutlery or silverware, you should use a disposable paper cloth.

How to clean a work surface

- Wipe away food remains
- Wash with hot water and detergent
- Rinse with hot water
- Sanitize
- Rinse
- Dry with disposable paper cloth

How to clean a kitchen floor

- Sweep
- Scrub using hot water and detergent, with a scrubbing machine or tough brush
- Rinse with a mop and very hot water
- Air dry

How to clean kitchen walls and ceilings

- Wipe with hot water and detergent, using a clean cloth
- After cleaning, sanitize areas behind sinks and work surfaces

Task 4.10

Prepare a work card, giving a list of instructions, which explain how to clean a work surface in a kitchen.

The laws on food and food hygiene

Recently, the law relating to food and food hygiene has been revised and updated. There are three pieces of legislation that you need to know about. These are the:

1. Food Hygiene (General) Regulations 1970
2. Food Safety Act 1990
3. Food Hygiene (Amendment) Regulations 1990 and 1991

Food Hygiene (General) Regulations 1970 as amended by the Food Hygiene (Amendment) Regulations 1990 and 1991

These Regulations affect anyone who owns or manages a food business. This may be a café, boading house, canteen, school, hotel or restaurant. They also cover anyone who works in food premises as a food handler. This includes people who prepare or serve food, wrap it for sale or work at a service counter. The regulations apply to food and drink, including the ingredients used to prepare food. The Food Hygiene (General) Regulations 1970 ensure that:

Food premises

- Have good lighting and ventilation
- Provide clean lavatories for the use of catering staff only
- Are not infested with rats, mice and insects
- Have a hot and cold water supply at sinks and wash hand basins
- Put wash hand basins in cloakrooms and kitchens
- Hang 'now wash your hands' notices by wash hand basins and 'no smoking' notices where food is handled
- Supply liquid soap, nail brushes and hand dryers
- Include waterproof dressings in first aid kits
- Provide lockers for food handlers' clothing in food rooms

Equipment

- Is kept clean and in good condition

Good condition means without chips or cracks which harbour food and bacteria, making thorough cleaning difficult.

Food waste and refuse

- Is stored properly before disposal
- Does not accumulate in food rooms

Proper storage is in a bin with a lid.

Open food on sale

- Is screened or covered to protect it from dirt, food handlers and customers

Food hygiene is observed

- Food is not placed where there is a risk of contamination
- Cooked and raw food are kept apart
- Wash hand basins are used only for personal washing

Food handlers

- Keep their hands, arms, face and hair clean
- Keep their personal and protective clothing clean
- Cover cuts and grazes with a waterproof dressing
- Do not spit
- Do not smoke while handling food
- Report diarrhoea or vomiting to their supervisor
- Report septic cuts or sores, boils or whitlows
- Report discharges from eyes, ears and nose

Food temperatures

- Are properly controlled
- Keep food cool below 8°C or 5°C
- Keep food hot above 63°C
- Cool cooked food rapidly

Task 4.11

Make a list of all the ways the Food Hygiene (General) Regulations 1970 are being broken in the kitchen shown in Figure 4.16.

Figure 4.16

Guides, published by the Department of Health and Social Security are available to help you to understand the Regulations.

Food Hygiene (Amendment) Regulations 1990 and 1991

These Regulations came into force from 1 April 1991. They are concerned with the temperatures you can store food at, and replace those originally given in the Food Hygiene (General) Regulations 1970. Maintaining food at chill temperatures (8°C and 5°C) or hot (63°C) controls the growth of any harmful micro-organisms (Table 4.3).

Table 4.3 Maximum chill storage temperatures for different types of foods

Food	*Temperature*
Cheese	
• Whole ripened soft cheese	8°C
Portions of ripened soft cheese (e.g. Brie, Danish Blue, Stilton, Camembert, Roquefort, Dolcelatte)	5°C
• Cooked products containing hard and soft cheese to be reheated before eating	8°C
• Cooked products containing hard and soft cheese to be eaten without reheating	5°C
Cooked products	
• Containing meat, fish, eggs, hard and soft cheese, cereals, pulses, vegetables	5°C
• Cooked products to be eaten without reheating (e.g. cold meat, vegetable salads, scotch eggs, pork pies, quiches, sandwich fillings)	5°C
• Cooked products to be eaten reheated (e.g. meat pies, fish pies, pizzas, ready meals)	8°C

Catering businesses comply with the regulations by:

- Ensuring that food is always at the correct temperature
- Checking the temperature of food deliveries
- Knowing the time/temperature tolerances
- Checking and recording food temperatures

Task 4.12

Ask for a copy of a completed form used by your school or college to check the temperature of food deliveries. What refrigerator temperatures are used to store the following foods at your school/college?

- *Coleslaw*
- *Sandwiches*
- *Meat pies*
- *Pork pies*
- *Portions of Danish Blue/Stilton cheese*

Check the temperatures you have found against the list given in this section

Exemptions from the regulations

There are times when it is not practical to meet these temperature controls. Some of the times when you can allow the temperature to vary are:

1. When taking a local delivery, food which should be at 5°C may be up to 8°C. You must put this food into chill storage straight away.
2. When refrigerators are defrosting or break down, the chill temperatures of food (8°C or 5°C may rise up by 2°C (10°C or 7°C) for more than 2 hours.
3. When you are preparing food, the tolerance is also 2 degrees for a maximum of 2 hours.
4. When you are serving 'hot' food it may be held below 63°C, but for no longer than 4 hours before sale.

5 When you are serving 'cold' food it may be held above 8°C (or 5°C), but for no longer than 4 hours before sale.
6 When you are displaying food on a sweet trolley, cheese board, self-service or counter display, you may keep food outside its controlled temperature for a maximum of 4 hours. However, you must not display more food than is necessary. After the 4 hours, you must return the food to temperature control or throw it away.
7 When you take food from the service point (for example, at a large banquet) the food temperature need not be kept above 63°C.

Food Safety Act 1990

This Act ensures that our food meets food safety requirements. It covers food, drink, water, ingredients used in food preparation, even chewing gum. Food does not comply with food safety requirements if it:

- Has had anything done to it which makes it harmful to health
- Is unfit to eat
- Is heavily contaminated

Unfit to eat means bad or poisonous or containing dead vermin. Contaminated means containing a rusty nail or harmful chemicals. If you:

- Sell food
- Prepare food for sale
- Supply food for sale

which does not meet these requirements, then you have committed a criminal offence. You may be heavily fined or even imprisoned, for food hygiene and food safety offences.

The Food Safety Act 1990 means that food which is contaminated by food-poisoning micro-organisms fails to meet food safety requirements. If you prepare or sell such food, you may be prosecuted and convicted, even though you are not aware that the food is harmful. Responsibility for food safety belongs to companies, managers and food handlers.

Local authorities enforce the Act through EHOs. Their powers have been extended by the Food Safety Act 1990. EHOs may issue the following notices and orders.

Improvement Notices

If a fault is found, the EHO can set a time limit in which the fault must be corrected.

Prohibition Notices

If the Food Safety Act 1990 is being infringed, Prohibition Notices may be issued, which require that a process is stopped or a machine is not used.

Emergency Prohibition Order

Where there is a serious breach of food safety, the Emergency Prohibition Order stops the process or business immediately.

Emergency Control Order

This is served on unfit food, to withdraw it from sale.

The Food Safety Act 1990 has caused caterers to be much stricter about their hygiene practices. All reasonable precautions must be taken to avoid offences being committed by companies or their staff for:

1 Checking food deliveries
2 Ensuring that stock is used within its storage time
3 Checking refrigerator temperatures daily
4 Setting up cleaning schedules
5 Inspecting premises

Supervisors must ensure that these systems work, or take action if they do not. This is called 'due diligence'. You may use due diligence as a defence if you are prosecuted for a food safety offence.

There are also thirteen codes of practice issued as a result of the Food Safety Act 1990. They contain information for everyone concerned with food hygiene and safety. One of their purposes is to enable EHOs to achieve consistent standards of enforcement throughout the country.

Company codes of practice

Catering establishments may produce their own food safety codes of practice to help food handlers understand the procedures to be followed in order to comply with the current food legislation. They help staff to understand how to:

- Accept food deliveries
- Handle and store all types of food
- Temperature control foods
- Clean and sanitize
- Maintain equipment and premises
- Manage waste

They do not replace the legislation but set company standards for you to use in the course of your work.

Task 4.13

Chilled Beef Steak and Kidney Pie
Use by 01 Dec

Cooking Instructions
Place in preheated oven at 200°C/400°F
Gas mark 6
for 20 minutes
DO NOT REHEAT

The Food Safety Act introduced 'use-by-dates' for foods that can go off in a few days. What action would you take if you went to the refrigerator on 2 December and found the instructions on a beef steak and kidney pie shown above?

Cook–chill guidelines

Guidelines on how to operate cook–chill catering systems have been produced by the Department of Health, who took into account information from cook–chill catering units when updating these guidelines, to ensure that cook–chill food is safe to eat.

Cook–chill catering

Cook–chill catering has been developed as a way of producing high-quality food, while trying to keep the costs down. The meals are prepared in a central production unit, rapidly chilled after cooking, then stored in refrigeration until ready for distribution. The food is then taken to the place where it will be eaten, where it is reheated and served.

Cook–chill may be used on a single site, such as a hospital, ensuring that all patients receive a palatable, hot meal. In other cases, the central production unit may serve several outlets, over quite a wide area. Here, the food must be transported under temperature-controlled conditions in a refrigerated vehicle. Where it is received at the outlet kitchen, the food is refrigerated until it is required for reheating. Companies with several facilities in an area may use this type of system. Quite a small unit is capable of producing 35,000 meals per week.

Cooking operations of this type are more economical to run for a variety of reasons:

1. Expensive food-preparation equipment is concentrated in one kitchen.
2. Skilled staff are only required in the central kitchen.
3. Weekend and holiday working is reduced for skilled staff.
4. Energy is more economically used.
5. Food can be bought in bulk, saving money.
6. Portion size is controlled, so the food reheats thoroughly.

Meals produced by this system are of high quality since:

- Quality raw food must be used
- Standardized recipes ensure consistent products
- Strict hygiene guidelines are followed
- Reheating times and temperatures produce food which is hot

Hygiene in cook–chill units is very strictly controlled. Clean protective clothing is provided for each shift. Staff cannot transfer from preparing raw to cooked food without a complete change of protective workwear and a thorough wash.

Often there is a wash hand basin situated just outside the preparation areas, where hands have to be washed for 15 seconds before entering the kitchen. Recipes also indicate the stages in food preparation when the hands must be washed.

Task 4.14

Using the following recipe, indicate at what stages during the preparation of the quiche you would wash your hands.

Recipe and method for producing Quiche Lorraine for a cook–chill system

Quiche pastry
plain flour
lard
margarine
salt
cold water for mixing

Make up the pastry, allow it to rest for 20–30 minutes, roll out the pastry and line the quiche tins with it.

Filling
cooked, smoked, streaky bacon chopped
cheddar cheese, grated
eggs
milk
salt and pepper

Place the chopped bacon and grated cheese in the pastry case. Beat the eggs thoroughly, then whisk the milk into them and season with salt and pepper. Pour this mixture over the filling. Bake at 180°C for 30–40 minutes.

The raw materials are checked for temperature on delivery and then stored in separate refrigerators for meat, fish and vegetables.

Each area of the kitchen may be colour coded according to the food prepared there, by using coloured flooring and coloured strips around the walls. The people preparing the food are also identified by coloured, plastic aprons. Even cleaning cloths and brushes are the correct colour.

Sandwiches are prepared in separate chilled areas. The staff need to wear body warmers and are given regular breaks so they do not become too cold.

After cooking, the food is rapidly chilled. *Air blast chillers* are often used but *cryogenic chillers*, using liquid nitrogen, may be used for dense foods like meat, to enable it to chill rapidly.

Definition

- ***Air blast chillers*** *blow cold air over the food and operate at –10°C.*
- ***Cryogenic chillers*** *blow nitrogen gas from liquid nitrogen over the food and operate at –190°C.*

After chilling, the food goes into chill storage. These stores are often quite large, with the food

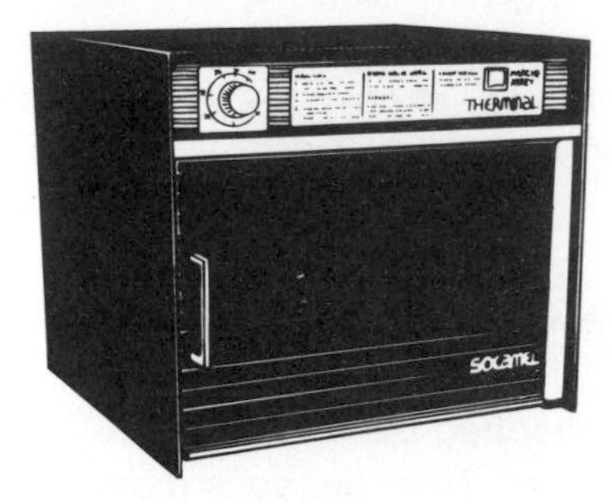

Figure 4.17 A forced-air convection oven

being dated and labelled. The temperature in the chiller is usually +3°C, but some are as low as –20°C.

Reheating is done with forced-air and steamer convection ovens (Figure 4.17), infra-red units or special chill–reheat trolleys (Figure 4.18).

Figure 4.18 A chill–reheat trolley

Effect of cook–chill on micro-organisms

Each stage of the cook–chill system has to control harmful bacteria:

1. Raw food should not be heavily contaminated.
2. Cooking should kill harmful bacteria (but not spores).
3. Post-cooking rapid chilling controls the growth of bacteria.
4. Storage and distribution temperatures must also control the growth of bacteria.
5. Reheating must be hot enough to make the food safe.
6. Service procedures should ensure that the food is safe to eat.
7. Cross-contamination must be avoided.

The cook–chill guidelines

To operate a cook–chill unit, you should:

When buying food

- Purchase food materials to a good quality specification

When preparing food

- Store food materials at the appropriate temperature
- Prepare uncooked food in separate areas
- Provide separate surfaces for raw meat, poultry and fish
- Keep raw-food-preparation staff in that area
- Identify and dedicate machines and utensils, especially knives, for raw or cooked food

Table 4.4 Temperature and time controls for cook–chill food

Process	*Temperature*	*Time*
Cooking	70°C (core temperature)	Maintain for 2 minutes
Portioning	+10°C	Within 30 minutes after cooking
Chilling	From 7°C to +3°C	Within 90 minutes
Storage	0°C to +3°C	Five days
	If over +5°C but under +10°C	Use within 12 hours
	If over 10°C	Destroy
Distribution to outlets	0°C to +°3C	–
Distribution to reheating points	0°C to +3°C	–
Reheating	70°C	Maintain for 2 minutes
Service	Minimum 63°C	Fifteen minutes of reheating

When cooking food

- Cook food thoroughly to the centre and check the temperature with a probe thermometer
- Prepare cooked food for chilling under strict hygiene conditions, handling it as little as possible. Hands must be washed frequently
- Portion food within 30 minutes of it being cooked
- Place cooked food portions in stainless steel, aluminium or porcelain trays, not more than 50 mm deep. Disposable containers may also be used.
- Clean and disinfect all equipment used

When chilling food

- Chill food within 30 minutes after cooking has finished
- Chill food to between 0°C and +3°C within 90 minutes
- Buy a chiller which will chill a 50 mm layer of food from 70°C to +3°C in 90 minutes when it is fully loaded, which has a temperature indicator

When chill storing food

- Dedicate a refrigerated store to cook–chill foods only
- Refrigerate the food between 0°C and +3°C
- Use a recorder to log the refrigerator temperature
- Have a temperature control alarm to indicate when the air temperature in the store is too high
- Label each food container with date of production and date of expiry
- Control food stocks so they are used in rotation and not kept for more than 5 days
- This includes the day of production and the day of eating
- Destroy any food which is over the expiry date

When reheating food

- Reheat food where it is to be eaten
- Reheat food within 30 minutes of it being taken from chill storage
- Reheat food thoroughly, using the standard times and temperatures required by the recipe
- Serve food immediately it is reheated, no longer than 15 minutes after reheating.
- Keep the reheated food above 63°C
- Serve cold food within 30 minutes of taking it out of chill storage
- Destroy any food that is not eaten

How to maintain hygiene standards when preparing and serving food

You will be expected to prepare and serve food to the strict hygiene standards we have been talking about in the previous sections. This section is to remind you what to do.

Preparing food

- Wear clean protective clothing.
- Take off jewellery and nail varnish.
- Wash your hands before handling food.
- Keep raw food separate from cooked food.
- Wash your hands after touching raw food.
- Wash your hands before touching food that will not be cooked again.
- Use colour coded boards.
- Use separate equipment and utensils for raw and cooked food.
- Keep food either hot or cold.
- Thaw food in a separate refrigerator.
- Cook food thoroughly.
- Store hot food for short periods of time only.
- Taste food with a clean spoon.
- Reheat food until the centre is at least 70°C.
- Throw away left-over reheated food.
- Avoid reheating food if possible.

Serving food

- Wear clean uniform although you need not cover your hair.
- Remove your jewellery and nail varnish.
- Wash your hands before serving food.
- Do not touch food with your hands.
- Use clean equipment and utensils to serve food.
- Handle plates by the rims.
- Pick up glasses by the bases.
- Pick up cups and cutlery by the handles.
- Keep hot food above 63°C.
- Keep cold food below 8°C.
- Remember that you are allowed to relax temperature controls when you are serving food.
- Clear away dirty crockery and cutlery regularly.
- Use a separate trolley for dirty crockery/cutlery.

Good practices for health and safety

We are also concerned about the *health and safety of people at work*. The hospitality and catering industry employs quite a large proportion of staff in kitchens, which are potentially dangerous places. Accidents happen all too easily due to thoughtlessness or carelessness or neglect. *Safety awareness is necessary wherever you are working.*

Failure to be concerned about health and safety is very expensive. Accidents and ill health cost employers up to 16 per cent of their wages bill. Most risks can be avoided if management sets out to reduce accidents and health hazards. Not only is money saved, but employees are saved unnecessary suffering.

Health and safety at work is *everybody's* responsibility. Your employer is responsible for your safety, also that of guests, customers, people making deliveries. You are responsible for your own health and safety, and that of the people you are working with. Forgetting to do something is just as serious as unsafe actions.

How accidents are caused

It is essential that people who are working in the hospitality and catering industry know how to carry out their duties in a safe way. You should be aware of the causes of accidents and how to deal with any which occur.

Excessive haste is one cause of accidents. When you are in a hurry, you take chances that inevitably lead to mishaps. However busy you are, never run.

Distraction also contributes to accidents. If you do not concentrate on what you are doing, whether through being worried, distracted by someone else, or simply not interested in the job, then you are more likely to have an accident. Always keep your mind on your work.

Safety rules are made to help you avoid accidents. When you start work, your induction programme should train you in safety procedures. If you fail to apply these rules, then you are much more likely to injure yourself.

Task 4.15

Complete the following safety checklists.

DEPARTMENT:

Date of check: *Name and signature of person making the check:*

	YES	NO
Kitchens:		
Are the floors kept clean and dry?		
Is there any equipment which does not work properly?		
Are there guards on dangerous machines?		
Is the firefighting equipment in position, unobstructed and clearly identified?		
Are notices on display (e.g. use of machinery)?		
Are knives stored correctly?		
Do staff wear appropriate protective clothing?		
Are chemical cleaning agents stored in a locked cupboard?		
Restaurants:		
Are the work areas and escape routes clear and free from rubbish and obstructions?		
Are escape doors clearly identified?		
Do escape doors open easily?		
Is all firefighting equipment in position?		
Are fire alarm points unobstructed?		
Are floors kept clean and dry, especially in service areas?		
Is equipment stored tidily so it is unlikely to fall on people?		
Are electric flexes, plugs, sockets and switches undamaged and working correctly?		
Is a closable metal container provided to hold contents of ash trays?		

Many of the thousands of accidents that occur each year in the hospitality and catering industry are due to people either burning themselves, slipping or tripping over.

What to do in case of an accident

- Look after the person who is injured.
- Remove the danger if you are able to do this without injuring yourself.
- Call a first aider, doctor or ambulance.
- Inform your supervisor.
- Observe the accident area and anything that may have contributed to the accident.

How to treat minor injuries

First aid is given immediately on the spot to a person who is injured or ill. A business must provide first aid equipment, facilities and people trained to give first aid. If the injury is serious, then a nurse or doctor must treat the injured person as soon as possible. You should know how to deal with an accident situation until trained help arrives.

Shock

You can tell if a person is suffering from shock because they are faint and cold, with a white, clammy skin. You should lie the person down, make them comfortable. To keep them warm, cover with a blanket. Do not use a hot water bottle.

Fainting

People may faint after standing for a long time in a hot, steamy kitchen. If a person is about to faint, they will look pale, feel giddy and start sweating. Lie the person down and put something under their feet, to raise them slightly above the level of the head. When the person recovers, take them outside for some fresh air and check they have not injured themselves in fainting.

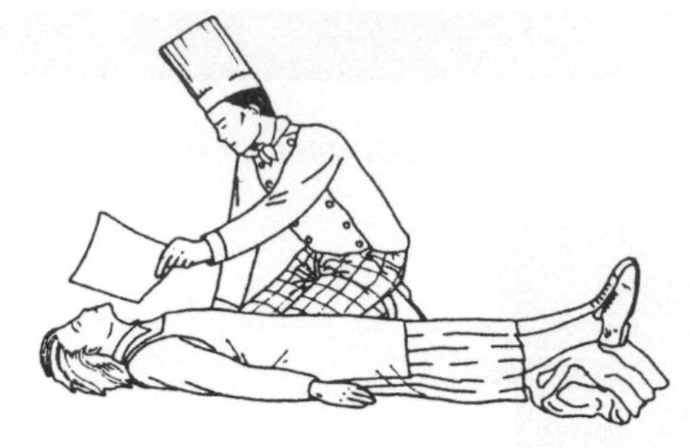

Figure 4.19 Fainting may occur after a long period of standing in a kitchen

Fractures

You should never move anyone you suspect has a broken bone until the injured part has been secured so that it cannot move.

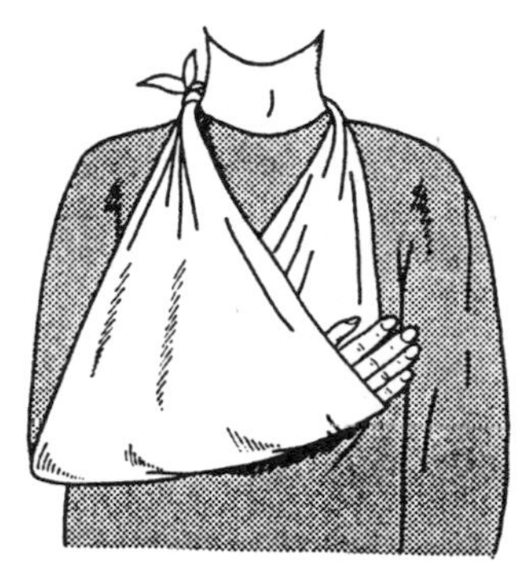

Figure 4.20 Injured parts of the body must be secured so that they cannot move

Cuts

You should cover cuts with a waterproof dressing, after washing the skin around the cut. If the cut is bleeding badly, you should stop it

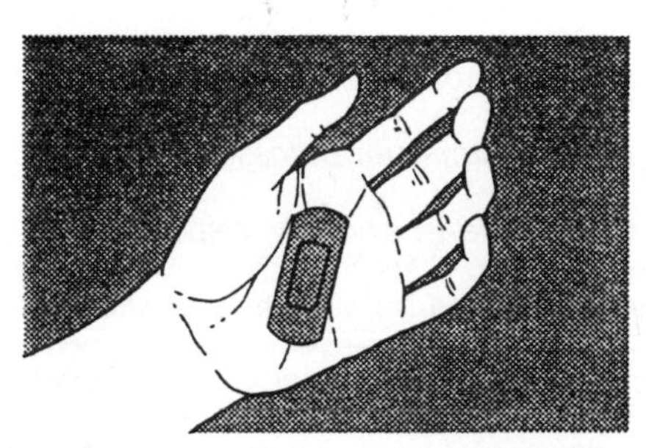

Figure 4.21 Cuts should be covered immediately with a waterproof dressing

as soon as possible. You can control bleeding by applying direct pressure. Bandage a dressing firmly on the cut. If the cut is on the hand, then also hold it above your head.

Burns and scalds

In this case, you should place the injured part under slowly running cold water, or immerse it in cold water. You will need to keep up this treatment for ten minutes or until the pain has been relieved. Should the burn or scald be serious, then cover it with a clean dressing and send the person to hospital for treatment.

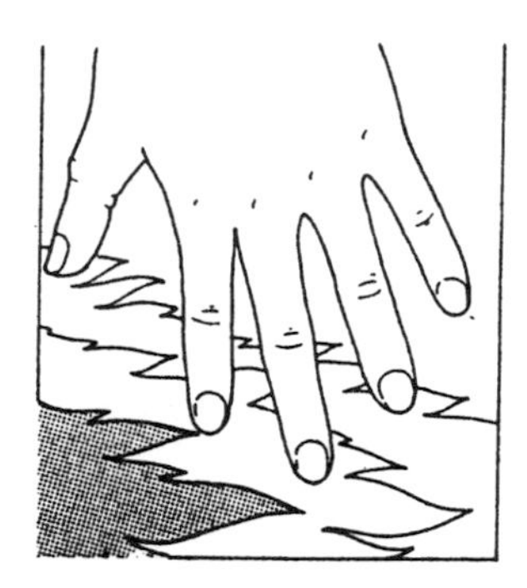

Figure 4.22 Burned or scalded parts of the body must be placed gently under slowly running water or immersed in cool water

Electric shock

Switch off the electric current. You must know where the main switch is located. If you cannot do this, separate the person from the appliance using a wooden brush handle. Take care not to touch the person with your own hands or body, otherwise you will receive a shock. If they have stopped breathing, a trained person should give artificial respiration, while an ambulance is called.

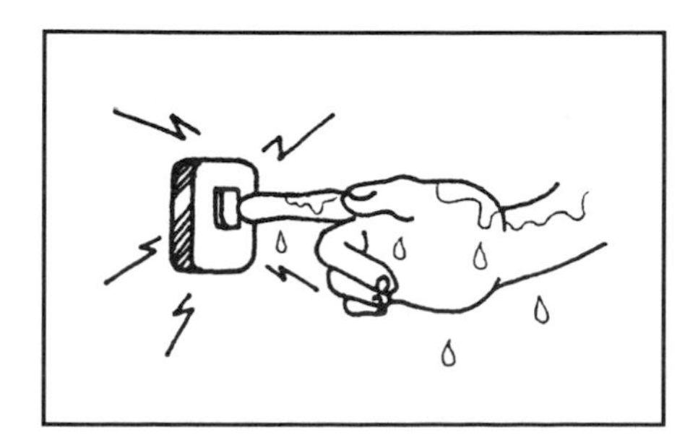

Figure 4.23 In the case of an electric shock switch off the current

Gassing

You should switch off the gas first. Then carry the gassed person into the fresh air. Do not let them walk. If breathing has stopped, then again give artificial respiration and send for an ambulance.

First aid provision

First aid provision depends on the hazards involved. Most hospitality and catering activities are considered to be low/medium risk. *Catering kitchens are high-risk areas.* Your employer has to provide the following for a high-risk area:

- A person appointed to take charge of an accident situation
- First aider(s) trained, with a current first aid certificate
- An occupational first aider, with a current occupational first aid certificate, who knows about catering hazards
- First aid boxes
- First aid room

How to prevent personal injury

During the course of your work in the kitchen or restaurant you may have to lift heavy equipment. Using correct lifting techniques will help to prevent injury to your back (Figure 4.24). When you are lifting a heavy object the best method is to:

1. Clear the route first
2. Grasp the object with the palms of the hands
3. Hold it close to your body
4. Bend your legs so they take the strain
5. Keep your back straight
6. Avoid jerking
7. Do not twist your body when picking up a load
8. Lift in easy stages
9. Do not over-reach

Figure 4.24 Lifting correctly

Fire

You should also know what action to take in case of fire. You are responsible for ensuring that your guests or customers are able to leave the building safely. People with a hearing disability may not hear a fire alarm. Anyone who has a physical disability could need extra help. A notice which explains fire rules to staff should be on display. Remember that fires often start in the kitchens.

Task 4.16

Draw a plan to show the escape routes and fire exits from your school or college kitchen and restaurant. Mark the points where you could raise the alarm and the outside assembly points. Put in where the fire extinguishers and fire blankets are situated.

FIRE RULES

In the event of a fire:

RAISE THE ALARM by operating the nearest fire alarm
CALL FOR HELP
EVACUATE THE BUILDING by the nearest safe route and exit
ATTACK THE FIRE with equipment provided – if you can do so without undue risk

If you hear the fire alarm:

ROUSE THE GUESTS under your charge or make sure they have been roused
LEAVE THE PREMISES with your guests by the nearest available exit. Give special help to the elderly or people with disabilities
REPORT TO THE PERSON in charge at the assembly point at ....

Your responsibilities

Know how to find the escape routes provided.
Know how to operate the fire alarm.
Know how to use the firefighting equipment.

DO NOT

Use lifts as a means of escape.
Shout or run, this tends to cause panic.

How to work safely in the kitchen

When you are working in the kitchen, you are responsible for your own safety and the safety of the people you are working with. By putting into practice the following rules you will prevent injury to yourself and others.

Your personal safety

Food preparation

- Carry knives by the handle, point the blade towards the floor
- Do not leave knives in sinks of water
- Place knives with the handle towards the edge of your work surface
- Do not place containers of boiling liquid, such as soups and stews, on high shelves or the tops of ovens
- Dry food before putting it in a deep fat fryer, wet food causes the fat to boil over and is a fire risk
- Use steamer doors as a shield when you open them, open slowly to allow steam to escape before removing trays
- Dry hands before handling electrical equipment or fitting/removing plugs
- Report faults on electrical equipment, such as worn cables or loose/broken plugs, to your supervisor
- Never use a piece of equipment which has a 'Danger, do not use' notice on it
- Report gas leaks to your supervisor

General safety

- Always walk in the kitchen, never run
- Clean up spills immediately to avoid slipping
- Never leave equipment and containers on the floor, where other people can trip over them
- Store knives in a separate drawer
- Do not leave drawers, oven or refrigerator doors open, for people to walk into
- Put broken glass and crockery into a container kept for it, never in a plastic bag
- Keep fire doors closed to prevent flames and smoke spreading

How to work safely in the restaurant

In the restaurant you have the additional responsibility of taking care of the safety of your customers. You can prevent accidents by:

1. Ensuring tables do not tip or wobble as hot food or liquid may spill on customers
2. Putting flex round the edges of the room and not allowing it to trail, causing people to trip
3. Remembering decorations like candles are a fire risk
4. Securing coat stands to prevent them falling onto customers
5. Never blocking fire exits
6. Reporting broken equipment or fittings which may injure you or your customers
7. Mopping up immediately any food or drink spilled by you or your customers
8. Reporting frayed carpet which is a tripping hazard
9. Never place furniture or equipment where people will fall over it
10. Reporting loose electrical sockets
11. Never carry glasses piled inside each other, they may shatter causing you a serious injury
12. Holding glasses by the stem or handle, especially if reaching
13. Avoiding stacking glasses, they fall over easily, or break when you try to separate them

How to store equipment safely

Equipment for food preparation or food service must be stored safely in the place allocated to it. It should be stored on shelves, not on the floor, where it makes cleaning the floor difficult and is a tripping hazard. Make sure you do not stack shelves too high, or overload racks and shelves. You may find everything topples down on to you. When stacking shelves, do not over-reach. To reach high shelves, always use a step ladder, which should be provided for you. Never stand on the bottom shelf.

How to handle and store cleaning equipment and sanitizers safely

However pretty and harmless they may look, many chemicals are caustic and dangerous.

They will burn your skin deeply. If swallowed, they cause very serious injuries. Oven cleaners, beer pump cleaners and alkaline degreasers are particularly nasty.

The Control of Substances Hazardous to Health Regulations 1988 (COSHH, 1988)

These regulations aim to reduce the health risk to employees who use such substances and prevent serious accidents happening. Cleaning chemicals carrying warning signs like those given in Task 4.17 are covered by COSHH.

The dangers may be from cleaning chemicals coming into contact with our skin, breathing them in or eating them. Employers must substitute less harmful substances where possible, provide safety equipment and keep cleaning processes separate, if this is practical.

The hospitality and catering industry buys cleaning chemicals in bulk. These stocks should be kept in a locked store, separate from the kitchen and used only for that purpose. You will find instructions on the container label on how to use the chemical. These must always be followed. If necessary, the label will carry a hazard warning sign (Figure 4.25). Oven cleaner and beer pump cleaner are corrosive.

Figure 4.25 Corrosive hazard sign

When chemicals are transferred to spray bottles for use, the bottle should also have on it a label stating the type of chemical, instructions for use and any hazard sign required. If chemicals are to be used in the kitchen, they should be stored in a special area set aside for them. They must not come near food-preparation or service areas, otherwise food may become contaminated.

Manufacturers of chemicals often supply a card for each of their products. These also give instructions for use and tell you whether you need to wear rubber gloves, goggles or protective clothing. There are also details of what you need to do if they come into contact with your skin or are swallowed (Figure 4.26).

Employers are required to train their staff on the safe handling and use of chemicals. The important things for you to remember are:

- Use cleaning chemicals for the job they are made to do, never anything else
- Read the instructions on the label
- Use them at the correct strength
- Handle containers with care, in case of drips down the side
- Replace lids immediately
- Wipe up spills at once
- Do not leave chemical containers on the floor
- Do not transfer chemicals to unlabelled bottles
- Never mix cleaning chemicals
- Wash spills off the skin with plenty of cold water
- Immerse your eyes in a bowl of cold water if chemicals splash in them
- If you swallow caustic cleaners, you need hospital treatment, never make yourself sick
- Wear rubber gloves, goggles and protective clothing when using alkaline/caustic cleaners, like oven cleaners

Sanitising Powder

Product Name: Sanitising Powder

Substance Identification Number: - - - -

Health and Safety Classification: J830 or J30

Product Colour: Purple

SAFETY

IN THE EVENT OF:-

INGESTION:
Discourage vomiting.
Give plenty of milk or water to drink.
Obtain medical attention immediately, showing this card.

EYE CONTACT:
Wash thoroughly with clean water for at least 15 minutes and seek immediate medical attention.

INHALATION:
Remove affected person to the fresh air, keep warm and if badly affected seek medical advice showing this card.

SKIN CONTACT:
Wash thoroughly with water and apply a soothing cream if irritation persists.
Seek medical attention if any adverse affects remain.

SPLASHES ON CLOTHING:
Wash thoroughly.

SPILLAGE
Wash away with copious quantities of water.

RISK

Contains

Chlorinated
Tri-Sodium Phosphate

ADDITIONAL INFORMATION

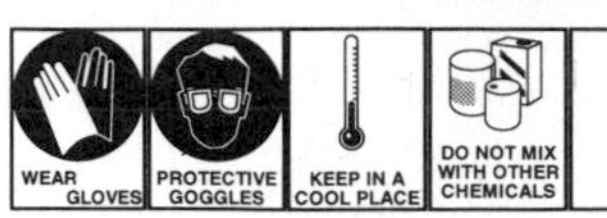

- Contact with combustible material may cause fire.
- Harmful if swallowed.
- Keep out of reach of children.
- Irritating to eyes and skin.
- Wear suitable gloves and eye/face protection.
- Do not mix with any other chemical cleaner.
- Keep in a cool place.
- In case of contact with the preparations or its solutions with the skin or eyes, rinse with plenty of water and seek medical attention for eye contact.

SAFE HANDLING DATA

- Do not take by mouth.
- Avoid skin contact - wear protective gloves.
- Avoid eye contact

ROTHERSTHORPE AVENUE, NORTHAMPTON NN4 9JH
TEL: 0604 764027 FAX: 0604 701238 TLX: 311732

ENVIROCLEAN
SANITISING POWDER **16**

ON

TABLING &
PREPARATION
SURFACES

USE

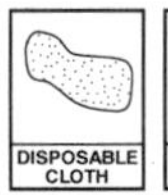

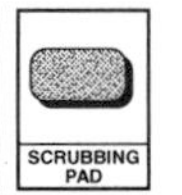

SAFETY

MEASURE

2

INSTRUCTIONS

ALL SURFACES SHOULD BE CLEANED WITH DISPOSABLE MATERIALS WHICH SHOULD ONLY BE USED ONCE, AND NEVER ON MORE THAN ONE SURFACE.

1. Add the number of measures indicated to one gallon of hot water.
2. Using a cloth or scrubbing pad clean all surfaces thoroughly with the solution, paying particular attention to surfaces used for the preparation of raw meat and poultry.
3. Supporting stands should be scrubbed ensuring that no food deposits are left.
4. Allow to air dry.

SEE FIRST AID, CAUTIONS AND STANDARDS OVERLEAF

HEALTH AND SAFETY CLASSIFICATION J830

FIRST AID

EYE CONTACT – WASH THOROUGHLY WITH CLEAN WATER AND SEEK IMMEDIATE MEDICAL ATTENTION.
(TAKE THIS CARD WITH YOU)

CAUTIONS

SPILLAGES WILL CAUSE SLIPPERY PATCHES, RINSE AWAY IMMEDIATELY WITH COLD WATER.

DO NOT MIX WITH OTHER CLEANING AGENTS.

STANDARDS

NO FOOD RESIDUES LEFT ON EQUIPMENT.

ALL SURFACES SHOULD BE THOROUGHLY DRY BEFORE USE.

DETERGENT EFFECTIVENESS MUST BE MAINTAINED.

BUCKETS SHOULD BE LEFT CLEAN FOR NEXT USER.

ENVIROCLEAN Enviro Clean
IS A MEMBER OF MIDKEM GROUP
ROTHERSTHORPE AVENUE, NORTHAMPTON NN4 9JH
TEL: 0604 764027

Figure 4.26 Enviroclean cards

Task 4.17

For each of the following hazard signs, find out a substance used by the catering industry which has one of them.

Oxidizer

Harmful

Toxic

Highly flammable

Irritant

How to store flammable liquids

Sometimes methylated spirits is used in the restaurant to fuel the spirit lamps used for flambé work. It is a flammable liquid, which should be stored in metal drums in a cool, dark, well-ventilated, fireproof, flammable liquids store. Smaller quantities may be transferred to labelled glass bottles. Other flammable materials such as paper and plastics should not be left around stores of methylated spirits. Fires caused by methylated spirits require a carbon dioxide fire extinguisher.

The laws on health and safety

Two of the laws concerning the health and safety of people who are employed are the:

Health and Safety at Work etc. Act 1974
Offices, Shops and Railway Premises Act 1963

The Health and Safety at Work Act 1974 (HASAWA 1974) includes all previous safety legislation, such as the Offices, Shops and Railway Premises Act (OSRPA 1963). HASAWA 1974 aimed to give the protection of the law to all employers and employees, and to make managers and staff more safety conscious.

Health and Safety at Work Act 1974

- Your employer has a duty to ensure the health, safety and welfare of all employees
- Your employer has a duty to ensure the health and safety of people affected by the work or who are using the place of work, but are not employees.
- You, the employee, must take reasonable care of the health and safety of yourself and other people who may be affected by your work
- It is a criminal offence to contravene the HASAWA

Your employer must provide:

- A safe workplace – walls, floor, stairs, lifts
- Safe ways of entering the workplace
- Safe equipment
- Safe materials
- Safe methods of carrying out jobs
- Training and supervision to ensure health and safety
- Training in the use of cleaning chemicals

- A first aid box
- Accident report forms
- A poster explaning the HASAWA
- A written safety policy
- Welfare provision – washing and toilet facilities
- A safe environment – lighting, heating and ventilation

You, as an employee, should:

- Cooperate with your employer concerning health and safety
- Not interfere with anything provided for your health, safety or welfare

Local authorities also enforce HASAWA in most of the hospitality and catering industry through EHOs. They may:

1 Advise
2 Issue an Improvement Notice
3 Issue a Prohibition Notice
4 Prosecute
5 Remove or make harmless dangerous items

Advice

EHOs give valuable advice on health and safety matters.

Improvement Notice

EHOs issue these when you are required to correct a breach of the health and safety law in a given time.

Prohibition Notice

EHOs issue these when they want to stop an activity likely to cause serious risk of personal injury.

Prosecutions

EHOs prosecute both people and companies who are breaking the law.

Removals

EHOs may take away or make harmless anything that is causing imminent danger or risk of serious personal injury.

Under the HASAWA there are powers to make regulations to safeguard the health and safety of working people. These regulations may be supplemented by codes of practice, which explain how to keep within the law. Breaking the health and safety law may result in a fine, prison sentence or both.

Offices, Shops and Railway Premises Act 1963

The reason for this Act was to protect the health and safety of people working in the retail sector. Office premises include the office accommodation in a hotel. Shop premises include restaurants, wine bars, hotel dining rooms and take-aways. A canteen, which is part of an office or shop, is part of the premises. If the HASAWA 1974 is enforced, then the standards set out in OSRPSA 1963 will be used. For example, the minimum working temperature in an office is 16°C.

It is illegal for anyone under 18 years of age to clean any machine, if this exposes them to risk from moving parts of the machine. You may not use a prescribed dangerous machine until you have been trained how to do so safely. During training, you must be supervised by an experienced, trained member of staff. Prescribed dangerous machines are:

Power driven

- Food mixing machines when used with attachments for mincing, slicing, chipping, cutting, crumbling
- Rotary knife bowl chopping machines
- Worm-type mincing machines
- Dough mixers

Power driven/manual

- Circular knife slicing machines
- Potato chipping machines

EQUIPMENT:

Staff trained to operate this equipment:

____

____

____

____

____

____

____

____

____

____

No staff other than those listed are permitted to use this equipment

Figure 4.27 List for staff allowed to use dangerous machines

Dangerous machines should be fitted with a guard, to protect employees from accidents. A warning notice should be placed on or near dangerous machines. Some companies display a list of people who are trained to operate and clean dangerous machines (Figure 4.27).

Safe working practices for large equipment

How to light a gas oven

- Make sure the gas is switched *off* before trying to light a gas oven
- If the gas is on, but not lit, *switch off immediately*, open the oven door and wait 5 minutes for the gas to escape before trying to light the oven
- Switch on the gas supply to the pilot light and light it, keeping your face and body *away* from the jet
- Switch on the main gas supply, keeping your face and body as far away from the jets as possible
- Wait for the pilot light to ignite the gas jets
- If the jets do not light *immediately*, switch off the gas supply and inform your supervisor

Figure 4.28 An exploding oven

How to use an electric oven

- Make sure all control switches are in the *off* position before turning the isolator switch *on*
- Set the oven temperature using the temperature control switch
- Load the oven when the correct temperature is reached, *closing* the door properly
- Check the oven temperature
- Never throw water into an electric oven
- When cooking is finished, open the oven door, taking care to avoid any steam that might shoot out
- Use an oven cloth to remove food from the oven
- Avoid possible accidents, by calling out if someone is in the way, when you are carrying hot food
- Close the oven door
- Switch all controls *off*
- Switch *off* isolator
- If you suspect that there is an electric fault, report it to your supervisor at once

Mixing machines

- Switch machine off at isolator switch/unplug the machine
- Fix the bowl securely to the machine, at its lowest position
- Fix the beater/hook/whisk to the machine
- Add the food to be mixed, do not overfill
- Adjust the bowl to its highest position
- Start the machine at its lowest speed, increasing the speed when necessary
- Never put your hands or arms near the mixing bowl while the machine is *on*
- When mixing is finished, switch the machine *off*, turn isolator switch *off*/unplug, lower the bowl and remove attachment
- Remove any food debris from the mixing machine immediately after use
- *Only one person* should operate a mixing machine at a time

Deep fat fryers, bratt pans, fritures

- Never fill any of these pieces of equipment more than two thirds full with oil or other liquid

- Set the thermostat to the correct temperature
- Dry the food before placing in hot fat
- Do not overload with too much food
- If there is a danger of overflowing, switch off the heat and cover pan with lid
- Never leave these pieces of equipment unattended while the heat is switched on
- Drain the oil when cool each time the equipment has been used

Bain-marie

- Before lighting/switching on check the tap is at *closed* position. Fill half-full with water
- Electric: switch on main switch and appliance switch
- Gas: turn on pilot light and ignite, then turn on main gas burners

Emptying and cleaning

- Ensure power supply is switched/turned off on both appliance (both gas and electric) and mains (both gas and electric)
- Drain off the water into a metal container, do not overfill
- Remove the false bottom and wash the whole bain-marie with hot, soapy water
- Rinse and drain
- Turn drain taps *off*

Cleaning cutting/mixing machines

- Only *one* person should do this to avoid the machine being switched on unexpectedly
- Switch the machine switch *off*
- Switch the isolator switch *off/remove* plug
- Remove slicing/cutting/mixing attachments
- Do not leave slicing/cutting/attachments unattended, someone may cut themselves
- Wash the attachments in a dish-washing machine
- Wash the machine with hot, soapy water
- Rinse with clean, hot water
- Sanitize, following the instructions on the container of the sanitizer
- Rinse
- Dry with a disposable paper cloth

Recognizing hazardous situations

One way to prevent accidents is to train staff to recognize any hazards they may meet in the course of their work. You need to be able to recognize hazards and identify how to make them safe. You must also be able to decide if you can carry out the appropriate action or if you need to report the situation to your supervisor.

Task 4.18

Complete two hazard-spotting exercises, one for a kitchen and one for a restaurant (Figure 4.29). Look at each picture for about a minute. Write a list of the hazards you have spotted. Say how each hazard could be corrected. Who would be responsible for removing the hazards?

Test your knowledge

1 You have been asked to prepare and chop the meat for a beef casserole. You are due to go on duty at 10.00 a.m., so arrive at college/school by 9.30 a.m. Make a list of the:

- Hygiene
- Health and safety precautions you would need to take for this job.

2 Read the following case study about an outbreak of food poisoning and then answer the questions set.

Figure 4.29

Case study – a reheated meal

On Saturday afternoon, the midday meal served in an old people's home offered a choice of chicken or ham as the main course. Those people who had the chicken remained well, but of the seventy-two people who ate the ham, forty-one suffered from severe gastro-enteritis. Two died on the day of the meal and a third a few days later.

The illness began twenty-four hours after the meal. The symptoms were diarrhoea and abdominal pain but only four patients vomited.

The ham had been boiled for three hours on Friday and allowed to cool in the kitchen for one hour. It was then skinned and bread-crumbed and put in the refrigerator at 4 p.m. It was taken out on Saturday morning at 11.30 a.m., sliced or minced and sent to the wards in trolleys to be served for lunch from 12.00 to 1.30 p.m.

As none of the ham had been kept after the meal a similar ham was cooked in the same way and a thermometer placed in it with its temperature probe at the centre of the ham. The digital read-out recorded 72.2°C. During the hour the ham lay in the warm kitchen the thermometer fell to 58.8°C; the outer layers cooling more quickly. It took two hours in the refrigerator to get the temperature at the centre down to under 20°C.

The trolleys used to convey the food to the ward had an upper hot section and a cold lower section. The insulation was found to be defective. The temperature at the time the food was inserted was 4.4°C but rose to 18.3°C in one hour and to 28.8°C in two hours. Most of the patients who became ill had their lunch between 1.00 and 1.30 p.m.

Questions

(a) List the stages in the food preparation at which (i) infection and (ii) multiplication of micro-organisms might have occurred.
(b) List the details of the outbreak which suggested that it was due to *Clostridium perfringens*
(c) What was the temperature of the centre of the ham during cooking? Would this kill (i) vegetative bacteria, (ii) spores of bacteria?
(d) How long did it take to get the temperature of the centre of the ham down to below 20°C? What might be happening during this time?
(e) What defect was found in the insulation trolley?
(f) What temperature did the lower section of the trolley reach after two hours? What might be happening during this time?
(g) Suggest a number of ways in which this outbreak of food poisoning could have been avoided.

3 How have the

- Food Safety Act 1990
- Food Hygiene (Amendment) regulations improved food safety and food hygiene?

4 What are the main measures which can be taken by caterers, to ensure that a cook–chill system produces food which is safe to eat?
5 What precautions can you take to make sure the customers who are using your restaurant are able to eat in a safe environment? Prepare a checklist of the safety measures you would take while setting up the restaurant for service.

Assessment

Unit title	Providing Food and Drink (Intermediate)
Assessment title	Investigating methods of food and drink service

Assessment details
You have been asked to look at the various methods of food and drink service that are in use within the hospitality and catering industry, for a foreign company who are breaking into the popular restaurant/pub market.

What they want from you is the following information:

- The results of your findings in a clear uncomplicated report.
- Your recommendations for the method of service you feel would be best suited. It may be possible to have more than one in use at the same time and your reasons for recommendation.
- What standard of work force would be required.

Your findings and recommendations must be presented in typed form and appropriately bound.

Element 4.1	*Core*
Investigative methods of providing food and drink services see below	2.1 – 1,2,3,4 2.2 – 1,2,3,4 2.4 – 1,2

Performance criteria

- Different methods of providing food and drink services in current use are identified
- Methods of providing food and drink services are matched to various outlets in the different sectors
- Skills required for the different methods of providing food and drink services are described
- Good practices for hygiene, health and safety are identified

Unit title	Providing Food and Drink (Intermediate)
Assessment title	Production skills in food and drink service

Assessment details
You are to complete the service of a meal for four covers within the college restaurant on a predetermined date.

- Carry out all mise-en-place tasks required to enable an organized service period
- Undertake all duties as station waiter showing at all times your skills and attributes to the best advantage
- Make sure that hygiene, health and safety standards are maintained at all times

A brief evaluation of service will be required the following date to be presented in an appropriate manner.

Element 4.3	*Core*
Production skills in food and drink service see below	2.2 – 1,2,3,4

Performance criteria

- Practical, social and manipulative skills required by a server of food and drink are explained
- Skills for service of food and drink are demonstrated
- Hygiene, health and safety standards are demonstrated

Core skills which you should experience

	Working with others	*Improve own learning and performance*	*Problem solving*
Level 1	1 Work to given collective goals and responsibilities. 2 Use given working methods in fulfilling own responsibilities.	3 Agree short-term targets. 4 Follow given activities to learn and to improve performance.	5 Select standard solutions to fully describe problems.
Level 2	1 Work to given collective goals and provide feedback to help with the allocation of responsibilities. 2 Use given working methods in fulfilling own responsibilities, and provide feedback to others on own progress.	3 Contribute to identifying strengths and learning needs, and agree short term targets. 4 Make use of feedback in following given activities to learn to improve performance.	5 Use established procedures to clarify routine problems. 6 Select standard solutions to routine problems.
Level 3	1 Work to given collective goals and contribute to the process of allocating individuals' responsibilities. 2 Agree working methods and use them, and provide feedback to others on own progress.	3 Identify strengths and learning needs, and agree short-term targets. 4 Seek and make use of feedbacks, follow given activities to learn and to improve performance.	5 Select procedures to clarify problems with a range of possible solutions. 6 Identify alternative solutions and select solutions to problems.
Level 4	1 Contribute to determining collective goals and to the process of allocating individuals' responsibilities. 2 Agree working methods and use them, and contribute to the process of maintaining standards of work.	3 Identify strengths and learning needs, and propose and agree short term targets. 4 Seek and make use of feedback, select and follow activities to learn and to improve performance.	5 Extend specialist knowledge in order to clarify complex problems with a range of possible solutions. 6 Identify alternative solutions and select solutions to complex problems.

Core skills which you should experience (continued)

	Working with others	*Improve own learning and performance*	*Problem solving*
Level 5	1 Lead the process of determining collective goals and allocating individuals' responsibilities. 2 Agree working methods and use them, monitor overall progress of own and others' work.	3 Identify strengths and learning needs, and propose and agree long term targets. 4 Seek and make use of feedback, select and follow a wide range of activities to learn and to improve performance.	5 Extend specialist knowledge in order to clarify complex problems with a range of possible solutions which include unknown/unpredictable features 6 Identify alternative solutions and select solutions to complex problems which include unpredictable features

▪ IDENTIFY AND USE SKILLS REQUIRED TO PREPARE FOOD ▪

In this section we look at the skills required by staff involved in the preparation of food as well as the cookery processes used in the preparation of food to be consumed by the customer. Hygiene, health and safety are also addressed. You need to know the basic cookery skills such as handling cutlery, weighing commodities correctly, measuring liquids, and knife skills such as peeling, chopping, slicing and carving, as well as the basic cookery processes, i.e. boiling, stewing, poaching, frying, roasting, grilling, microwave and baking.

The following will look at the cookery skills and basic cooking processes. This section will give you the theory background behind these skills areas, but you will need to practise them in order to understand them more fully.

Cooking techniques

Boiling

Definition

- ***Boiling*** *is a method of cooking where prepared food is cooked in a liquid which contains water (water, aromatic cooking liquor, stock, milk). The boiling action may be quick and rapid (as when cooking green-leaf vegetables); or slow, with a gentle surface movement known as simmering (used when boiling most foods).*

You boil food in order to

- Make foods tender, by breaking down and softening starch, cellulose, protein and fibrous material
- Make foods more palatable and digestible
- Make foods safer to eat, by destroying bacteria which can cause food poisoning
- Produce a particular quality in food, of colour, flavour and texture (e.g. boiled cabbage)

Boiling methods

Food is placed into cold liquid, which is brought to the boil and cooked. You would use this method to create a clear cooking liquid. Scum and impurities will rise to the surface as the liquid comes to the boil and can be skimmed off. This is important when preparing stocks and clarified liquids such as consommés and jellies. Work as carefully as possible. It is wise to cover food with cold liquid then bring to the boil.

Food is placed into boiling liquid and cooked to:

- Keep cooking times as short as possible
- Retain nutritional value and colour, by keeping the cooking time short
- Reduce vitamin loss when cooking vegetables by destroying oxidative enzymes
- Reduce the risk of burning cereals and starch mixtures such as rice and pastas

Suitable foods for boiling

1. *Dried cereals and pulses* Common examples are rice, barley, oats, marrowfat peas, lentils and various dried beans.
2. *Eggs and pastas* Common examples are boiled eggs and fresh and dried pastas (e.g. noodles, spaghetti and macaroni)
3. *Fish and shellfish* It is more desirable to poach most fish, but there are some classic dishes which are boiled. Lobsters, for example, are usually cooked by boiling.
4. *Fresh and frozen vegetables* Common examples are cabbage, cauliflower, turnips, peas, green beans and potatoes.
5. *Meat and poultry* Boiling is used for the tougher joints and birds (e.g. silverside of beef, rolled brisket and hams). It is a suitable method for producing plain dishes (e.g. boiled gammon with cabbage and parsley sauce).

When boiling food:

- Always keep liquid content to a minimum when boiling food to ensure that valuable nutrients are not lost. Also serve the cooking liquor with the food whenever possible.
- Arrange saucepans of boiling food on the stove so that the correct cooking speed is maintained (i.e. rapid boiling or simmering). Also check saucepans regularly to ensure the correct speed of cooking and to determine degree of cooking.
- Avoid soaking or storing vegetables in water (except pulses). Also start the cooking of vegetables in boiling liquid whenever possible.
- Be careful when draining foods with boiling liquid. Stand back from the saucepan, avoiding splashes of hot liquid.
- Cook vegetables in batches and as near to service as possible. Avoid cooking and reheating vegetables.
- Many boiled dishes have long cooking times (e.g. stocks, boiled meats and pulses); you will need to allow for this in your time plan.
- Remove fat from the surface of stocks and sauces as it forms.
- Soak out as much salt as possible from salted joints prior to cooking (e.g. hams and gammons).
- Store boiled foods at temperatures below 5°C/40°F, for as short a time as possible.
- Thoroughly cook dried beans, as under-cooked beans contain a poison which can cause sickness. Dried beans should therefore be boiled rapidly for a minimum of 10 minutes and then simmered for the remaining cooking time.
- To avoid food poisoning, cool liquids and foods quickly then store chilled until required for use. Never leave boiled foods and liquor sitting in a warm kitchen.

Poaching

Definition

- ***Poaching*** *is a way of cooking whereby food is cooked in a liquid containing water (court-bouillon, milk, stock, water or wine). The food is cooked at temperatures below boiling point (75–93°C/167–200°F) with little or no liquid movement.*

Poaching is a gentle method of cooking foods which would otherwise break up or lose shape if boiled. Food is poached:

1 To make foods more palatable and digestible
2 To make foods tender, by breaking down starch, cellulose and protein
3 To make foods safer, by destroying bacteria which can cause food poisoning

Poaching methods

In deep-poaching food is covered with the minimum quantity of liquid, mostly very hot and then gently cooked. Large whole fish are an exception: e.g. salmon, which is covered with cold liquid then brought to poaching temperature (to reduce the distortion of the fish when applying heat). Deep-poaching is a method of cooking, producing dishes such as poached fruits.

In *shallow-poaching* food is partly covered with the poaching liquor (to two-thirds the height of the food item) and then cooked gently under cover in an oven. This is a more involved method of cooking because the cooking liquor is reduced down and forms the base of the accompanying sauce. Many classic fish dishes are produced in this way (Figure 4.30).

Key points to follow when poaching are:

1 Allow sufficient time to prepare poached foods which are to be cooked and served cold. A whole salmon for a cold buffet has to be cooked then thoroughly cooled before it can be moved from its poaching liquor. After this it must be skinned, decorated and garnished.
2 Always keep liquid content to a minimum when deep-poaching food to avoid losing valuable nutrients.
3 Check regularly to ensure that the food is being poached and not boiled; this is important to maintain good quality.

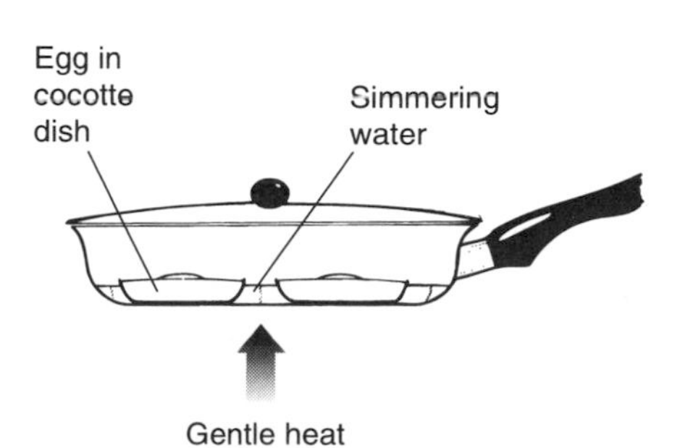

Figure 4.30 A poaching pan

Oven temperature chart

	°C	*Regulo*	°F
Slow (cool)	110		225
	130		250
	140	1	275
	150	2	300
	160	3	325
Moderate	180	4	350
	190	5	375
	200	6	400
Hot	220	7	425
	230	8	450
Very hot	250	9	500

Steaming

Definition

- ***Steaming*** *is a moist method of cooking where prepared food is cooked in steam (water vapour) at varying degrees of pressure.*

Food is steamed to:

- Keep the loss of soluble nutrients to a minimum (e.g. in vegetables)
- Make foods more palatable and digestible
- Produce a particular quality in food of colour, flavour and texture (e.g. steamed sponge pudding)
- Make foods safer to eat, by destroying bacteria which can cause food poisoning
- Make foods tender, by breaking down and softening starch, cellulose and protein

Suitable foods for steaming

- Eggs
- Fish and shellfish
- Savoury and sweet puddings (low-pressure steaming only)
- Vegetables (including potatoes)

Steaming equipment

- Atmospheric and low-pressure steamers
- High-pressure steamers and jet steamers

Key points when steaming

1. Be careful when opening the door after use. Stand behind the door and use it as a shield against escaping steam.
2. Turn off the steam before opening the door unless using a low-pressure steaming cabinet (which is not switched off during cooking).
3. Overcooking food, especially with high-speed steaming where even short periods of overcooking will destroy nutrients.
4. Cook vegetables as near to service time as required. A high-speed steamer is ideally designed for this purpose.
5. Switch on the machine in good time if preheating is required.

Stewing

Definition

- ***Stewing*** *is a method of cooking where prepared food (cut into pieces) is cooked in a minimum quantity of liquid. Both the food and the liquid form the stew, so they are always served together. Stewing is an ideal method of cooking for the tougher cuts of meat, poultry and game; and since you are cooking and serving them in their cooking juices, the process also saves valuable nutrients. It is also a term used when slowly cooking fruits to a pulp (e.g. stewed apples).*

Stewing methods

Methods of stewing are grouped according to the following factors:

- Colour of stew (e.g. white and brown stews)
- Method of preparation:
  Stews cooked in a prepared sauce (e.g. fricassées)
  Stews where the liquid is thickened at the end of the cooking process (e.g. blanquettes)
- Type of commodity (e.g. fish, meat, vegetable stews)

Suitable foods for stewing

- Fish and shellfish
- Fruits – cooking of apples, pears and rhubarb to form a coarse pulp
- Poultry and feathered game (e.g. chicken, duckling, partridge and pheasant)
- Red and white meats (e.g. beef, mutton, lamb, veal and pork). The tougher cuts of meat are used for stewing
- Vegetables are usually cooked together to form the stew (e.g. onions, garlic, courgettes, aubergines and tomatoes in a ratatouille)

Blanching

This is done to remove impurities from meat when preparing blanquettes as follows:

1. Cover the prepared meat with cold water and bring it to the boil.
2. Drain, then prepare the stew.
3. Remove from the stove and place under cold running water to rinse off all the scum which has formed.

Braising

Definition

- ***Braising*** *is where prepared food is cooked in a covered container with a quantity of stock or sauce in an oven. The food to be braised is usually placed on a vegetable base (mirepoix) or sautéd chopped vegetables and the liquid or sauce added to approximately two-thirds the height of the food item. This rule does not apply when braising small cuts of meat and offal such as chops, rump steaks and sliced ox liver, where the food is completely covered with the cooking liquor or sauce to maintain even cooking. When the food is cooked it is portioned and served with the finished sauce or cooking liquor.*

Reasons for braising foods

- To cook and serve foods in their own juices, thus conserving valuable nutrients
- To make foods more palatable and digestible
- To make foods safer to eat by destroying bacteria which can cause food poisoning
- To make foods tender, by breaking down and softening starch, cellulose, protein and fibrous material

Methods of braising are grouped according to the colour of the finished dish and the foods to be braised:

- Braising rice
- Brown braising of meat, poultry, game, offal and vegetables
- White braising

Suitable foods for braising

- Butcher meats – including beef, veal and venison
- Offal – including ox liver and sweetbreads
- Pickled meats and offal – including ham and pickled tongue
- Poultry and feathered game – including duck, duckling, pheasant and partridge
- Rice
- Vegetables – including cabbage, celery, leek and onion

Special care is required when removing braising pans from the oven, especially when they contain large joints. The pan should be lifted carefully (with correct body posture and movement) using a thick, dry, folded oven cloth on each handle, remembering that the joint may move about as the pan is lifted.

Roasting

Definition

- ***Roasting*** *is a dry-heat method of cooking, where prepared food is cooked on a spit or with fat in an oven.*

Food is roasted to:

- Make foods more palatable and digestible
- Produce a particular quality in food, of colour, flavour and texture (e.g. roast venison)
- Make foods safer to eat, by destroying bacteria which can cause food poisoning
- Make foods tender, by breaking down and softening mainly protein, but also starch, cellulose and fibre

Oven roasting

This is the cooking of food in an oven, mainly by convected heat or forced-air convected heat. However, other forms of heat application may also play an important function when roasting (e.g. conducted heat from a roasting tray when roasting potatoes, and radiated heat from the sides of an oven, both of which help to develop colour on the surface of the food). In addition, combination ovens which combine microwave energy or steam with forced air convected heat are also used when roasting.

Pot roasting (poêler)

This is a form of casserole cooking. The food is cooked under cover in an oven with (traditionally) butter as the cooking fat. Using this method of cooking the removal of the lid during cooking allows the food to develop colour. After cooking, the vegetable base together with the cooking juices provide the basis of the accompanying sauce.

Spit roasting

This involves cooking the food by dry heat on a spit which is slowly turned over a heat source such as a charcoal fire, electric elements or gas flames. The main form of heat application is direct radiated heat, but convected heat (hot air) is also present. Conducted heat from metal spit bars may also aid cooking in some instances.

Suitable foods for roasting

Good-quality joints must be used when roasting meat, poultry and game.

- Butcher meats and furred game (e.g. beef, veal, lamb, mutton, pork and venison)
- Potatoes and parsnips
- Poultry and feathered game (e.g. chicken, turkey, duckling, grouse and pheasant)

Pot roasting

Use good-quality butcher meats, poultry and game for this type of cooking.

Resting, standing or settling a roast

Remove a roast from the oven after cooking and leaving it in a warm place for a short period (5–15 minutes depending on size). This is to reduce the risk of someone being burned when portioning or carving the joint. The food is also easier to carve or portion after resting.

Key roasting points

1 Keep your hands well protected and wear your sleeves long to avoid burns from spurting hot fat. Take care when removing roasts from the oven. Special care should be taken with large roasts which may move when the tray is lifted.
2 Roasts are served at a particular degree of cooking, i.e. underdone, medium, well done. This must be carefully considered when preparing your time plan.
3 Where possible, use lean joints such as rump and good-quality topside, and trim off surface fat before serving.

Task 4.19

Describe the preparation of a chicken required for 'spit roasting'. How does this type of roasting differ from other foods roasted in an oven?

Microwave cooking

Microwave cooking is a method of cooking or heating of prepared food by using high-frequency power. This radio wave, when applied to the cooking of food, acts like a 'cocktail shaker'. It shakes all the molecules in the food causing 'friction' which in turn gives off heat and either heats or cooks the food depending on how long the process is carried out. Food in a microwave is cooked 'whole', that is, it is not cooked from the outside to the inside like traditional ovens but all through at the same time, hence it is so quick.

Grilling

Definition

- ***Grilling** is a dry heat method of cooking where prepared food is cooked mainly by radiated heat in the form of infrared waves.*

Foods are grilled to:

- Make foods more palatable and digestible
- Make foods tender, by breaking down and softening mainly protein, but also starch
- Make foods safer to eat, by destroying bacteria which can cause food poisoning

Grilling methods

- Between electrically heated grill bars
- Over a heat source which can be fired by charcoal, electricity or gas (e.g. steak grills and barbecues)
- Under a heat source fired by gas or electricity (e.g. salamander-type grills)

Good-quality cuts must be used when grilling meat, poultry and game. Other foods include:

1. Butcher meats – various types of steaks, chops, and cutlets
2. Fish and shellfish: various small whole fish (sole, plaice, trout); cuts of fish (fillets and steaks); and shellfish such as lobster, large prawns and scampi
3. Made-up items and convenience foods (e.g. burgers, bitokes, sausages and sliced meat puddings)
4. Offal and bacon – sliced liver, kidneys and gammon steaks
5. Poultry and feathered game: various small birds prepared ready for grilling – spring chicken, grouse and partridge
6. Vegetables – mainly mushrooms and tomatoes

Brushing

Brushing with oil involves lightly brushing the item with fat before and during cooking. It is done to prevent the surface of the item drying out and becoming hard. Basting with fat (coating the item) should be avoided as this increases the fat content.

Flouring

Coating foods with flour prior to grilling only applies to items which do not develop a good colour when cooking. Whole fish, cuts of fish and liver are usually lightly coated with flour when they are to be cooked under a salamander.

Turning

Foods being grilled should be turned with tongs or a palette knife. Never stab or pierce foods with a fork at any stage of preparation or cooking. This applies to all foods including sausages.

Key points

Thoroughly cook foods which can cause food poisoning (e.g. chicken, pork and made-up items such as sausages). Knowing when food has reached a specific degree of cooking is an important skill which must be learned. One way of quickly determining the degree of cooking is to use a temperature probe.

Grilled foods are served at a particular degree of cooking depending on the type of food item and customer choice; i.e. rare, underdone, medium and well done (Figure 4.31). The time at which you should begin to cook these items is therefore dictated by the service requirements.

Beef grills

Approximate weight per portion 100–150 g (4–6 oz); in many establishments these weights will be exceeded.

Figure 4.31 A grill (courtesy of Marwood Vulcan Ltd)

Rump steak	–
Point steak	–
Double fillet steak	chateaubriand
Fillet steak	fillet grillé
Tournedos	tournedos grillé
Porterhouse or T-bone steak	
Sirloin steak	entrecôte grillée
Double sirloin steak	entrecôte double
Minute steak	entrecôte minute

All steaks are lightly seasoned with salt and pepper and brushed on both sides with oil. Place on hot preheated greased grill bars. Turn half-way through the cooking and brush occasionally with oil and cook to the degree ordered by the customer.

Degrees of cooking grilled meats

Rare	au bleu	Just done	à point
Underdone	saignant	Well done	bien cuit

Task 4.20

Find out the correct temperature to cook red meats to the following degrees:

- *Underdone*
- *Just done*
- *Well done*

Shallow-frying

Definition

- ***Shallow-frying** is a dry-heat method of cooking, where prepared food is cooked in a preheated pan or metal surface with a small quantity of fat or oil. It is a fast method of cooking because heat is conducted from the hot surface of the cooking pan directly to the food.*

Foods are shallow-fried in order to:

- Make foods tender, by breaking down and softening protein, fat, starch, cellulose and fibre
- Make foods more palatable and digestible
- Make foods safer to eat, by destroying bacteria which can cause food poisoning

Good-quality cuts must be used when shallow-frying meat, poultry and game. Other foods include:

- Batters and doughs (e.g. crêpes, scones and pancakes)
- Butcher meats and furred game (e.g. various types of steaks, chops, cutlets, escalopes and medallions)
- Eggs: mainly scrambled eggs and omelettes
- Fish: various small whole fish (sole, plaice, trout) and cuts of fish (fillets and steaks)
- Fruits (e.g. bananas, peaches, apple and pineapple slices)
- Offal and bacon (e.g. sliced liver, kidneys and gammon steaks)
- Poultry and feathered game: cuts for sauter and supremes
- Vegetables: sliced potatoes, mushrooms, onions, tomatoes and courgettes

Key points

1 Always preheat the frying utensil to reduce both fat absorption into the food and the risk of the food sticking to the pan.
2 Ensure that the presentation side of the food item is fried first so that the item does not become discoloured or marked with sediment.

3 Keep the frying fat to a minimum and if possible dry-fry on a non-stick surface.
4 Place the foods with the longest cooking times into the pan first (e.g. chicken legs before wings).
5 Remember that certain shallow-fried foods (e.g. beef dishes) are served at a particular degree of cooking; i.e. rare, underdone, medium and well done. The decision on when to start cooking a particular item must be made in keeping with service requirements.
6 Use lean cuts of meat and trim off excess fat before cooking. Also drain the food to remove as much surface fat as possible prior to service. To reduce fat content, cook foods by grilling rather than shallow-frying. This applies to meat, poultry, game and made-up items such as sausages and hamburgers.

Deep-frying

Definition

- ***Deep-frying** is a dry-heat method of cooking, where prepared food is cooked in preheated fat or oil. It is a fast method of cooking because all the surfaces of the food are fried by being cooked at the same time, with temperatures of up to 195°C (383°F) being used.*

Figure 4.32 A deep-fryer (courtesy of Marwood Vulcan Ltd)

Foods are deep-fried in order to:

- Make foods more palatable and digestible
- Produce a particular quality in food, of colour, flavour and texture (e.g. apple fritters)
- Make foods safer to eat, by destroying bacteria which can cause food poisoning
- Make foods tender, by breaking down and softening fat, starch and fibre

Deep-frying methods

Partial cooking or blanching is the deep-frying of foods until tender, but without developing colour. The reason for blanching foods is that they can be stored on trays until required for service then fried quickly in hot fat until crisp and golden brown. Chips are usually blanched in this manner; fruit fritters and battered vegetables may also be blanched prior to service.

Complete cooking is the deep-frying of foods until fully cooked, where serving takes place immediately, to maintain a crisp, dry product.

Suitable foods for deep-frying

- Batters and doughs (e.g. choux paste (fritters), bun dough and doughnuts)
- Chicken or turkey: portions of poultry
- Fruits (e.g. bananas, peaches, apple and pineapple slices)

- Made-up items and convenience foods (e.g. scotch eggs, savoury cutlets, croquettes and cromesquis)
- Potatoes
- Vegetables: raw (e.g. aubergines, courgettes); or cooked (e.g. prepared celery, fennel and cauliflower)
- White fish (e.g. some small whole fish (haddock) and fillets of fish)

Basic techniques

Foods should be drained and dried as much as possible before being cooked. It is very dangerous to place wet foods into hot fat because the fat reacts violently and rapidly increases in volume. Many fried foods are coated with batter or bread crumbs prior to frying. This not only produces a crisp, coloured surface but also reduces the juices and fat from the item entering and contaminating the frying medium.

Foods which are battered are passed through the batter (usually after coating with flour), and then placed directly into the hot fat. They should be placed carefully into the fat to avoid splashes of fat which can cause burns. A basket should never be used when frying battered foods.

Foods coated with bread crumbs are usually fried on trays or in baskets. Most foods are fried at a temperature which will cook, colour and crisp the food all at the same time. Avoid low-temperature frying as this increases fat absorption in the food.

Fried foods should be drained thoroughly after cooking to remove surface fat. In addition, it is standard practice in many establishments to serve fried food on dish papers which absorb surface fat.

To produce high-quality fried food for the customer the food should be served immediately after frying. Never use a lid to cover fried foods as this produces condensation and softens the crisp coating.

Key points

1. Always use a well-designed fryer with a thermostat and never an old-fashioned friture.
2. Never exceed a maximum frying temperature of 195°C (383°F).
3. Never fry too much food at once as this is not only dangerous but will also reduce the frying temperature and increase fat absorption.
4. Strain the fat regularly to remove food particles. Keep the number of fried foods offered to a minimum.

Stir fry

This method of cooking vegetables originated in the Orient. It requires a deep pan with sloping sides and a high, fierce flame to create sufficient heat. The pan is oiled and then finely chopped raw vegetables are added and tossed until they are glazed, slightly softened and just beginning to colour. At this point they are removed and served immediately. Peppers, mangetout, onions, carrots, Chinese lettuce, mushrooms, courgettes, bean sprouts and parsnips can all be cooked using this method.

Baking

Definition

- ***Baking*** *is a dry-heat method of cooking where prepared food and food products are cooked by convected heat in a preheated oven.*

Foods are baked in order:

- To make foods more palatable and digestible
- To make foods safer to eat, by destroying bacteria which can cause food poisoning
- To make foods tender, by breaking down and softening fat, starch and fibre

Methods

1. *Baking fruits, vegetables and potatoes* This is a form of simple oven cooking where the food

Figure 4.33 A baking oven (courtesy of Blodgett Ovens Ltd)

items are cooked in an oven until tender (Figure 4.33).

2 *Baking within a bain-marie:* This involves placing the item to be baked in a water bath, so that low temperatures may be maintained during cooking. The baking of egg custard mixtures is an example of this type of cooking, where a gentle oven heat is maintained by a bain-marie, reducing the likelihood of the mixture curdling.

Suitable foods for baking and oven cooking

- Eggs which are oven cooked
- Flour products (e.g. cakes, sponges, pastries and yeast goods)
- Fruits (e.g. apples and pears)
- Meat and vegetable hot pots which are oven cooked
- Milk puddings and egg custard products
- Potatoes
- Vegetables prepared in vegetarian bakes

Gilding or coating with egg wash

Foods which are baked, especially pastry and yeast goods, can be lightly brushed with egg wash just prior to baking so that a good colour will develop on the surface of the item.

Speed of heating

Foods are baked so that the product rises, develops colour and cooks through at the same time. It is important that the oven is set to the correct temperature and preheated before inserting the food.

Proving

Proving is the final fermentation of yeast goods after they have been shaped and placed on the baking tray. It is usually carried out at 28–30°C (82–86°F) in a moist atmosphere to prevent the surface of the goods developing a skin.

Cooling

Many baked foods are very delicate when hot (cakes and pastries, for example) and should be allowed to cool slightly prior to use. This is usually done on a cooling wire tray which allows the air to circulate under the food and prevents condensation and softening of the product.

Key points

Allow sufficient time for the oven to reach the correct baking temperature. Do not have, for example, a sponge ready for the oven but which cannot be cooked because the oven is not hot enough.

Task 4.21

Suggest the most suitable method of cooking the following items:

- *Silverside of beef*
- *Breast of chicken (served with cream sauce)*
- *Fresh leeks to be served as a vegetable course*
- *Sirloin steak with a cream and brandy sauce*
- *Cheese fritter*
- *Pancake with an apple purée filling*
- *Lamb cutlet for serving at a buffet*
- *Vegetables (cut thinly) for serving with a boiled rice dish*

Knife skills and safe handling

Introduction

It is very important that you learn to handle, maintain and care for your knives from the beginning of your training as a chef. Given time and practice they will become an extension of your hands.

You will also need to learn how to select the correct knife for the job in hand, such as a filleting knife for filleting fish. During your training you may well come across a great number of cutting, shredding and chopping machines, but none of these can produce the same fine quality of work you will be able to achieve with a sharp knife.

Knife skills

- Always use the knife best suited to the job
- Maintain your knives in a clean and sharp condition
- Handle all knives safely and in a methodical manner
- Once you have chosen the knives you are going to use, place them flat on the work surface with the blades facing inwards
- Never try to catch a knife if it is falling to the floor
- Never leave knives in a sink
- Only ever have one knife on the chopping board at any one time
- Never leave knives on the edge of the table or board
- Never allow knives to become hidden under food items

Choosing the correct knife

Failure to do this can be dangerous because:

1. Too large – you will not have adequate control over it and you are therefore more likely to have an accident
2. Too rigid – when you need a flexible blade you will not be able to work as quickly or as efficiently as possible, and you may even have an accident

Always keep your knives clean because:

- You have less control over a dirty, greasy or wet knife
- Cutting raw and cooked produce with the same unwashed knife can cause cross-contamination

Always keep knives sharp because:

- A blunt knife requires more pressure to allow it to cut through a food item; this extra pressure can cause loss of control and therefore accidents
- A blunt knife will take longer than a sharp knife to complete a task and the finished result will not be as neat and accurate as when done with a sharp knife

Always handle knives safely and methodically:

1. Careless handling of knives causes accidents.
2. Carry knives carefully, by holding the handle, pointing the knife downwards towards the floor with the sharp edge pointing behind you. Keep it slightly away from the body.
3. Never threaten anyone with a chef's knife (even in jest) however small its blade may be.
4. Never transport knives around the kitchen by placing them on a board and then carrying the board. They could easily fall off and cause an accident.

Different types of knives

1. *Boning knives* – the blade sizes of these ranges from 13–17 cm (5–6½ inches). They are used to remove bones from joints of meat. The blade can be straight or curved to suit large and small butchery. The blades are generally rigid but it is possible to buy boning knives with a slightly flexible blade.
2. *Cooks' knives* – the blades of these knives range in size from 10–30 cm (4–12 inches). All cooks' knives have a rigid blade and are used for a wide range of jobs including shredding, dicing and chopping. They are always used for trimming vegetables, meat,

poultry or game. The larger cooks' knives can be used to chop through young porous bones of meat or poultry.

3 *Deep-freeze knives* – these are specially designed with a serrated blade to saw through frozen meat or fish. This type of knife is very specialized and is not part of every knife set.
4 *Filleting knives* – the blades of these can range from 15–20 cm (6–8 inches) or even longer. They have a very thin and flexible blade and are used to fillet fish.
5 *Palette knives* – these vary in length and width; some are plain edged while others have serrated edges. The blade is always flexible and rounded at the top. They are used for:

- Moulding and shaping items, such as puréed potato
- Turning items over while cooking, such as shallow-fried fish
- Applying icing/cream to pastries and gateaux
- Carving (serrated-edge palette knives only)

6 *Paring knife* – this is a small knife with a thin, slightly flexible blade. It is used for all small hand-held work, such as shaping vegetables.
7 *Steak knives* – these range in size from 20–30 cm (8–12 inches). A steak knife has a curved end and is specially designed to cut through raw meat (e.g. sirloin and rump steaks).
8 *Fork* – a fork used by a chef has long and very sharp prongs. It is used to lift meat and poultry out of trays without piercing the flesh (which would allow the natural juices to escape).

Holding knives

When practising your knife skills it is important to learn how to hold a knife in the correct manner (Figure 4.34). If you were to hold a cook's knife in the same way that you hold a knife when eating you would have your hand around the handle and your first finger pointing down the blade. This is not the way to hold a cook's knife as it would not give you enough control. Instead, place the knife into your hand so that your thumb and first finger are grasping the blade but are not underneath the heel of the knife (or you will cut yourself). This may feel uncomfortable until you get used to it. When holding the knife correctly the blade should not be able to wobble about in your hand. You would hold a filleting knife in the same way, but you should work with it keeping the blade horizontal (rather than vertical) in your hand most of the time.

The most notable exception to this method is the boning knife, which is generally held like a dagger (Figure 4.34). Note that the holding method depends on the joint being boned out.

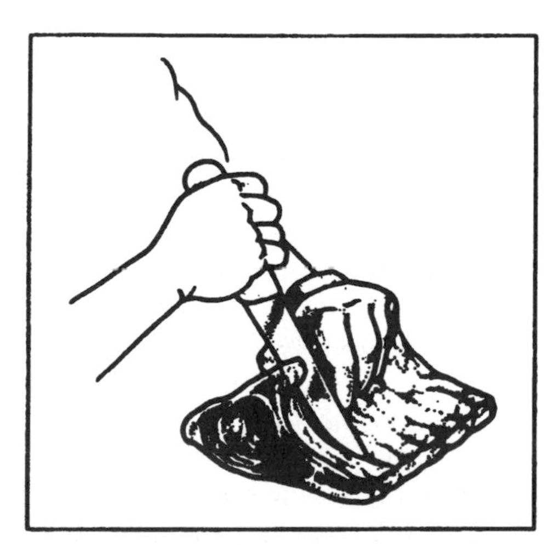

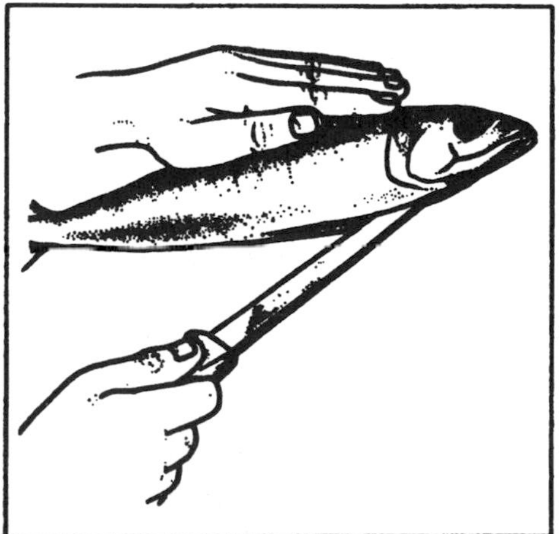

Figure 4.34 Cutting techniques

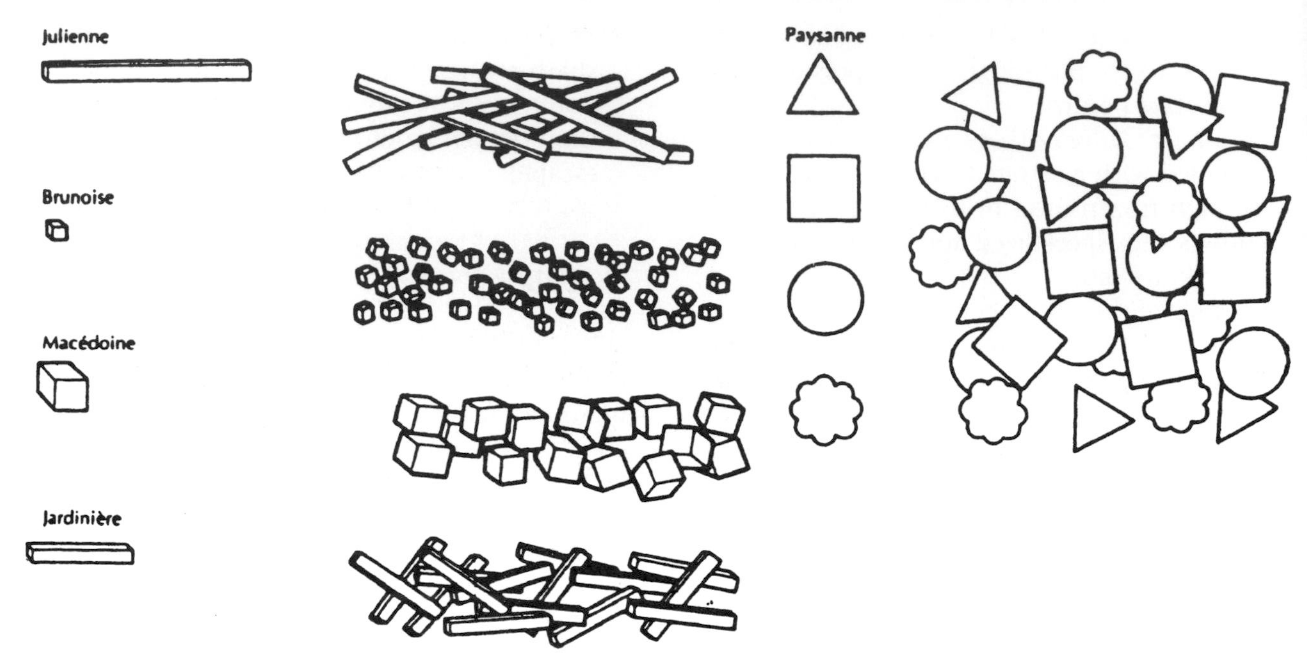

Figure 4.35 Vegetable cuts

Sharpening knives

The most traditional method of maintaining a sharp edge on a knife is by using a steel. Sharpening a knife can be a dangerous exercise if not done with care. Sharpen your knife each time you come to use it or if it goes dull during use.

Vegetable cuts

There are five traditional vegetable cuts that are frequently used either to create a vegetable garnish or to prepare vegetables for cooking (Figure 4.35):

1 Julienne – vegetables are cut to 3 cm × 2 mm thin strips and used for garnishing
2 Brunoise – vegetables are cut to 2–5 mm dice and used for broths and garnishing
3 Macédoine – vegetables are cut to 5 mm dice and used as mixed vegetables
4 Jardinère – vegetables are cut to 5 × 5 × 25 mm batons and used with mixed vegetables
5 Paysanne – vegetables are cut to thin shapes, a mixture of circles, triangles, rectangles and edged rounds (used in soups where the vegetables are not passed through a sieve)

Knife types (Figure 4.36)

1 Vegetable peeler (vegetables)
2 Vegetable preparation knife (vegetables)
3 Filleting knife, 6-inch flexible blade (filleting fish)
4 Medium large knife, 10-inch blade (shredding, slicing, chopping)
5 Carving knife (carving – butchery)
6 Boning knife (carving – butchery)
7 Palette knife (spreading, turning and lifting)
8 Trussing knife (trussing poultry and game)
9 Fork (lifting and holding meat)
10 Steel (sharpening knives)

Points to remember

1 Select a steel and the knife you wish to sharpen.
2 Hold the steel in one hand with its point away from you and pointing slightly upwards.

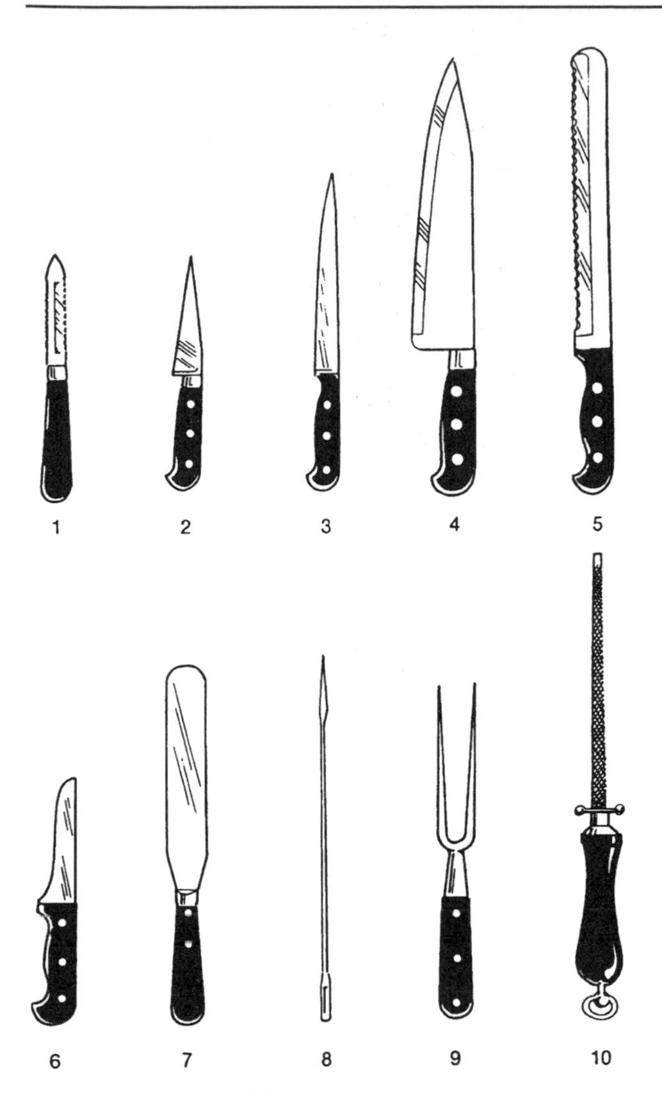

Figure 4.36 Types of knives

3 Holding the knife firmly in the other hand, start by placing the hilt of the blade at the base of the steel.
4 Angle the knife at approximately 18° then firmly draw the blade across the steel.
5 Repeat this process by placing the knife on the underside of the steel.
6 Repeat steps 4 and 5 several times.
7 To test for sharpness, carefully and gently draw your finger over the blade. It should feel slightly abrasive.
8 Now wash the knife to remove any filings that might be on the blade.

Maintaining knives

Good maintenance of your knives is essential for many reasons, from health and safety aspects to prolonging the life of your equipment. The following points need to be considered when maintaining knives:

- Always keep knives clean, as you may be using them on both cooked and raw foods
- Always wash knives in hot water with detergent and then rinse them well
- Make sure the handles of knives are clean: if they are greasy they could cause the knife to slip during use
- Store the clean knives safely by placing them back into their carrying wallet or a case specially adapted to hold them in individual compartments
- When drying your knives, always make sure that the sharp side of the blade is facing away from you and that your fingers are not over the cutting edge

Never just throw your knives into a box, drawer or locker. They should always be placed into some form of compartmental holder to prevent you having an accident while searching for a particular knife. Searching through a pile of knives for the one that you want is also time wasting.

Smoothing and spreading

The skill of spreading and smoothing mixtures to fill sponges or gateaux requires practice and patience. The technique of spreading is best learnt by watching an expert. Notice how they hold the palette knife. How do they place the mixture to be flattened onto the cake surface? What technique is used to distribute the icing or cream or topping onto the cake evenly?

Use the following simple procedures when smoothing or spreading on soft surfaces.

1 *Blending* – always blend and work coatings and fillings before trying to achieve a smooth surface.

2 *Clean buttercream* – if you are trying to obtain a clean buttercream or icing finish, with no air bubbles or scratches, first prepare the mixture by stirring and working with a small cake palette to remove the air.
3 *Cleanliness* – work cleanly – always wash your tools when they become sticky.
4 *Fondant* – when spreading fondant or chocolate mixes, the action must be swift and skilled to spread and smooth such mixtures before they set. If some areas begin to set before you have finished smoothing, they will drag and spoil the finish.
5 *Fresh cream* – if using fresh cream, never overwhip the cream. Softer semi-whipped cream will smooth easily when worked. If area is overwhipped, the action of smoothing will cause further coagulation of the butter fats, producing a rough and unsightly finish.
6 *Quantities* – never use too much or too little filling or coating to spread and smooth.
7 *Spreading* – spread mixtures with an even pressure of the hand using a small palette knife.
8 *Tools* – make sure that any tools you will need to use are clean and ready to hand.

Piping

Piping bags and tubes

Bags are available in nylon, plastic or cloth. Of these, the plastic bags have a definite advantage in that they are not porous and when used for creams etc. no liquid can seep through. Whatever their composition, savoy bags require to be sterilized before each use, especially when used for fresh cream and jelly concoctions. After sterilizing in a suitable solution or by boiling they should be thoroughly dried and stored in a very clean place. Tubes are made of either plastic or tin-plated metal. In the latter case rust must be guarded against.

- *Icing or chocolate* – piping icing or chocolate from a nylon savoy or paper bag requires control, balance and coordination. The skills required to pipe a shape with flair and speed can only be learned through practice.
- *Bag handling* – once the bag is filled, fold the top tightly inwards and down towards the point of the bag. Make certain the paper of a paper bag is not creased, as this can cause problems in both making the bag and keeping a fine sharp point.
- *Chocolate* – chocolate can be thickened with a little glycerine, alcohol or stock syrup and piped onto silicone. These decorations set quickly and can be stored until required. When you have some spare time, prepare some of these mixtures and practise creating neat rows of designs, both large and small: try making some little birds, butterflies or palm trees.
- *Coordination* – hand coordination is essential. Always use your spare hand to guide the bag: it is not possible to produce high-quality piping without using both hands.
- *Design* – always try the design first on paper. When writing a name or message on cakes, check the balance of the words by sight by writing the name on paper and comparing the spacing with your cake surface.
- *Icing* – try piping icing onto waxed paper, allowing it to dry and then transferring it to the cake. This is a good way of decorating and will give you practice.
- *Overfilled bag* – never fill the bag more than half-full. If the bag is overfilled the chocolate will leak and become a problem, as you will tend to concentrate on the leaking liquid rather than the design being piped.
- *Preparation* – ensure that basic preparations are carried out before piping starts.
- *Royal icing* – make sure that royal icing is not too stiff, and that the nozzle used is not too small. Otherwise your hand can become cramped if the pressure is constant even for a few minutes

Cream piping

Fresh or non-dairy cream can be used to finish cold desserts, cakes puddings and pastries. Never overwhip fresh cream, as this will cause it to lose its buttermilk, resulting in liquid dripping from the piping bag and spoiling the product. It will also become difficult to pipe.

The cream will look pale yellow and have a coarse texture.

Piping can be carried out using a plain or star tube made of plastic or metal, and a nylon piping bag (this is more hygienic than cotton). Do not place too much whipped cream in the bag: half-fill the bag and then twist at the same time working any trapped air from the bottom of the bag to the top.

When the bag feels comfortable to hold, pipe the shells by squeezing the bag with an even and steady pressure to shape the forms. Use your spare hand to guide the savoy bag. You can usefully practise with meringue and choux pastry on a workbench to develop control and accurate design.

Weighing

Unless automatic balances are used, weighing of small quantities of materials will usually be done on what are termed counter scales. This is where materials are placed in a scale pan and balanced by putting weights on a plate. Some are fitted with a sliding weight which makes it easier to weigh small quantities, and provides less risk of small weights becoming lost or accidentally added to mixtures.

Before weighing on such scales, they should first be made to balance. This will ensure that the wrong scale pan is not mistakenly used (if there is more than one pair of scales). It will also indicate if dried food, material or dirt has adhered to either the scale pan or the weight platform, and so altered the balance.

Having ensured before the weighing operation that the scales balance perfectly, also check that the correct amount of material is weighed by observing that the scales balance again (not down on one side). Such accuracy is very important in the weighing of very small quantities of vital ingredients such as baking powder. Never attempt to guess at weights even if these are very small. It is impracticable to attempt to weigh a quantity of less than 5 g or ¼ oz.

Metric equivalents

	Approx. equivalent	Exact equivalent
¼ oz	5 g	7.0 g
½ oz	10 g	14.4 g
1 oz	25 g	28.3 g
2 oz	50 g	56.6 g
3 oz	75 g	84.9 g
4 oz	100 g	113.2 g
5 oz	125 g	141.5 g
6 oz	150 g	169.8 g
7 oz	175 g	198.1 g
8 oz	200 g	227.0 g
9 oz	225 g	255.3 g
10 oz	250 g	283.0 g
11 oz	275 g	311.3 g
12 oz	300 g	340.0 g
13 oz	325 g	368.3 g
14 oz	350 g	396.6 g
15 oz	375 g	424.0 g
16 oz	400 g	454.0 g
2 lb.	1 kg	908.0 g
¼ pt	125 ml	142 ml
½ pt	250 ml (¼ litre)	284 ml
¾ pt	375 ml	426 ml
1 pt	500 ml (½ litre)	568 ml
1½ pt	750 ml (¾ litre)	852 ml
2 pt (1 qt)	1000 ml (1 litre)	1.13 litres
2 qt	2000 ml (2 litres)	2.26 litres
1 gal	(4 ½ litres)	4.54 litres

If it is a powder, quantities less than this can be weighed as follows. Let us suppose we require 1/16 oz. The best method is first to weigh ¼ oz, place this quantity onto paper and with a knife or scraper physically divide into four and use a quarter part. Alternatively, use a level teaspoonful.

Always endeavour to keep the scale pan as clean as possible. Fat, for example, should be weighed onto either the sugar or the flour of the recipe and not on its own. This would unnecessarily soil the scale pan which would require washing in hot detergent water before other materials could be weighed.

For liquids it is best to weigh a container first empty and then weigh the liquid by pouring it into the container on the scale pan. Critical amounts of liquids should always be weighed, never measured in a calibrated vessel like a quart pot.

Knife skills and examples

Ail (garlic)

There are many types of garlic readily available, the best of which is the smaller 'red garlic', so-called because of the reddish colour of the skin. Garlic affects foods in different ways depending on how it is cut and used. You can roast a chicken with three full heads of garlic (about 40 unpeeled cloves) and serve them with the chicken. Guests can pick up the cloves and suck the tender insides out of the peel. Prepared this way, it is astounding how mild and sweet garlic is. The scent and taste are barely noticeable. However, the smell of one clove of garlic, peeled, crushed, chopped fine and added at the last minute to sautéed potatoes or string beans, or to a salad, can permeate a whole room and remain on your breath for hours.

The same crushed chopped garlic – when cooked slowly for a long time, as in a stew – loses most of its pungency and harmonizes, quite modestly, with the other herbs and ingredients. Crushing the garlic releases more essential oil and gives more flavour than slicing it or leaving it whole. Raw garlic chopped to a purée is the most powerful. Mixed with olive oil, it becomes the garlic-loaded mayonnaise of Provence (atoll or ailloli), known as beurre de Provence (the butter of Provence).

One important point: When making scampi, escargots, sautéed potatoes, zucchini or any dish where the garlic is added at the end and slightly cooked, be careful not to burn it. Burned garlic hopelessly ruins a dish.

1 Holding the 'head' on a bias, crush with the heel of your hand to separate the cloves (Figure 4.37a).
2 Using the flat side of a heavy knife, smack the clove just enough to crack the shell open (Figure 4.37b).
3 Remove the clove from the shell and cut off the root end (Figure 4.37c).
4 Place the blade flat on tile clove and smack it down and forward to crush the clove to a pulp (Figure 4.37d).
5 Chop to a purée (Figure 4.37e).

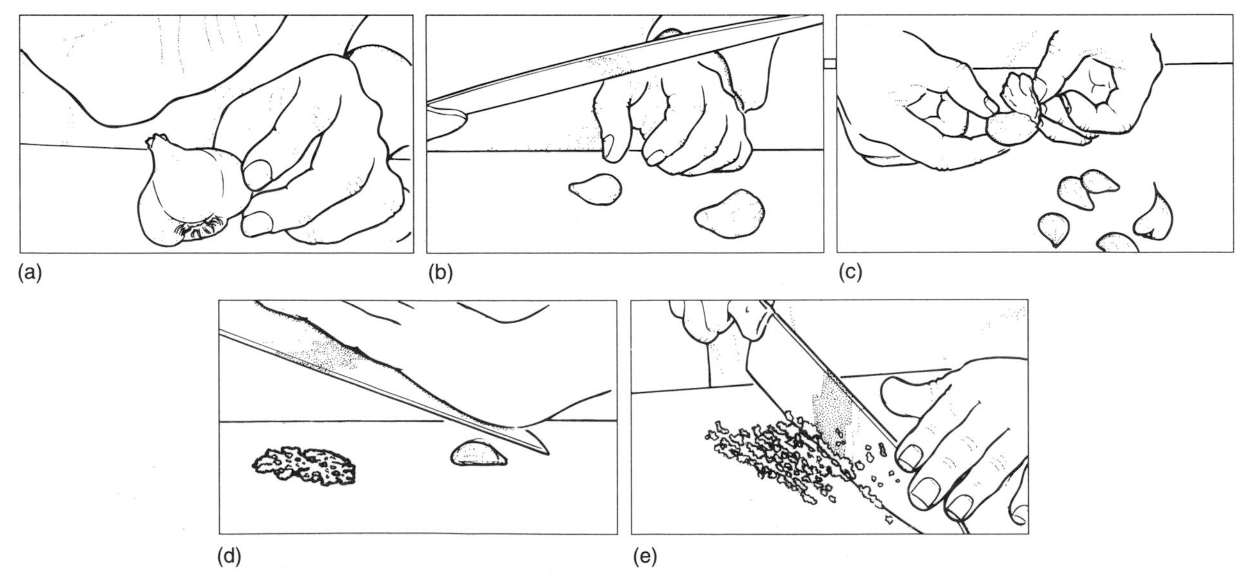

Figure 4.37 Preparing garlic

▪ IDENTIFY AND USE SKILLS REQUIRED TO SERVE FOOD AND DRINK ▪

In the previous sections we have looked at investigating the various forms of food and drink service and the skills required in the process of preparing food. In this section we shall look at the skills required in the *service* of food and drink and the hygiene, health and safety legislation that goes with it. Skills required by food and drink staff can be categorized as

- Practical skills
- Social skills
- Technical skills

First, we shall look at the *practical skills*, which could include:

1. Preparation of the service area such as dining room or restaurant/cafeteria
2. Serving and clearing of food from the customer's table
3. Serving and clearing of drinks from the customer's table
4. Clearing down:
   In front of the customer
   After the customer has left

Let us look at this more closely.

Service styles

There are several types of service depending on:

1. The type of catering establishment
2. The type of customer
3. The time available for the meal
4. The amount of business expected
5. The type of menu offered
6. The cost of the meal
7. The size of the establishment

Family service

Not to be confused with the image of a large family at home in Victorian England but more of a concept that the meat, fish, poultry or vegetarian dish is plated from the kitchen and the supporting vegetables, potatoes and sauces are placed on the table in bowls. The customers then help themselves. This creates a more relaxed atmosphere and actually allows the waiter/waitress to serve one or more additional tables, thus reducing costs. This type of service has been with us in many guises from the Chinese restaurant where the selection of dishes is put on a hot plate near the customers and they help themselves and the more modern derivative of the 'relish tray', 'French fries' and 'onion rings' of the non-chain fast-food restaurant. Family service is seen as a more sociable method of combining the service of food and, at the same time, encompassing the time spent with the customer by the waiter.

Full Silver service

This method of service requires a good degree of skill as dexterity is needed in the use of Silver service such as a table spoon and table fork or fish knives in certain cases, as well as good organizational skill in bringing hot or cold food from the kitchen. The chef is reliant on the skill of the waiter to present the food just as he would if plated by him. Timing, too, is important. If the waiter takes too long in the service, no matter how hot the crockery is, the food will go cold. The waiter will often work from a sideboard or adjacent table in the service of the food and it is quite common to have a hot table or flare lamp to keep food hot or to reheat in the case of the flare lamp. The waiter must have good presentation skills as it is important the food looks attractive on the plate. This method of service may be used in a restaurant using a table d'hôte menu (meal with a set price) or à la carte (individually priced and cooked to order).

Modified Silver service

This type of service involves a combination of plating the meat, fish or vegetarian dish and serving the vegetables and potatoes from separate dishes as well as the accompanying items such as sauces and condiments. It is often used on table d'hôte menus. There is some skill in the service and presentation of the food similar to that for Silver service.

Counter service

This form of 'self-service' has seen many developments and is often regarded as a method of speeding up the service in areas where there is a high volume of meals being offered.

The basic concept involves the use of a service area by way of a counter or counters where hot and cold items are separated (Figure 4.38). There is a tray for the customer and the food is displayed in a logical sequence (i.e. cold items and 'starters', main dishes (hot), potatoes and vegetables, hot desserts, cold desserts, beverages hot and cold). Very often accompaniments, such as sauces and gravies, can be in a separate area to avoid congestion. Cutlery, too, is often in a separate area for the same reason.

Depending on the type of operation, cash points will be at the end of the sequence in order to collect payment. However, some operations such as industrial canteens may provide the food free of charge or via a token or card system where no money is exchanged.

The service of food via the counter service can involve staff serving the food from behind the counter of each stage or, as in some operations, the customers help themselves. In the latter case 'portion control' is an imperative. This is often addressed by use of individual portion dishes or scoops, ladles or crockery of a prescribed size and beverages will involve portion-dispensed drinks or individual coffee or tea pots with milk or cream. Portions of butter, margarine and jam may also be served.

The basic concept of customer service has been around for many years. What has changed is its layout in relation to the type of operation and the space available and also how the crockery/glassware used for the service of the food, once consumed, is cleared from the eating area.

Carousel system

This involves a revolving food dispenser unit where the food is in tiers (e.g. cold on the top layer, hot in the middle and desserts on the bottom). The customers see the food rotating and help themselves to the pre-plated item or items while standing in one spot. This system optimizes the variety of food which can be served while at the same time minimizing space.

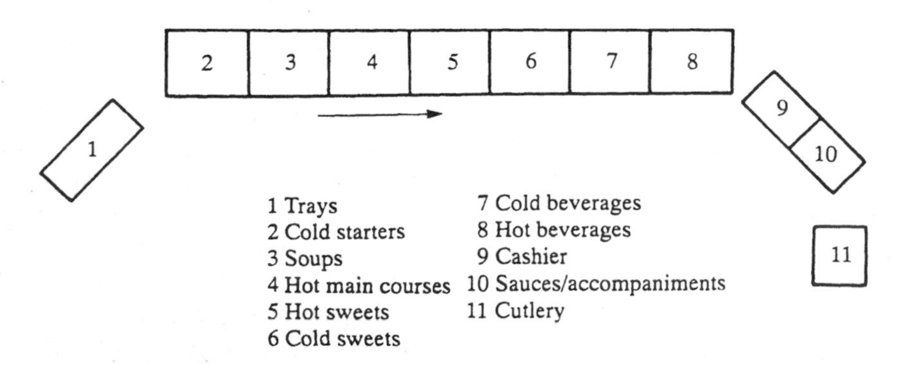

Figure 4.38 A traditional counter system

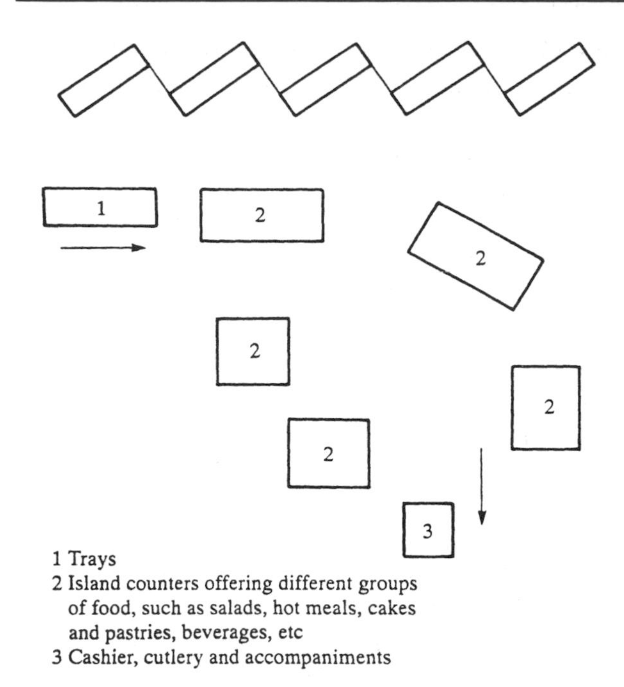

Figure 4.39 An echelon counter system

Echelon counters

This form of counter service involves a series of smaller counters, self-contained, but offering different choices such as cold and hot dishes with accompanying potatoes and vegetables as well as salad counters, drinks and desserts (Figure 4.39). These counters are often given codes such as letters A, B, C, or D etc. and the items on these respective counters are indicated under the letter and displayed outside the service area. Thus the customer can make his or her choice and heads for the appropriate counter, therefore saving time queuing in what could have been the case using a traditional counter.

Note

Counter service relies on the customer to make quicker decisions on choice of food to be eaten and is also reliant on how they assist in the clearing of the food. Systems today are based on the customer eating off the tray and, when finished, placing the tray into a slotted trolley. When this does not happen, labour is required to conduct a 'mopping-up' exercise.

Vending

This has increased as a form of customer service as it does not require a high cost in 'labour'. The labour is only required to clean and replenish the stock of the vending unit.

A full meal provision to include beverages can be offered by way of prepared meals using 'cook–chill' production. This system can provide a full 24-hour service without needing staff in attendance. The food is also at its optimum best, as it is refrigerated and does not require being hot as with a conventional counter service.

Very often disposable containers, cutlery and plates are used for service of the food so no washing up is required. The system can be geared to a coin-, card- or token-operated system so no money is exchanged with cash tills, thus further reducing staff requirements. The food is often pre-coded or colour coded in order for the customer to reheat the food for the correct length of time, using a microwave oven. The customer merely selects the item from the refrigerated food display, pays via a coin, card or token and places the food in a microwave oven. The code or disk on the item will indicate the correct length of time the food is to be heated. These vending areas can be situated near to the workplace, thus reducing the time the customer has to travel and erosion of their break time.

There are, of course, some drawbacks in this form of service, the main one being loss of interaction between the customer and catering staff and its 'impersonal' nature. But there is no doubt as to the operation of a 24-hour service within the industrial sector and the provision of a similar daytime service in a large city-centre office block, if it is clean, effective and convenient for the customer. The spender can also split the operation to provide drinks and snacks actually in the work area, thus reducing or negating the need for break times, which is a useful feature in 'flexi-time' hours for workers.

The carvery

This is less in use these days except in large restaurants. However, it was a feature in public house operations a few years ago but has recently lost favour because it ties the chef to one area thus losing his or her skill elsewhere.

This skill, too, is an integral feature of a carvery. It takes a lot of skill to carve meat or fish properly and also ensure correct portion control (Figure 4.40).

Figure 4.40 A carvery counter (courtesy of Victor Manufacturing Ltd)

The carvery has been operated in two forms:

1 In large hotels or restaurants the carving is done via a trolley at the customer's table then the remaining vegetables and potatoes and accompaniments are Silver served (Figure 4.41).
2 In public houses or smaller restaurants it was done via a form of 'counter service' where the chef would carve the meat and place it on the customer's plate (often on a small round wooden tray). Then the customer would choose their own vegetables, potatoes and accompaniments from the counter areas.

The carvery has been a traditional feature in the UK but its demise has been due to changing trends, i.e. eating where more choice or vegetarian or lighter dishes are required to cater for the variety of eating habits now in place. Time available, too, is a feature, as it was a time-consuming form of service and costly. The skill of staff required needed to be reflected in the salaries paid.

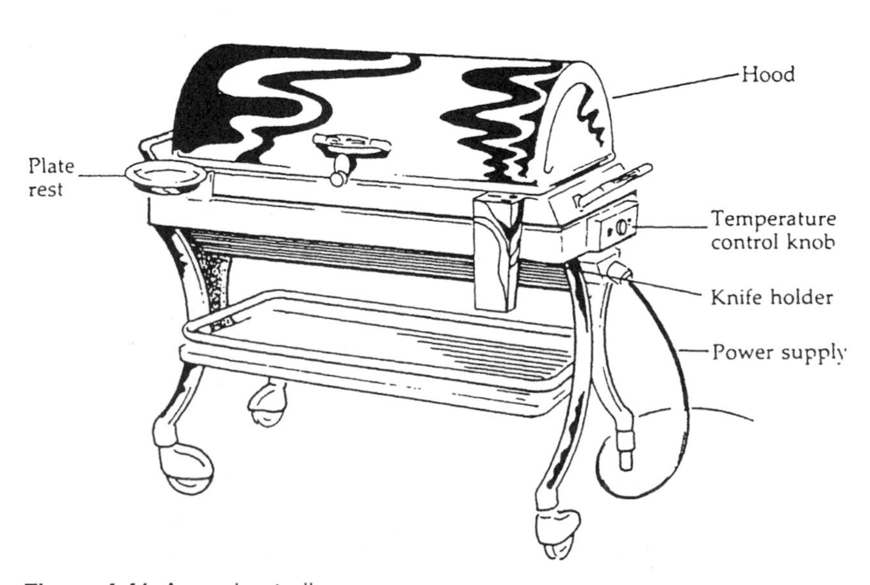

Figure 4.41 A carving trolley

Take-away

This form of service has been in the UK for many years since the beginning of 'fish and chip' shops. It embraces the concept of counter service but allows the customer to eat the food elsewhere, whether that be in the home or on the park bench. In recent years, take-away food has had an aggressive marketing strategy with the advent of McDonalds, Burger King and Wimpy operating in the UK. This has seen the demise of many fish and chip shops because they simply could not compete against the multinational companies with their high street locations and television advertising.

We have seen, however, the fish and chip shops fighting back by forming networks for advertising and some of the large fish importers investing in the more modern approach of high street locations with waiter service, bar and relaxed pleasant atmosphere. Rooney's, Hungry Fisherman and Harry Ramsden's are examples of this.

There has also been an expansion in types of take-away operations to include Mexican, Italian, Chinese and Tandoori. Because of the image portrayed by companies such as McDonald's and the practice of strict hygiene codes in service and cleanliness of their products the non-chain take-away operations have responded accordingly by upgrading their premises to fit in with customer expectations. We have seen, too, the take-away service expanding into door-to-door service via 'Dial a Pizza', for example.

The take-away area will continue to develop as long as the large chains see a market in it. Recent developments in the UK include 'Drive Thru' operations often situated in modern retail parks where there will be a high volume of people in transit, due to their out-of-town situations.

Preparing the service area

Linen

Linen having been obtained from the linen room, a waiter should check the number and sizes of all the pieces to ensure that they are all in good condition. The linen should then be sorted according to sizes and neatly stacked on the side-table.

Sideboard cutlery arrangement

Silver should be obtained from the silver pantry, care being taken that every piece is clean. These should be sorted into knives, forks, spoons, etc., and placed in the respective drawers of the side-table, the handles being kept towards the outer part of the drawer, the prongs of forks and spoons facing sideways. Other items such as ice bowls, rolls of bread, butter, water, doilies should also be obtained from the appropriate room and placed in readiness on the side-table. *Note*: Butter should be kept fresh and cool, on ice, or in ice and water.

Preparing tables

Table laying is usually an exercise for a team of waiters. Each waiter will take an allotted task throughout the room. However, the procedures involved in laying the cloth and setting the table are as follows.

Tablecloth or mats

Establishments offering waiting service usually fall into two main classes: those which use dining tables covered with a cloth: and others using tables, generally polished or glass-topped on which plates are placed with or without a table mat.

The waiter first obtains the cloths or mats. If mats are to be used they should be placed on the table exactly where the plate, bowl, glass, etc. are to be set. When tables are to be covered with a cloth they should be of the type fitted with baize or felt. This is a soft covering which;

- Deadens noise of plates, cutlery and glass placed on them
- Keeps the cloth in position

Laying tables

Most restaurants will use either heat-resistant place-mats or linen table cloths on wooden tables. Fast-food establishments are more likely to have tables topped with a heat-resistant material, such as Formica that does not need a covering, enabling the staff merely to wipe the tables as they are cleared. Table mats should be cleaned with a damp cloth and placed centrally on the cover, about 10 mm (½-inch) from the edge of the table.

Checking the cloth

The tablecloth should be the right side up: this side is always more highly laundered and the hem is always on the underside of the cloth. Tablecloths are normally screen folded (that is, to form a W) with the face side (more glossily laundered) outside. The aim in laying a cloth is to cover the four table legs with the four corners hanging about 8 or 10 cm (3 or 4 inches) from the floor.

On square and rectangular tables the corners of the cloth should be mitred to produce a neat finish. This is done by creasing between the thumb and forefinger along the natural crease of the cloth.

On round tables the corners of the cloth should cover the table legs. Where two or more cloths are needed on a rectangular table the overlaps should face away from the main entrance to the room and the central creases in the cloths should join to produce the effect of one continuous line.

Laying the cloth

Tablecloths will be collected from the linen room, usually on a one-for-one basis, that is, one clean cloth supplied for one dirty cloth returned. Exchanges of linen are recorded in a

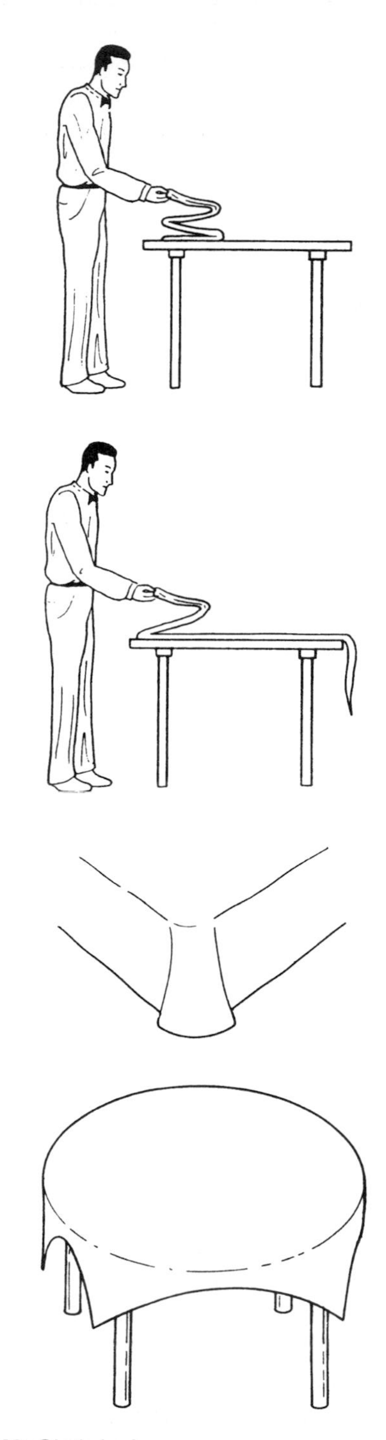

Figure 4.42 Cloth laying

linen book, so that strict control can be achieved. The table should be steady and in position before the cloth is laid, and the procedure for laying a cloth is as follows (Figure 4.42):

1 Check that the table is correctly positioned and firm.
2 If a felt is not already fitted, place felt over the table.
3 Choose the correct size of tablecloth.
4 Stand centrally between two legs of the table.
5 Place the folded cloth on the table with both open edges towards you and the main folds facing away from you.
6 Open the cloth across the table so that its woven edges (the selvage edges) and its inside double-fold lie facing you and with the two double-folds facing away from you.
7 With thumbs uppermost, take the top flap of cloth between your thumbs and first finger and take the central folds between the first and second fingers.
8 With arms spread out the width of the table, move the cloth to the far edge of the table away from you.
9 Release and drop the bottom flap (which is lying loose) over the far edge of the table.
10 Allowing the rest of the cloth to lie on the table, release your hold on the centre folds.

Laying the cover

All cutlery, china and glassware should be polished before being placed on the table. When laying the tables, the waiter will carry cutlery in the service cloth or on a salver, giving the cutlery a final polish before placing it on the table. All items must be placed neatly on the table; it is important that the appearance of the table creates a good impression to the customer. Covers should be evenly spaced around a circular table and on square or rectangular tables they should be directly opposite one another. Cutlery should be placed approximately 10 mm (½-inch) from the edge of the table and be positioned, where appropriate, close to one another but never touching. Plates with a badge or crest should be positioned so that the crest is at the top of the cover. Glasses should be placed on the table upside down to prevent dust dropping into them, and turned the correct way just prior to service.

The cover laid will vary according to the requirements of the establishment, but there are two generally accepted covers used for lunch and dinner menus.

Types of place setting

Table d'hôte cover

This cover would be used in restaurants offering a table d'hôte or a set menu and provides cutlery for all courses. This comprehensive cover means that the waiter will have to adjust only minor items at the beginning of the meal to provide the customer with the correct cutlery requirements for the whole meal (Figure 4.43(a)).

A la carte cover

This cover is used by establishments offering an à la carte menu where the customer's choice is much more extensive and it is not possible to predict what dishes are to be served. This simple cover can be adjusted by the waiter prior to the service of each course with the cutlery required for that course (Figure 4.43(b)).

These standard covers may be adapted according to the requirements of the restaurant. A steak house, for example, may use a simplified table d'hôte cover, omitting the fish knife and fork and the soup spoon.

In addition to the items in Figure 4.43, others are required on the table.

1 Cruets: consisting of salt, pepper and mustard. These are placed centrally on the table, cleaned and filled before service.

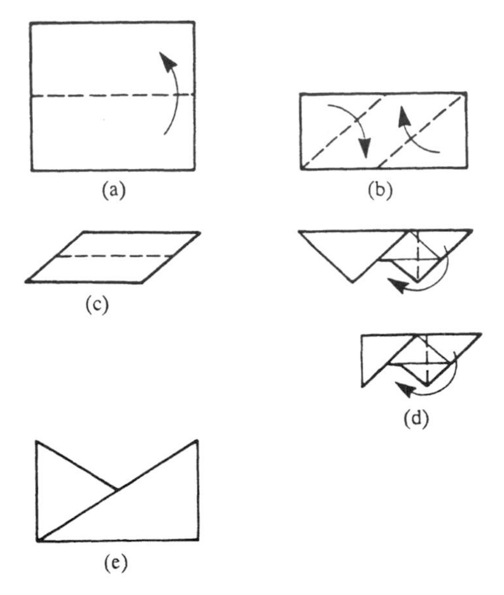

Figure 4.46 The bishop's mitre

(c) Turn the napkin over so that the flaps are underneath and a folded edge is towards you. Fold in half
(d) Release the points. Fold one end over and tuck under the flap.
(e) Turn the napkin over and repeat (d)

Triple wave (Figure 4.47)

(a) Fold the napkin in three to form a rectangle
(b) Fold the bottom edge under
(c) Fold to form three steps or waves and tuck the end under the back

This is a popular fold because it requires little handling.

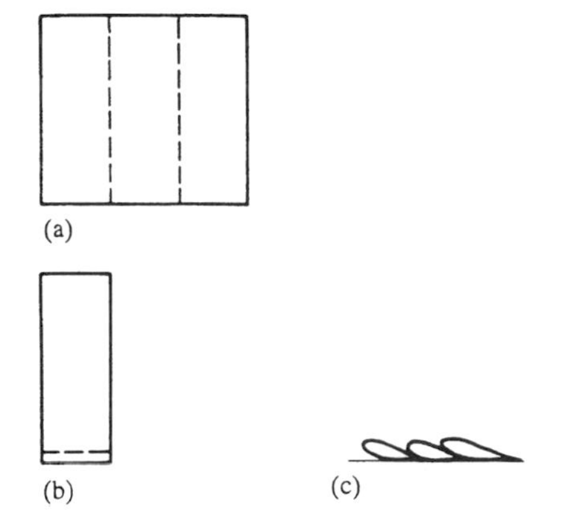

Figure 4.47 The triple wave

Sideboard preparation

The sideboard is the base from which the waiter works; it holds all the items the waiter may need during service. It is important that the sideboard is well prepared before service so that everything needed is at hand. Items normally held on the sideboard include:

- Service cutlery
- Spare linen
- Matches
- Checkpads
- Spare china
- Water jug
- Trays
- Spare cutlery
- Salvers
- Menus
- Pen
- Accompaniments and condiments
- Bread, melba toast, etc.

Let us now stop and recap on what we have looked at up to now.

1 Service styles
2 Linen and how it should be used
3 Preparing the customer's table
4 Types of cutlery the waiter uses
5 Types of place settings
6 Napkin folding
7 What to look for when checking your laid-up table
8 The waiter's sideboard and how it is stocked

Practical task

Take two linen napkins and prepare the following folds:

- Cone
- Bishop's mitre

Remember, 'Practice makes perfect'.

Serving and clearing food and drink

In this section we look at the skills involved in the serving and clearing of food from the customer's table. The most important skill the waiting person must master is 'holding the spoon and fork. Let us look at this skill more closely.

Note: practice on a regular basis is required in all the skills we shall cover in this section.

Holding a service spoon and fork

Expertise in this technique can only be achieved with a great deal of practice. The purpose of the service spoon and fork is to enable the waiter to serve food from a flat or dish onto the guest's plate quickly and present it as the chef would wish (see Figure 4.48).

1 The ends of the service spoon and fork should be positioned in the centre of the palms of the serving hand. This allows for more control when serving various foods.
2 The service spoon is held firmly in position by the fingers of the serving hand other than the forefinger.
3 The forefinger or index finger is used together with the thumb to hold the handle of the service fork.
4 Using this method you are able to pick up food items from the serving dish in between the service spoon and service fork.
5 There are occasions where two service forks may be used, or a slice, as this makes the service of the food item more efficient.

Holding the spoon and fork correctly is one of the most important skills, as we have said and the other practical skills required of the waiter are:

- Carrying plates
- Using a service tray
- Carrying glasses
- Carrying trays (such as a breakfast tray)

Let us look at these skills in more detail.

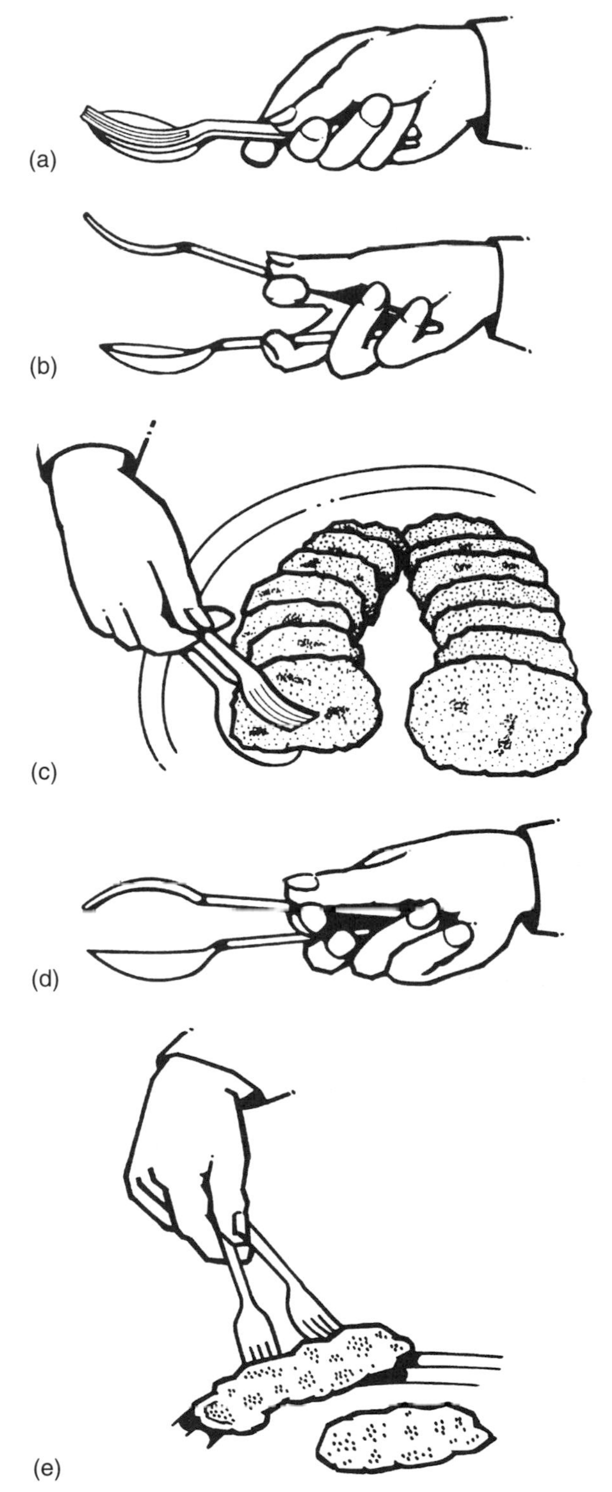

Figure 4.48 Service with fork and spoon. (a) Service fork positioned on top of the service spoon: (b) positioning of fingers to allow leverage of fork; (c) food secured between fork and spoon, with the fork uppermost; (d) fork is turned to hold the food more firmly and to give more control in serving; (e) using two service forks

Carrying plates

This skill is necessary in carrying plates of plated foods as well as for clearing. To be able to clear correctly

- Ensures speed and efficiency around the table
- Avoids the possibility of accidents
- Creates minimum inconvenience to guests

In turn it also allows the stacking of dirties neatly and correctly on the sideboard with the minimum delay. A correct clearing technique enables more to be cleared, in less time and in fewer journeys between sideboard and table.

Figure 4.49(a) illustrates the initial hand position for the first plate. Care must be taken to ensure that the first plate is held firmly, as dirty plates are built up from here. The second plate will rest firmly on the forearm and the third and fourth fingers. Figure 4.49(b) shows the second plate positioned on the left hand.

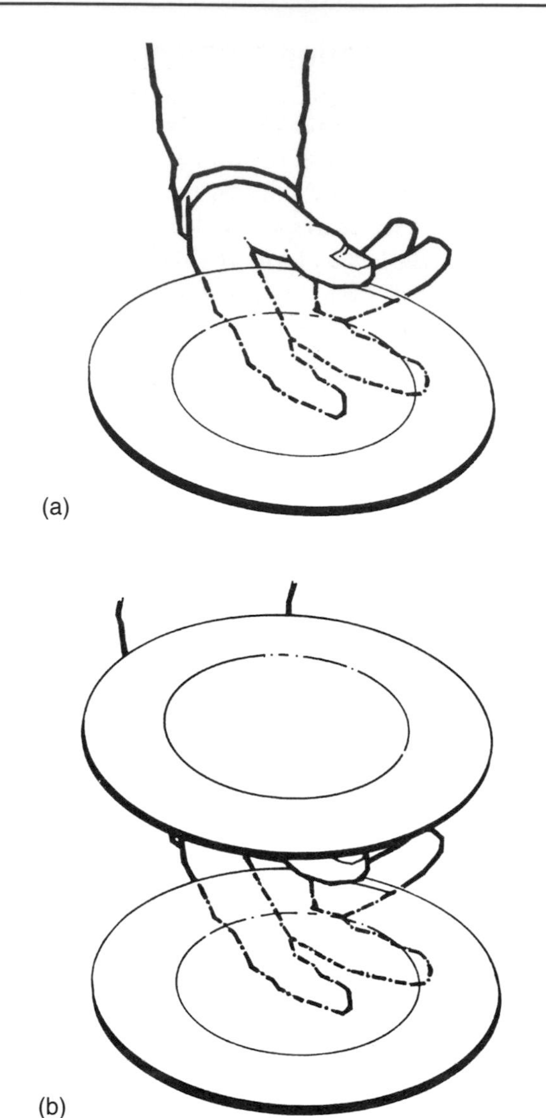

Figure 4.49 Carrying plates. (a) Initial hand position; (b) positioning of second plate

Using a service tray

A service tray consists of a round silver tray with a napkin set on it. It may be used in a number of ways during the actual meal service

- For carrying clean glasses and removing dirty glasses from a table
- For removing clean cutlery, flatware from the table
- For placing clean cutlery
- For placing coffee and tea services on the table
- As an underflat when Silver serving vegetables and other items.

Carrying glasses on a service tray

There are two basic methods of carrying glasses in the food and beverage service areas. These are either by hand or on a service tray.

The wine glasses are placed upside down on the service tray to avoid dirt settling in them (Figure 4.50). It is also easier to remove the clean and polished wine glass by the base, which is now readily accessible, and set it on the table without touching the bowl of the glass that is to hold the wine.

The wine goblets should be positioned between alternate fingers as far as is possible. The wine goblets should only be carried in one hand, allowing the other hand to remain free to steady oneself in case of emergencies or accident.

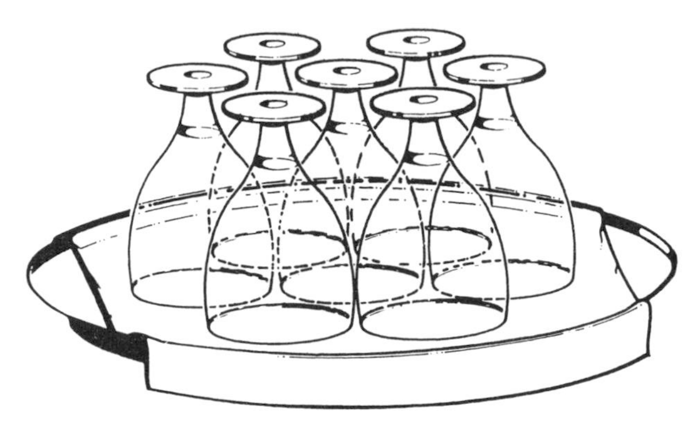

Figure 4.50 Carrying clean glasses on a salver

Carrying clean cutlery and flatware

When removing from or placing clean cutlery on a table they should be carried on a service tray (Figure 4.51). The blades of the knives should be placed under the arch in the middle of the forks, and if carrying dessert spoons and forks the prongs of the fork should go under the arch in the middle of the spoon. The reason for this is to help to hold the items steady on the service tray.

Carrying coffee services

When taking coffee services to a table (Figure 4.52):

1 The side plates may be stacked in one pile on the service tray

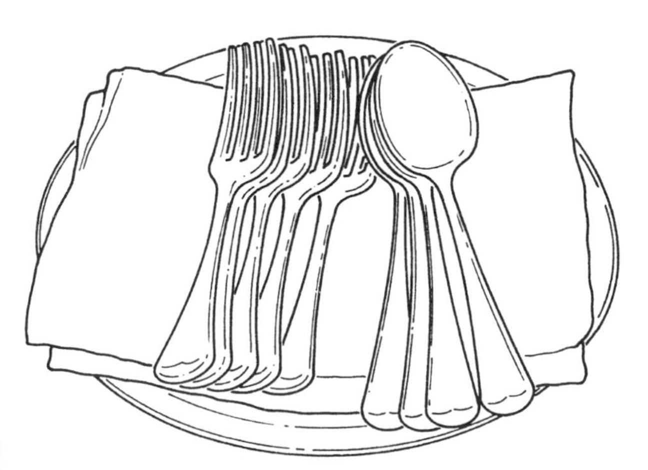

Figure 4.51 Carrying clean cutlery

Figure 4.52 Carrying coffee

2 The coffee saucers in another
3 All the demitasse together
4 All the coffee spoons laid flat on the service tray.

When the waiter is at the table:

1 Ensure that the table is clear and clean.
2 Place the cup, saucer and underplate slightly to the right of the guest. A coffee spoon should be placed on the saucer, with the handle pointing to the right. The cup's handle should also point to the right.
3 Place a pot of coffee, a jug of hot milk, and sugar with a spoon on to a napkin-covered salver. Carry the salver on a flat palm.
4 Enquire whether or not the guest takes sugar and whether they take coffee black or with milk (not black or white).
5 Serving from the right, place sugar as necessary into the cup. Serve the coffee and milk.
6 To assist with the service, the salver should be rotated on the palm of the waiter's hand so that service equipment is nearest to the cup.
7 The coffee pot and milk jug should not be lifted from the salver, but tilted almost as though they are hinged.

Figure 4.53 Serving vegetables

8 In some restaurants, sugar and cream are left on the table for the guests to help themselves.

Serving vegetables

When serving vegetables and potatoes at the table an underflat should be used to hold either one large vegetable dish or a number of smaller ones depending on the guests' order (Figure 4.53). The purpose of the underflat is:

- To give the waiter more control when using the service spoon and fork to serve the vegetables from the vegetable dish to the guest's plate
- To provide greater protection in case of spillage
- To give the waiter added protection against heat and possible spillage on the uniform or guest.

Using a service plate

A service plate is a joint plate with a napkin upon it. It has a number of functions during the meal service:

1 For removing clean cutlery and flatware from the table
2 For placing clean cutlery and flatware on the table
3 For clearing side-plates and side-knives
4 For crumbing down after the main course, or any other stage of the meal if necessary
5 For clearing accompaniments from the table as and when necessary

Clearing sideplates and knives

When clearing dirty side-plates and side-knives, the side-plates may be stacked one upon another with all the debris in a separate pile and the knives laid flat upon the service tray. This is a much safer and speedier method.

Crumbing down

'Crumbing down' is a procedure generally carried out by the waiter after the main course has been eaten and all the dirty items of equipment cleared from the table. The waiter then brushes any crumbs and other debris lying on the tablecloth onto the service plate with the aid of either the folded service cloth or a small brush (Figure 4.54).

Clearing accompaniments

The service plate is also used to clear such items as the cruet, pepper mill or other accompaniments which are not already set on an underplate.

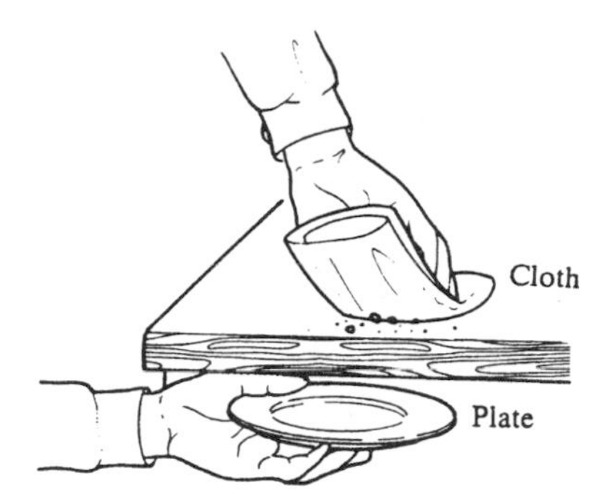

Figure 4.54 Crumbing down

Carrying glasses

There are two basic methods of carrying glasses in the food and beverage service areas. These are either by hand or on a service tray.

Carrying by hand

The wine goblets should be positioned between alternate fingers as far as is possible. The wine goblets should only be carried in one hand, allowing the other hand to remain free to steady oneself in case of emergencies or accident. Figure 4.55 illustrates wine glasses held in one hand showing how the base of each glass overlaps the next, allowing the maximum number to be held in one hand.

Carrying glasses on a service tray

The method of carrying clean glasses about the restaurant during the service period using the service tray is also used. The service cloth is placed on the palm of the hand, with the service tray upon it. The purpose of this is to allow the service tray to be rotated more easily in order to remove each wine glass in turn by the base and to set it on the table.

The wine glasses are placed upside down on the service tray to avoid dirt settling in them. It is also easier to remove the clean and polished wine glass by the base, which is now readily accessible, and set it on the table without touching the bowl of the glass that is to hold the wine.

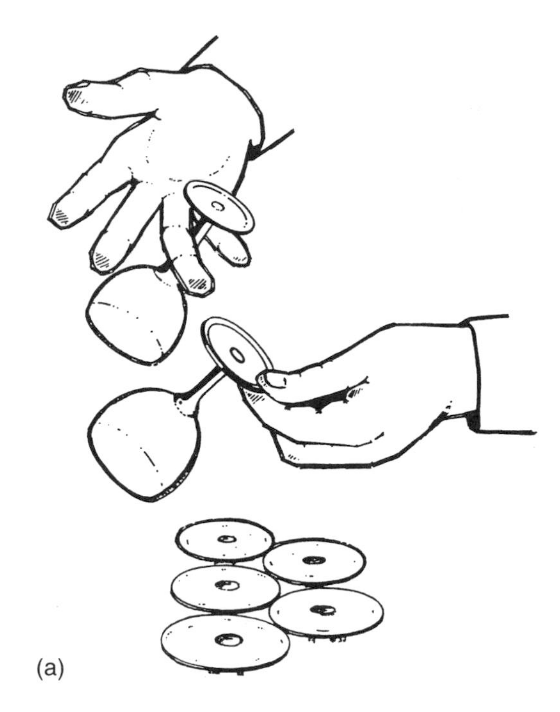

(a)

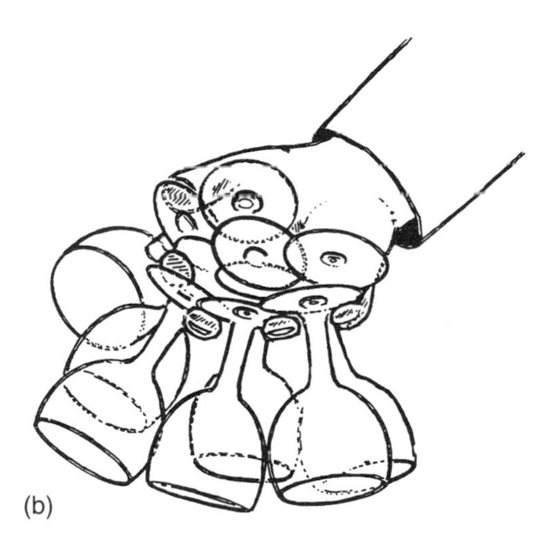

(b)

Figure 4.55 (a) Positioning glasses in hand; (b) carrying glasses

To summarize, trays are used for:

- Carrying food from the kitchen to the restaurant sideboard
- Service in rooms and lounges
- Clearing from sideboards
- Clearing from tables
- Carrying equipment

Serving from silver

The greatest skill required by the waiter or waitress is that when food is 'silver served' using a spoon and fork and transferring the food from a 'salver' (service tray) or service dish with items such as potatoes or vegetables. We looked at the technique of holding the spoon and fork earlier in the section. Now let us consider some of the uses of this technique.

In the following the term 'silver' may be taken to include stainless steel. Similar techniques also apply when serving in this style from copper and oven-proof crockery.

Before serving, always check carefully yourself the food you are about to serve and make sure:

1 It is the right order.
2 Portions are adequate.
3 The dish is neat and clean.

Sequence of hot and cold dishes

If at any time you have to serve some customers with hot dishes, and others with cold dishes, serve cold dishes first.

Presenting a dish

Present each dish at a table prior to serving from it. First show it to the host for his or her approval and to confirm it is the one ordered. If it is not visible to the rest of the party, present it also at the other end of the table.

Serving from a dish

With food already portioned on a silver dish, place on it a spoon and fork for service. Stand on the guest's left, with the dish on the palm of your left hand (protected by the pad of folded waiter's cloth). Bring the dish down to the level of the guest's plate just over the rim; the dish being perfectly level. Take the spoon and fork in your right hand to serve food onto the plate. Basically, food should be lifted with the spoon, with the fork gently keeping it firm. Skill in spoon and fork usage is readily acquired with practice.

Serving from silver trays (Figure 4.56)

When serving from a large flat dish remember to: Ensure that guests' plates are hot and clean. Protect yourself and the plates with a service cloth when carrying a pile of hot plates. Stand on the guest's left. Serve with care to avoid spilling gravy or sauce on the plate's rim.

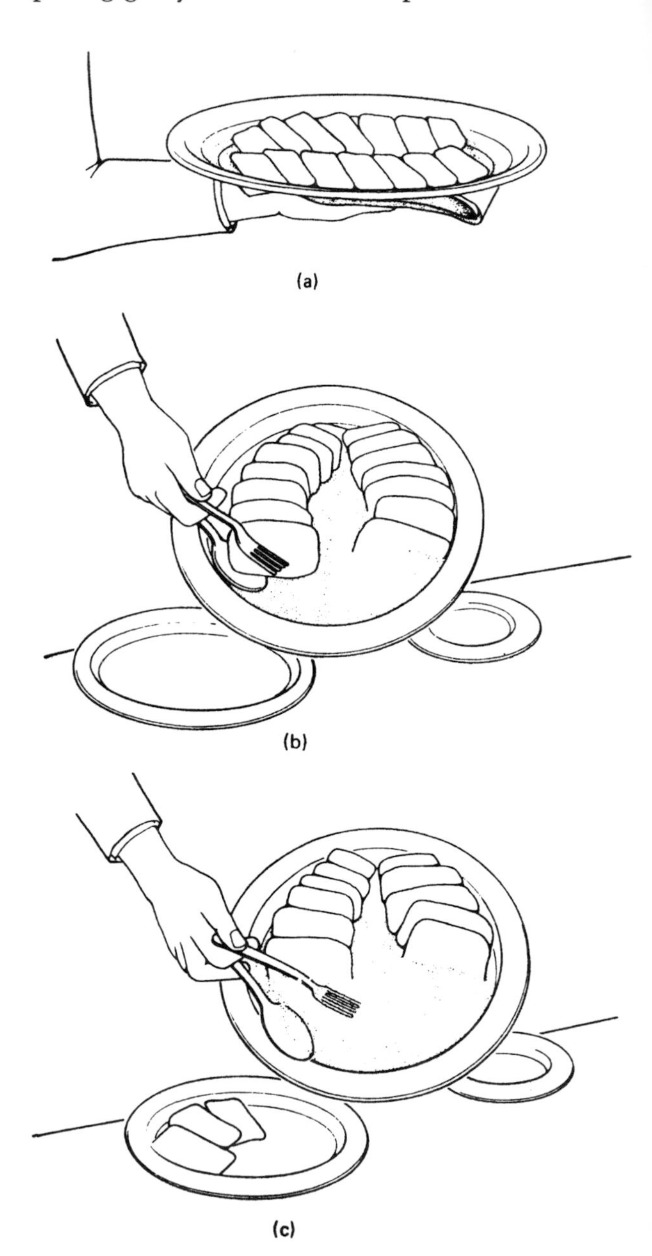

Figure 4.56 Serving from silver trays. (a) Carry a flat dish on the left hand and forearm with a service cloth in a pad in the left hand; (b) bring down the dish as near to the guest's plate as possible; (c) tilt the dish slightly forward so that gravy or sauce collects and can be served

Serving large items

If a fish portion is too large for easy service with spoon and fork, sever it across the middle with the spoon. When serving an omelette cut off the extreme tips with the spoon before serving. If an omelette, large fish fillet or other items must be cut into several portions, check beforehand exactly how many, to avoid unequal portioning to the customer.

Putting food on the plate

Arrange food appetisingly when placing on the plate. Generally, fish or meat is served lower-centre with vegetables on one side and potatoes on the other; separate sauces and/or accompaniments at the top right-hand side. When serving sauce, do not pour it over the food without asking a guest.

Using a salver

1 Salvers may be used to serve vegetables, to clear glasses and to serve drinks.
2 Lay a cloth on the salver to stop slipping and prevent conduction of heat thus avoiding burning the palm of the hand.
3 Carry clean cups, glasses, etc. on a salver and lift them by their handles or stems and not by putting your fingers inside them.
4 Remove dirty glasses on a salver and not by hand.

Note: A salver is a round service tray made of silver or stainless steel, and may be of different sizes in order to suit various tasks.

Serving skills

The skill of serving food is equally matched by that of knowing from which side of the customer to serve from. There is always confusion about this and it does differ from establishment to establishment. In general terms the following traditions apply.

Continental tradition

The main rules are:

1 Place clean plates and glasses from the guest's right.
2 Place coffee cups and saucers (with underplate) from the guest's left.
3 Serve food from the guest's left.
4 Serve drinks (including wine and coffee) from the guest's right.
5 Clear all used items, that is, plates, cups and glasses, from the right.

These rules conform with conventional styles observed in most establishments in Europe, particularly France and Switzerland, and are the basis of teaching in most Continental hotel and catering schools.

English version

The main rules are:

1 Plates or utensils for food are placed from the left.
2 Food is served from the left.
3 Used food plates are cleared from the left.
4 Glasses are placed from the right.
5 Drink is served from the right.
6 Used glasses are cleared from the right.

Drinks and coffee service sides

Drinks are served from the right but further detail regarding wine service is given later. Coffee cups (on saucers and underplates), sugar (unless it is on the same salver as the coffee itself) and bread are also placed before or offered to the guest from the left. Because coffee, as other beverages, is served from the right some people consider it illogical to place coffee cups and saucers from the left. But, again, it is adopting one practice and keeping to it that is important. Coffee service is described later.

Clearing skills

Clearing skills are important as they ensure speed and minimum inconvenience to the guest by cutting down the number of journeys to and from the sideboard.

1 Where possible, clear plates from the right.
2 Collect plates with the right hand and transfer them to the left.
3 Hold the plate with the first two fingers underneath and the thumb on top. The remaining two fingers stand upright to help balance further plates.
4 Secure the fork under the thumb and slide the knife underneath. This prevents the cutlery sliding and the knife being dropped.
5 The next plate is balanced on the forearm, thumb and two upright fingers.
6 Scrape any debris from the second to the first plate and place the cutlery on to the first plate.
7 Continue with further plates.
8 Side-plates and cruets should be removed when the main course is cleared.
9 Clearing bowls with underplates.

Clearing bowls with underplates (Figure 4.57)

1 The first bowl and underplate is collected and the underplate is held as described above.
2 The second bowl and underplate is collected and balanced on the thumb, forearm and fingers as before.
3 The spoons are transferred from the lower bowl to the upper bowl.

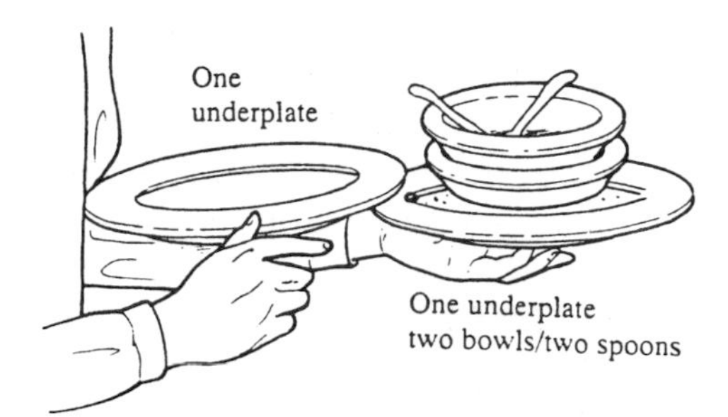

Figure 4.57 Clearing bowls with underplates

4 The upper bowl is placed into the lower bowl, leaving a clear plate to repeat the procedure.

An alternative hold which may prove more comfortable involves the first three fingers being positioned under the plate, the thumb on top and only the little finger standing upright. At wash-up, clear cutlery from soiled plates and place in the appropriate receptacle.

Crumbing down

This clearing skill was described earlier.

Service of tea and coffee

There are many traditions and 'rituals' associated with the service of tea and coffee and it depends on the country you are visiting on how it will be served (and how it will taste!) but in general terms the following would apply for service in the UK. The following equipment would be required for the service of tea and coffee.

- Tea tray
- Coffee tray

Silver service of coffee (Figure 4.58)

1 Ensure that the table is clear and clean.
2 Place the cup, saucer and underplate slightly to the right of the guest. A coffee spoon should be placed on the saucer, with the handle pointing to the right. The cup's handle should also point to the right.
3 Place a pot of coffee, a jug of hot milk, and sugar with a spoon onto a napkin-covered salver. Carry the salver on a flat palm.
4 Enquire whether or not the guest takes sugar and whether they take coffee black or with milk (not black or white).
5 Serving from the right, place sugar as necessary into the cup. Serve the coffee and milk.
6 To assist with the service, the salver should be rotated on the palm of the waiter's hand

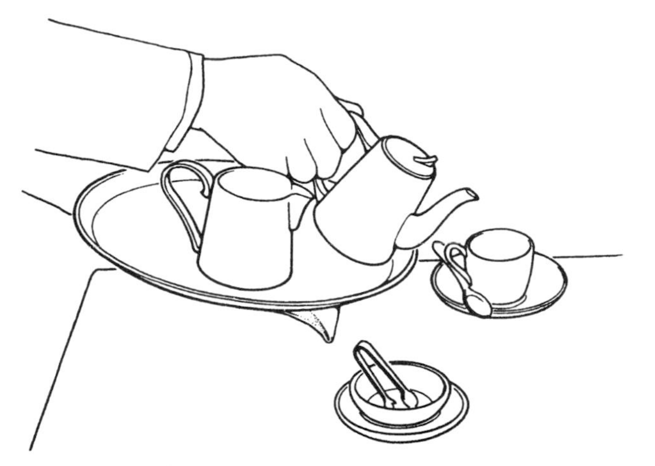

Figure 4.58 Silver service of coffee

so that service equipment is nearest to the cup.

7 The coffee pot and milk jug should not be lifted from the salver, but tilted almost as though they are hinged.
8 In some restaurants, sugar and cream are left on the table for the guests to help themselves.

Clearing checklists

Once the restaurant service is over the area has to be cleared and all items of equipment put away in its respective place. It is important to leave the dining area clean and tidy as cleanliness in the eating areas is vital as well as being part of hygiene regulations.

The following checklists would be suitable for most establishments but remember, the range and type of equipment as well as where it is stored will depend on the type of service offered and the type of establishment such as restaurant, cafeteria, hotel restaurant or function catering establishment.

Table and assisted service

The supervisor should ensure that all the clearing up is completed and that it is done properly. Duties might include:

1 Clearing the cold buffet to the larder; collecting and washing all carving knives; assisting generally in clearing the restaurant.
2 Collecting all linen, both clean and dirty; checking that the correct quantities of each item of linen are returned. The serviettes should be tied in bundles of ten. All linen should be placed in the linen basket and returned with the linen list to the linen room.
3 Switching off the hotplate; clearing away any service silver remaining; restocking with clean china.
4 Returning all the silver, together with the tableware trolleys, to the silver store. Silver should be arranged and put away neatly as shown by the shelf labels.
5 Collecting all cruets and accompaniments; returning sauces, etc. to their original containers.
6 Checking that all the sideboards are completely empty. Hotplates should be switched off and the dirty linen compartment empty.
7 Clearing down the bar top; putting all the equipment away; washing and polishing used glasses. These should be put away in their correct storage place; removing all empty bottles, etc. completing consumption and stock sheets; locking up.
8 Putting away all equipment that has been used; emptying all coffee pots and milk jugs; washing and putting away. All perishable materials should be put away in their correct storage places. The still set and milk urns should be emptied, washed out and then left standing with cold water in them.
9 Emptying and cleaning all trolleys and returning them to their appropriate place. Any unused food items from the trolleys should be returned to the necessary department. Any silver used on the trolleys should be cleaned and returned to the silver room.
10 Emptying the liqueur trolley; returning stock to bar cupboard; restocking bar from the cellar. Bar shutters and doors should be properly locked.

Clearing down counters

1 Turn off the electricity supply to the hot-food counter.
2 Clear the hot-food counter and return all left-over food to the kitchen.
3 Turn off power supply to oven at the wall.
4 Clear the oven of any remaining food.
5 *Important*: Write down on the day sheet the number of portions of each type of regenerated meal that is left over as waste. This exercise is essential for portion-control monitoring and should give a helpful indication of the popularity or otherwise of any one particular dish. Hand in the day sheet to the supervisor who will then prepare a reconciliation of what was taken out and what is not left. This will then be entered into the analysis book.
6 Clean all kitchen utensils such as serving spoons, ladles, fish slices, knives and trays that have been used during the course of the day in hot-food preparations and service. Wipe dry.
7 Return all cleaned and dried kitchen utensils to the appropriate storage places ready for the next day's use.
8 Check the stock of plates needed for the next day's service of hot food.

Remember: as stocks are used up they have to be replenished.

Manipulative skills

In this section we shall look at some examples and techniques of manipulative skills. (These are the practical skills which involve precision and care in carrying them out!)

Serving soup

When serving soup use an underlayer plate. Hold the underplate in the left hand, place the soup plate on it and then serve the soup from the tureen using a silver soup ladle. This is normally done from the sideboard. Should any soup be spilled on the soup plate's edge, wipe it with the service cloth before serving to the customer (from the customer's left).

Figure 4.59 Serving soup from a tureen

Serving soup from a tureen (Figure 4.59)

- If brought really hot from the kitchen, use of a lamp or rechaud should not be necessary (overheating can spoil the soup).
- Ensure that soup plates are hot and clean.
- When carrying a pile of hot plates protect yourself and the plates with your service cloth.
- Stir and ladle with care to avoid drips on plate rims. The lid should be inverted when removed to avoid drips.
- Serve plates of hot soup on underplates with great care to avoid spillage on plate rims. The underplate also prevents any possibility of soup contacting a waiter's thumb. Its use is even more important when soup is plated in the kitchen and has to be carried a distance by the waiter.

Service from individual bowls

Alternatively, individual portions of soup may be presented in silver soup bowls. In this case, set soup plates and underplate before the guest. From the left, carefully tilt the silver bowl to transfer the soup, away from the guest, into the soup plate. For many soups, croutons, grated cheese and flutes are then separately passed. Serve these from sauceboats using a ladle or a spoon.

Service in cups (en tasse) (Figure 4.60)

Clear soup (consommé) is usually served in consommé cups, i.e. cups with two handles. A dessert spoon is used by the guest for clear soup en tasse instead of a soup spoon. The en tasse set consists of an entrée plate as the underplate, a saucer and a cup. Serve all three at one time. Serve the soup from the tureen into a cup with a silver soup ladle and place the complete set from the left.

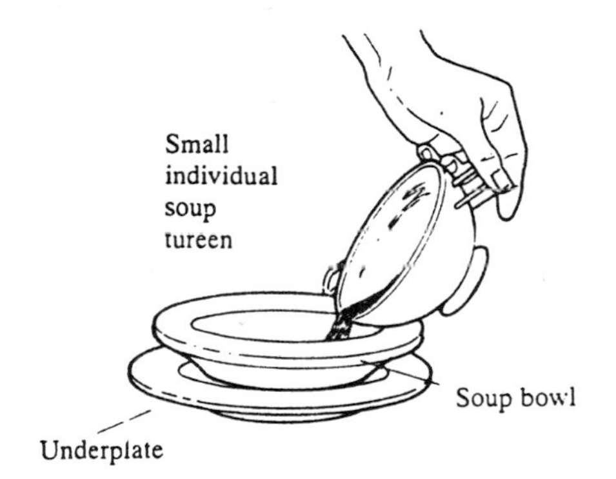

Figure 4.60 Serving soup from an individual tureen

Serving special coffees

Cona coffee

Conas operate on the vacuum infusion principle. Water is placed in a lower bowl made of heat-resistant glass. A glass infuser with a long tube is put on top with the tube passing into the lower bowl. Coffee is placed in the infuser and heat is applied to the water, which, when boiling, rises into the coffee-filled infuser. The heat is removed and the infused liquid coffee now descends into the lower bowl again. (It may be infused a second time for additional strength if requested.)

Conas are available in various sizes and combinations for use in a stillroom and also for making coffee 'in the room' on a sideboard or central service point for pour'n'serve service. Table models for individual service to a guest's table are particularly popular in up-market operations. Once made in a table mode the coffee may be served by the waiter direct from the glass bowl.

Cona machines are normally heated by electricity but the individual table service models are best used with the small spirit heater as it is not practicable in most cases to connect to an electric point sufficiently adjacent to the table.

Serving spoon and fork

Do not regard one-handed manipulation of service spoon and fork as a holy ritual. Some items such as small boiled potatoes, peas or some other vegetables are served better using only a spoon. Fragile sole fillets, for example, may be better transferred using two splayed-out forks.

Some modernists have scorned 'spoon and forkery' and urge 'rationalization' of serving techniques. Yet the skill required to manipulate a spoon and fork is quickly acquired (most achieve dexterity in minutes rather than hours). Further manipulation skills have been covered earlier in the chapter.

Task

List five examples of manipulative skills other than the ones we have covered so far. From your list check the correct procedure for one of them for (e.g. changing an ashtray at a customer's table). Write out the procedure on a card and use as a teaching aid for a fellow student. Conduct the task in your practical session (you may require permission from your instructor).

▪ SOCIAL SKILLS ▪

Social skills are extremely important in the role of waiter/waitress in the dining area. Very often the waiter/waitress is the first point of contact for the customer, and how he or she is dealt with (no matter what age) will affect the overall impression of the establishment. Social skills are not just about 'manners', they involve the whole sphere of the work situation, personal attributes as well as personal practices, while in work examples would include:

- Personal hygiene
- Time keeping
- Menu knowledge
- Communication with customers and colleagues
- Personal presentation
- Awareness of customers' needs and requirements

Personal presentation

Lasting opinions are formed from first impressions when the diners walk into the establishment. The atmosphere and decor should create a feeling of comfort and luxury. To be greeted pleasantly and with *good humour* is very reassuring, especially in a strange environment. The appearance of the staff, with *smart attire* and *personal grooming*, gives immediate confidence that the service given will also be of a high standard.

All staff clothes should be well pressed and of a proper fit. Each business has its own rules about uniforms. In some cases staff are provided with properly laundered clothing, while others are more informal. But every employer who takes a *pride* in their enterprise will expect the staff to dress smartly, with clean hands and finger nails, and well-styled hair. Extremes of fashion usually restrict the job opportunities available. The service staff should not be the centre of attraction but should quietly blend in with the surroundings. Heavy make-up should be avoided and jewellery either non-existent or restricted to a minimum.

Good *deportment* gives confidence and body language is important. Front-of-house staff should display an upright posture and all movement should be purposeful and positive. Lounging and leaning, chewing gum, sitting around, and generally negative attitudes do nothing to help to sell the products and services available.

Speech is an immediate and vital method of communication. Moods and temperamental outbursts by food and beverage workers can lose good customers. The tone of voice, the speed of speech, as well as the pitch and volume, can all make the waiter or bar staff sound disagreeable. Every effort should be made to improve the vocabulary and the utmost discretion should be used to avoid words and phrases which might give offence to the customers. Bad language and crude expressions do nothing to enhance the image of the person using them or the establishment to which they belong. Staff should be *articulate* and should pronounce their words clearly so as not to be misunderstood.

Personal attitudes and behaviour are usually acquired at a very early age. The hospitality and service industries require people who are able to demonstrate *courtesy* and *civility* at all times, and *tactfulness* on occasions when disagreements or arguments arise, or when you have information about events or people which it is wiser to keep to yourself.

You may have to exercise great *patience* in dealing with people who continually complain, or with whom you find it difficult to communicate. Great *sensitivity* is needed, especially in establishments where guests are from abroad and where language barriers may prove to be a handicap to good communication. The effect of social factors in a multi-racial society requires from the staff an awareness of separate cultural differences, and an acceptance and understanding of the habits and traditions of other religions and races. Good humour and a pleasant manner help to break down barriers and make communications easier.

Anticipate the moment when you can refill the wine glasses, or produce the matches at the appropriate time when the cigar needs to be lit. Attention to such details leads to consumer satisfaction and may be just the final touch which is needed to ensure repeat business. Each diner, whether a regular or a chance caller, must be made to feel at all times that they are the focus of your attention.

The importance of *teamwork* cannot be overstated. A pleasant atmosphere between you and your colleagues will reflect itself around the tables and in your bar. A sense of *calm* will prevail. A willingness to help a fellow worker who is as some time under pressure, or who is unwell, will be amply repaid when you yourself need help.

A *smiling*, relaxed attitude to work, coupled with a willingness to make the maximum effort towards the improvement in the service, and the success of the business with infinite customer satisfaction, will inevitably lead to promotion for you and expansion for your company.

Customer contact

Welcoming guests is often overlooked. People just drift into the restaurant instead of being met by a smiling member of staff. A few phrases of pleasant conversation after a sincere, 'Good evening, Sir/Madam' can help to relax and unwind even the most nervous visitor. If the customer is a regular then they should be addressed by name when first greeted. For the rest of the visit they should be called 'sir' or 'madam', as appropriate.

Compliments from customers should be accepted gracefully and reported to the management, and also to the kitchen staff and the cleaners if they are included in the comments. Complimentary customers are very likely to return and will certainly speak highly of you to prospective diners.

Elderly members of the community may not be able to react quite so quickly as younger folk, and it is always necessary to show tolerance and understanding. Staff should show an interest in the lives of customers, so helping to establish good relationships. The wealth of experience possessed by older customers can be of great benefit. It is better always to try to show an interest, even if the conversation in the bars seems boring.

Children need firm but friendly control. If they are encouraged by way of special menus, non-alcoholic cocktails, and a room full of interesting activities, the parents are more likely to frequent your premises.

Members of the public with disabilities are to be treated as far as possible in the same way as the other customers. As service staff you may find yourself in a position to help; for instance, to explain the content of a wine list to an unsighted visitor. A little thought would inspire you to place the wheelchair occupant on the side of the table away from the main thoroughfare.

Complaints must be dealt with promptly, so that customers are not lost forever. If the complaint is justified, it may be necessary to invite the customer back on another occasion. Most people who complain think that they are justified and that the customer is *always* right. You may have your own views but all complaints should be referred to the supervisor. If you are the cause of the upset, apologize and make every effort to learn from your mistake.

▪ ASSIGNMENT ▪

Service skills in Food and Drink

This activity will no doubt be conducted differently from centre to centre. The following information is not intended to be prescriptive for this assignment but to give ideas for coverage of the PCs across the range.

Tasks could include coverage of the following:

- Table d'hôte cover
- A lá carte cover
- Use of spoon and fork
- Serving vegetables
- Carrying plates
- Clearing plates
- Carrying glasses
- Service of coffee
- Service from silver trays

Note: The sequence and tasks for preparation of the restaurant or dining area are covered and supported with illustrations in the text book. You may wish to record your activities in the Assembly of Evidence Log Book.

▪ FACTORS WHICH INFLUENCE THE COST OF FOOD AND DRINK ▪

This section gives us an introduction to calculating the cost, and eventually the selling price, of food and drink.

Different types of organization have different aims. Some aim to make a *profit*.

Definition

- ***Profit*** *is the money which an organization makes from selling its goods and services, after deducting the costs of providing those goods and services.*

Others aim only to cover their costs (and hence make no profit), while some are *subsidized* and have their costs covered from somewhere else (e.g. from the government).

Definition

- ***Subsidized*** *means that part or all of the cost is provided from somewhere else.*

Whatever the aim of the organization, it must be able to calculate the cost of the products it provides, otherwise it will be impossible to find out how much to sell the items for or how much subsidy is needed.

How 'cost' is made up

The cost of food and drink obviously includes the cost of buying in the *raw materials* in the first instance.

Definition

- ***Raw materials*** *are the ingredients which go into a product.*

Some products have only one raw material (e.g. a piece of fruit), others have several raw materials (e.g. an apple pie has fruit, pastry, sugar, etc.). However, the majority of items also need some work to be done on them to make them ready for sale or consumption, so they also include *labour costs*.

Definition

- ***Labour costs*** *are the costs of employing staff, including basic wages, overtime, and other costs such as uniforms and free accommodation.*

There are two types of labour costs which we need to consider:

- *Direct labour*
- *Indirect labour*

Definition

- ***Direct labour** is the cost of employing people who make the products (e.g. chefs).*
- ***Indirect labour** is the cost of employing people who do other tasks to assist those who make the products (e.g. storekeepers, kitchen porters and supervisors).*

Both these types of labour add costs to a product.

In addition, there are general running costs which any organization must pay for, such as heat and light, rent and rates, insurance, laundry, administration and maintenance costs. These are called *overheads*.

Definition

- ***Overheads** are amounts spent on items not classed as materials or labour.*

All these costs, i.e.:

- Materials
- Labour
- Overheads

need to be considered when working out the cost of a product.

As an example, suppose we sell a portion of soup. The cost will include:

1. An amount for the ingredients of the soup (the materials)
2. An amount for the chef's time (direct labour)
3. An amount for the kitchen porter, the waiting staff, the restaurant manager etc. (indirect labour)
4. An amount for heat and light, rent and rates, etc. (overheads).

All these costs need to be considered in some way. If we only calculate the materials cost and ignore the other items, then we are in danger of selling at too low a price or obtaining too small a subsidy.

Purchase price of commodities

All commodities will have a purchase price, which will depend on where they were purchased, when they were purchased, and the terms that were agreed at the time. This purchase price will change from time to time and will be different for different organizations. This is because some organizations can make special arrangements with suppliers by using different methods of purchasing. There are four main methods of purchasing, each suitable for different types of product and organization:

1. *Contract purchasing or purchasing by tender* is suitable for large organizations who can buy large quantities and be sure to use them up. An agreement (a contract) is made between the supplier and the organization for the regular delivery of a fixed amount, over a certain period. The price and other details are also agreed at that time. The advantages include the knowledge that the price is fixed, but this might also be a disadvantage if prices for that commodity go down after the price has been agreed.
2. *Centralized purchasing* is also suitable for large organizations, or ones with several outlets. The organization buys for the whole of its outlets at once, and then distributes items to the outlets as they need them. Because of the large quantities involved, the organization can usually negotiate lower prices. The organization needs to have plenty of suitable storage space, especially for perishable commodities.
3. *Purchasing by market list or quotation* involves getting several prices from different suppliers whenever the commodity is required. Some

suppliers deliver regular price lists to their customers, with the latest prices given. One advantage of this method is that the organization can choose the best price from several suppliers; another advantage is that the price is up to date, which means that advantage can be taken of special offers and seasonal bargains.

4 *Purchasing from a cash and carry* involves the organization in selecting its goods at a warehouse, paying for them immediately and arranging its own transport. Although cash and carries sell large packs of commodities, the organization needs only buy what it requires when it needs it. The price cannot be negotiated, it is whatever the cash and carry is offering at the time. Cash and carries are usually fairly local and therefore the organization does not need to keep large stocks of commodities itself.

In addition to the above methods, purchasing can also be done through wholesalers who sell only to traders. This method is often suitable for specialized goods such as wines and spirits, tobaccos, etc.

Each method is suitable for different types of commodities and organizations, and has different effects on the purchase price.

Task 4.22

Your organization will require the following products on the first day of next month:

- *Fresh parsley for garnishing*
- *Fresh chicken portions*
- *Tinned hot-dog sausages*
- *Liquid disinfectant*
- *Potatoes*

Suggest a suitable method of purchasing each of the products, for each of the following organizations:

- *A 30-bedroomed hotel with a 60-seater restaurant, open to the public at lunchtimes and evenings*
- *A hot-dog stand*
- *A city general hospital*
- *A 200-bed hotel, part of a national chain of hotels*

Using the invoice price

Once the commodities have been purchased, the supplier will issue an *invoice* which will detail the amount bought, a description of the goods, and details of the price to be paid.

Definition

- *An **invoice** is a document made out by the supplier and sent to the purchaser as a written record of the goods and services which have been bought.*

The price might have an amount included for delivery costs, or it might be reduced if a *discount* has been given.

Definition

- *A **discount** is a reduction in the normal price.*

This invoice price can be used to calculate the cost of the materials used.

Using an issue price

Many organizations keep stocks of commodities which may have been purchased at different times and at different prices. Unless the storekeeper is very careful to note the cost of every single item on the shelves, and knows exactly which are issued to the kitchen and used in the preparation of a particular dish or menu, it will be impossible to tie up the commodities with their original invoice price.

Therefore, most organizations have a separate system of calculating the *issue price* of commodities used from stores.

Definition

- *The **issue price** is the price given to commodities taken from stores.*

For example, if a commodity has been bought in on two occasions, at two different prices, the organization might use the earliest price for issues, or the latest price, or an average of the two. Whatever value is used, it will be given to the kitchen and the costing clerk in order to work out the cost of the dish or menu.

Control of commodities used

It is common for many dishes to be made in bulk, i.e. several portions or dishes at a time. For example, soup might be made in 5-litre lots, each lot producing 25 portions of 200 ml each. The ingredients will therefore be costed out for the whole batch of 5 litres, and then divided by 25 portions to find the cost of one portion.

The same is true of liquor – for example, spirits are bought by the bottle and dispensed one measure at a time. The cost of the whole bottle is easy to find, so it is then divided by the number of measures in the bottle to find the cost per measure.

Weights and measures

Before we start to look at the different units, we need to know some basic rules regarding measurements of weight, length, volume, etc. Many of the quantities and other units of measurements used in the hospitality and catering industry are expressed in a mixture of imperial and metric units. You should practise converting from imperial to metric and vice versa with a variety of different units of measurement, e.g.

- Weight (pounds and ounces: kilos and grames)
- Liquid measures (pints, gallons: litres, centilitres)
- Length (yards, feet and inches: metres and centimetres)
- Area and volume (square/cubic yards, feet and inches: metres and centimetres)

The following are some useful weights and measures:

Imperial measurements

12 inches	=	1 foot
3 feet	=	1 yard
16 ounces	=	1 pound (lb)
112 pounds	=	1 hundredweight (cwt)
20 fluid ounces	=	1 pint
4 gills	=	1 pint
8 pints	=	1 gallon

Metric measurements

100 centimetres	=	1 metre
1000 grams	=	1 kilogram
1000 millilitres	=	1 litre

and here are some useful *approximate* conversions:

1 pint	=	0.57 litres	1 litre	=	1.76 pints
1 yard	=	0.9 metres	1 metre	=	1.1 yards
1 lb	=	454 grams	1 kilogram	=	2.2 lbs

Note that the above are only *approximate* conversions. If you need more exact conversions (e.g. when measuring for a carpet) you will need to consult a tape-measure or a more accurate conversion chart.

You will note that sometimes even more approximate conversions are used. For example, in many recipes, 1 lb is converted to 500 grams for ease of weighing using scales.

Task 4.23

Using the above conversion guidelines, find the metric or imperial equivalent for each of the following:

10 pints	*15 fl.oz*	*3 kg*
4 metres	*350 grams*	*12 ounces*
2.6 gallons	*0.6 kg*	*3 lb 8 oz*
7 feet 8 inches	*2.4 cwt*	*1.6 litres*

As well as knowing the cost of commodities, we also need to know how much of a commodity is used in making a dish or a portion. This amount will depend on several things:

- The size of the portion required
- The number of portions required
- The amount which is lost in preparation and cooking

Portion control

It is important that the size of portions is exact. A portion which is too small will receive complaints from customers but one that is too large will cost more to prepare. If it is sold for the normal price this may result in a loss being made.

It might surprise you to realize how a small difference in the size of a portion can cost such a lot. Let us look at an example.

Suppose a normal portion of soup is 200 ml. This might be made in a container of 5 litres, and might cost £7.50 in ingredients to make. It will produce 25 normal portions, so each one costs 30p.

Let us say that a portion sells for £1. The total selling price of 25 portions of soup is £25 and the total cost of the ingredients is £7.50.

Therefore, £17.50 goes towards the labour and overheads and any left over will be the *net profit*.

Definition

- ***Net profit*** *is the profit remaining after* all other costs *have been deducted.*

Suppose that the serving staff are feeling generous, and give customers 250 ml in each serving. What difference to you think that would make to the cost of a portion, and the net profit to be made?

Well, there are only 20 portions of 250 ml in a 5-litre container. So the total selling price will be only £20. The cost of the ingredients is still £7.50, so only £12.50 goes towards the labour and overheads, which is £5 less than we had originally planned. This will mean there is reduced profit, or no profit at all, or even worse – not enough to pay for the labour and overheads. And all because of a few teaspoons of extra soup in a bowl!

Portion control can be difficult to maintain without proper equipment, so it is important that standard sizes of containers and serving tools are used (e.g. ladles, bowls, slicing equipment, etc.). Portion control is also difficult to maintain if the chef is adventurous and wants to try different ways of preparing foods!

Task 4.24

1. *Calculate the number of glasses of fruit juice of 120 ml to be obtained from a 2-litre container.*
2. *Calculate the number of glasses of fruit juice of 150 ml to be obtained from a 2-litre container.*
3. *Calculate the number of apple pies, each using 8 oz of pastry, which can be made from a 2 kg batch of pastry.*

Beverage control

Beverages require separate consideration because they usually come in large containers, from which small amounts are dispensed at a time. For items such as tea, coffee and sugar the use of single sachets makes it easy to determine a unit. If these items are bought in large tins, it is more difficult, but there are several different ways round the problem:

- To 'test measure' a number of portions, say 100 spoons of coffee
- To make up the beverages in large quantities, and then measure by individual cups
- To ensure that all cups used are of the same size
- To assume that all guests take a standard amount of milk and sugar

For alcoholic beverages the calculation depends on how the beverages are packaged.

Here are some useful standard measurements:

1 *Spirits:* 1 measure = 1/6 gill (1 standard bottle = 32 measures)
2 *Beers:* 1 firkin = 9 gallons (1 barrel = 4 firkins)
3 *Wines* = 6 glasses per bottle
4 *Fortified* wines = 1/5 gill per measure

Task 4.25

- *Calculate the number of cups of coffee which can be made from 500 grams, if 50 grams makes 30 cups.*
- *Calculate the number of pints of beer left in a firkin if it is three quarters full*
- *Calculate the number of measures of gin used up from a bottle which has 1 gill remaining.*

Yield and wastage

When foods are being prepared there is often *wastage*.

Definition

- ***Wastage** is the amount of material lost during storage, preparation, cooking or serving, due to shrinkage, evaporation, boning, cutting, etc.*

Wastage reduces the amount of food available to be served – this is the *yield*.

Definition

- *The **yield** is the amount of usable product from an item after it has been prepared, cooked and served.*

Wastage can occur in several ways:

- Carelessness
- Unusable parts of the food (e.g. bones, skin)
- Loss of weight during cooking
- Loss of weight after cooking (e.g. evaporation while a dish is cooling)
- Carving or portioning losses (e.g. where there is not enough for a full portion)

All these areas need to be looked at and carefully controlled, although some foods are more difficult to control than others. Tests should be carried out on foods to see how much wastage does occur, so that you need to know how much to buy in order to produce the number of portions you want. It would be unacceptable to buy a 3 kg chicken which 'shrinks' to only 1 kg of meat if you want 1.5 kg.

Calculating the yield

The following is an example of the loss which can occur during the preparation and cooking and serving of a turkey:

Original plucked and prepared weight of turkey	5.2 kg
including giblets	0.3 kg
Weight after cooking	4.3 kg
Weight when cooled	4.1 kg
Sliced weight	2.2 kg

You can see that the end weight of meat available (the yield) is only 2.2 kg, having lost 3 kg in the process of preparing, cooking and slicing. This loss is made up of:

Giblets	0.3 kg
Cooking and cooling	0.8 kg
Skin and bones	1.9 kg

The usable weight or yield is only 42.3 per cent of the original weight – less than half. This is found by the following formula:

$$\text{Yield} = \frac{\text{Usable weight}}{\text{Original weight}} \times 100$$

$$= \frac{2.2}{5.2} = 42.3 \text{ per cent}$$

There are several useful calculations which can come from the information regarding *yield* and *wastage*. Here are some of them:

1 *The number of usable portions* depends on the required weight of a portion and the yield of usable meat. The number of portions is

$$\frac{\text{Usable meat}}{\text{required weight per portion}}$$

If the required weight per portion is 0.14 kg, the number of portions is

$$\frac{2.2}{0.14} = 15.7 \text{ portions}$$

2 *Cost per portion of usable food.* Once we have calculated the yield, we can then calculate the cost of the usable food. This is calculated as:

$$\frac{\text{Cost of food as purchased}}{\text{Number of usable portions}} =$$

$$\frac{\pounds 6.24}{15.7} = 39.7\text{p per portion}$$

Task 4.26

The information regarding a leg of pork is as follows:

Original weight as purchased	–	*4.6 kg*
Price paid	–	*£2.50 per kg*
Weight lost in cooking	–	*14 per cent*
Weight lost in boning and slicing	–	*1.1 kg*

Calculate:

- *The percentage yield*
- *The number of portions at 0.14 kg per portion*
- *The cost per portion at 0.14 kg per portion*
- *The cost per portion at 0.125 kg per portion*

Calculating the materials cost of a dish or recipe

To find the materials cost of a dish or recipe we need to know the ingredients of that dish and the amount which it is expected to produce. This is more easily done if there is a laid-down method of preparing each recipe which can be followed every time it is made. This is called a *standard recipe*.

Definition

- *A* ***standard recipe*** *is one that has been tried and tested to produce exactly the dish required.*

It should be followed accurately to make sure that the cost of a recipe is properly controlled. The recipes are recorded on cards or in a file, with the ingredients and the method of cooking and preparation. The cost of standard recipes should be reviewed regularly, especially where they contain ingredients which change frequently in price.

Let us look at a sample standard recipe for watercress soup.

Standard recipe No. 49
Watercress soup 5 litres

Ingredients	Quantity	Cost at			
		28.9.94			
Potatoes, chopped	1 kg				
Chicken stock	5 litres				
Watercress, chopped	12 bunches				
Grated nutmeg	2 tsps				
Single cream	500 ml				
Total cost					
Cost per portion (200 ml)					

The blank columns are for the costs to be entered at different times.

Suppose we are given the following costs for the above ingredients:

Potatoes	£0.20 per lb
Chicken stock	£0.30 per litre
Watercress	£0.38 per bunch
Grated nutmeg	£0.03
Single cream	£1.10 per pint

We can then work out the cost of the recipe as follows:

1. *Potatoes* – we need 1 kg, at 20p per lb. 1 kg = 2.2 lb, so the cost of 1 kg of potatoes is 20p × 2.2 = 44p
2. *Chicken stock* – we need 5 litres, at 30p per litre = £1.50
3. *Watercress* – we need 12 bunches at 38p per bunch = £4.56
4. *Grated nutmeg* – this is given at 3p
5. *Single cream* – we need 500 ml (½ litre) at £1.10 per pint. 1 litre = 1.76 pints, so the cost of 1 litre is £1.10 × 1.76 = £1.94 and therefore the cost of ½ litre is £0.97

We can now slot these figures into the standard recipe to calculate the total cost and the cost per portion:

Standard recipe No. 49
Watercress soup 5 litres

Ingredients	Quantity	Cost at			
		28.9.94 £			
Potatoes, chopped	1 kg	0.44			
Chicken stock	5 litres	1.50			
Watercress, chopped	12 bunches	4.56			
Grated nutmeg	2 tsps	0.03			
Single cream	500 ml	0.97			
Total cost (25 portions)		7.50			
Cost per portion (200 ml)		0.30			

Task 4.27

From the following information for a standard recipe, calculate the materials cost of the recipe and the cost per portion, assuming 6 portions per recipe:

Apple Pie		
Cooking apples	*500 g*	*costing 48p per lb*
Shortcrust pastry	*200 g*	*costed at 45p per 250 g*
Demerara sugar	*125 g*	*costing 50p per kg*
Cloves	*4*	
Cinnamon	*pinch*	*add 2p overall*

Calculating labour costs

As mentioned earlier, there are two types of labour – direct (for employees who actually make the products) and indirect (for other employees).

Direct labour costs

Direct labour is usually the cost of wages for the chefs. It is usually possible to work out how long it takes a chef to cook a particular dish or batch of food, and then to divide out the wage costs between the dishes.

Let us say that a chef takes 30 minutes to produce 5 litres of soup. The rate of pay is £6 per hour. Therefore the direct labour cost of the 5 litres is £3. Earlier we said that this produces 25 portions, so this is 12p per portion.

Labour costs includes overtime. Overtime is often paid at a higher rate than normal. If an employee *frequently* works overtime, then the hourly rate used in costing dishes should be adjusted to take account of this. However, in most circumstances this is not necessary and the basic rate will be used.

Labour costs also include the cost of providing staff meals, uniforms and accommodation, etc. Again, an adjustment should be made to the hourly rate used to cost dishes. For the above chef, these costs might add another £2 to the hourly rate, making £8 per hour as the amount to be used. If the chef takes half an hour to make 5 litres of soup, this works out at £4 per batch, and for 25 portions this is 16p per portion.

Task 4.28

Calculate the direct labour cost of making a portion of the apple pie in the previous task if the chef makes 14 complete pies in 1 hour, at an hourly cost of £7.

Indirect labour costs

Indirect labour also needs to be considered. This might include labour costs of supervisors, kitchen porters, storekeepers, etc. It might also include the costs of restaurant serving and waiting staff, as well as the manager's salary. Some of these members of staff will be paid hourly, some weekly and some will be on an annual salary.

It is difficult to calculate precisely how much should be added to the cost of a product to allow for this kind of labour. It is common to simply add a percentage to the cost of the direct labour. So in the example earlier, where the cost of labour for the chef making the soup was 16p per portion, we might add a percentage (say 50 per cent) to cover the indirect labour. This means that 8p would be added to the cost of a portion of soup.

Task 4.29

Calculate the cost of indirect labour to be added to the apple pie at a rate of 40 per cent of direct labour.

Overheads

Overheads are all the other costs of running an organization. The list of overheads is almost endless, and is different for every organization. However, overheads can sometimes be classified according to their behaviour – i.e. the way in which they change:

1. *Variable overheads* are those which change as the level of activity changes. The more business the organization does, the greater are its variable overheads. Very few overheads change at *exactly* the same rate as the level of activity, but some change roughly in proportion (for example, power costs, laundry costs etc.). If there are 10 more guests, 10 more lots of laundry will need to be done. Some organizations might include heat and light with this category, although often a restaurant needs to be heated and lit even when it is half-empty.
2. *Fixed overheads* are those which do not change with the level of activity, or change only when there are major alterations to the business done. Examples include rent and rates and insurance. If there are 10 more guests, these will not change. If there were 100 more guests the insurance might rise, or larger premises might be needed and hence higher rent charges.

Many of these overheads are connected with the supporting operations of the organization – i.e. those operations which do not earn income but provide the 'back-up' services needed, such as maintenance, laundry, reception, housekeeping, etc.

As with indirect labour, it is often difficult to determine exactly how much should be added on to the cost of a product to cover these items, but obviously they cannot be ignored. Some organizations add on a percentage of the materials cost or an amount per dish. The actual calculations are beyond the knowledge you need for this qualification, but you should understand why these amounts are added.

Using our example of the watercress soup, we might add 40 per cent of the food cost to cover variable overheads, and 5p per portion to cover fixed overheads. The food cost was 30p per portion, so 40 per cent is 12p. We can now calculate the total cost of our portion of soup, as follows:

	£
Food cost	0.30
Direct labour	0.16 (including staff meals, etc.)
Indirect labour	0.08 (50 per cent of direct labour)
Variable overheads	0.12 (40 per cent of food cost)
Fixed overheads	*0.05* (given to us)
Total cost	0.71

This does not leave much out of the selling price of £1.00 for net profit – only 29p. There may well be other costs to be deducted such as the cost of bank overdrafts and borrowings, as well as tax.

Task 4.30

Calculate the total cost of a portion of apple pie, using the figures you obtained from the previous three tasks. Add 30 per cent of the materials cost for variable overheads and 6p per portion for fixed overheads.

▪ FACTORS WHICH INFLUENCE THE SELLING PRICE OF FOOD AND DRINK ▪

There are three main factors which influence the selling price of food and drink:

1 The cost
2 The profit required
3 The Value Added Tax to be included

Cost

The cost of the product is the starting point in calculating the selling price. Different organizations use different 'levels' of cost to assist them.

Total cost

We have already seen how the total cost of a product is made up. Some organizations take the total cost and add a percentage to it to obtain the selling price. In our example of a portion of soup, the total cost was 71p. We would need to add 41 per cent to the total cost to give a selling price of £1.00:

41 per cent × £0.71 = £0.29 net profit

Selling price = total cost plus net profit = £0.71 + £0.29

Task 4.31

Using the total cost which you calculated in the previous task for a portion of apple pie, find the selling price if 30 per cent net profit is required.

Materials cost

We have seen how difficult it can be to determine the total cost of a product, especially in calculating the value of indirect labour and overheads to be included in the cost. For this reason, many organizations prefer to use just the materials cost as a starting point for calculating selling price. There are two main calculations which might be performed.

Gross margin

Definition

- ***Gross margin*** *(also called* gross profit*) is the selling price minus the materials cost.*

Gross margin can be stated as an amount of money, or as a percentage.

The calculation of gross margin is usually used to determine how much profit should be made from a given selling price. Using our portion of soup again, the gross margin required would be 70p, which gives a selling price of £1.00. This can then be expressed as a percentage of selling price to give gross margin percentage:

$$\frac{\text{Gross profit}}{\text{Selling price}} \times 100 = \frac{0.70}{1.00} \times 100 = 70 \text{ per cent}$$

Mark-up

This is another word for gross profit, but this time expressed as a percentage of the materials cost.

Definition

- *The* ***mark-up*** *is the amount which is added to the materials cost to give the selling price.*

Using our portion of soup, the gross profit required was £0.70, and the materials cost was £0.30. The mark-up required therefore is:

$$\frac{\text{Gross profit}}{\text{Cost of materials}} \times 100 = \frac{0.70}{0.30} \times 100$$

$$= 233.33 \text{ per cent}$$

It is quite common for mark-up percentages to be very high, especially where the food and drink cost is a small proportion of the total costs – don't forget we still need to deduct labour costs and overheads before we arrive at net profit.

In this example we already knew the gross profit because we were given the selling price. But it is quite common for the selling price *not* to be known. In such cases it needs to be calculated by adding a given percentage onto the materials cost. This percentage will have been carefully worked out by senior staff to be the amount required to cover all the costs and produce the required amount of profit.

As an example, suppose a portion of beef casserole cost 50p in materials, and a mark-up of 250 per cent was required. The selling price would be the materials cost plus the mark-up. The mark-up is:

$$\frac{250}{100} \times 50\text{p} = £1.25$$

and therefore the selling price is 50p plus £1.25 = £1.75.

Task 4.32

Calculate the selling price of the portion of apple pie used in the previous task, given a mark-up percentage of 180 per cent.

Value Added Tax

This is a tax which is added to the selling price of most goods and services. It is imposed by the government. Only very small organizations and some goods and services do not add value added tax (VAT). The current rate of VAT is 17.5 per cent. The selling price is calculated as normal, and the VAT is added afterwards.

Using our portion of soup again, the selling price we determined was £1.00. The VAT to be added is 17.5 per cent of this, i.e. £0.175. This must be rounded up to £0.18 as we do not have half-pence, so the total selling price will be £1.18 to the customer.

The organization cannot keep this extra 18p – it must be passed over to the government. The organization is acting merely as a tax collector. Therefore the VAT does not affect the profit which the organization makes. It is worth knowing that the organization can also claim back from the government any VAT which it has to pay out when it buys goods and services from others.

Task 4.33

Using the selling price for a portion of apple pie which you calculated in the previous task, add on the correct amount of VAT to find the selling price to the customer.

▪ Assessment ▪

Costing and pricing food and drink

Scenario

Next week you have been invited to an interview for the position of Assistant Restaurant Manager with a new hotel to be opened in your locality. The job specification includes responsibility for costing and pricing, and you have been asked to submit a report to the interview panel to demonstrate your knowledge of this area.

Task

Prepare a report for the interview panel, which explains clearly in your own words:

- The factors which influence the cost of commodities
- The factors which influence the selling price of commodities

To illustrate your understanding, calculate the cost and selling price of a portion of bolognese sauce, from the information attached.

Assessment coverage:

Element 1 *Performance criteria* 1.3, 1.4.
Core skills:

Communication – 2.2. (all)
Information Technology – 2.1 (all), 2.2. (all)
Application of number – 2.2. (all)

Assignment – data for completion:

1 Recipe for bolognese sauce:

Minced beef	5 lb raw weight
Tinned tomatoes	5 14-oz tins
Onions	1 kg
Oregano	3 tsp
Basil	4 tsp
Sugar	1 oz
Wine vinegar	5 fl.oz
Garlic	5 cloves
Chicken stock	1.5 litres
Salt and black pepper to taste	

The raw ingredients weigh 12 lb, while the finished weight is 9 lb. Portion size is 8 oz per portion.

2 Prices:

Minced beef	£0.80 per lb
Tinned tomatoes	£0.25 per tin
Onions	£0.20 per lb
Oregano and basil	£0.20
Sugar	£0.90 per lb
Wine vinegar	£1.20 per pint
Garlic	£0.20 for 5 cloves
Chicken stock	£0.30 per pint

3 Chef's time to make a batch of sauce is 30 minutes, at an hourly rate, including all extras, of £6 per hour. Indirect labour is 10 per cent of direct labour.
4 Variable overheads are 20 per cent of food cost, while £3 is to be added to allow for fixed overheads.
5 A gross profit mark-up of 300 per cent is required.

ASSEMBLY OF EVIDENCE

In the following pages you will find activies which may be undertaken in support of evidence for this unit. The log book contains

Introductory notes
Action plan sheet
Core skills sheet
Performance criteria for the unit
Assessment activities

About this log

In order to obtain more than a pass grade for this unit you must show that you are capable of planning your approach to the assessment, gather the appropriate information and use it properly, and finally, show that you are able to learn from your experience in other words, that you can:

Plan

Gather information

This work log is divided into parts:

Part 1
This gives detailed information about what you need to do in order to obtain a Merit or Distinction grade for each of the above.

Part 2
This is for you to write down how you intend to tackle the assessment that has been given to you by your tutor, along with dates and deadlines for particular tasks to be completed.

Part 3
This is for you to record the activities which you undertake in order to complete the assessment. You should also record any difficulties which you encounter and any changes which you have made to your original plan.

Important

- This work log forms part of your portfolio and must be kept safe.
- Read the information in Part 1 carefully. If you are unsure about it in any way, ask your tutor.
- Complete Part 2 before starting the assessment and show it to your tutor.

Part 1: Grading themes and criteria for the Intermediate GNVQs

Theme 1: Planning: the way the student lays down how s/he will approach and monitor the tasks/activities undertaken during a period of learning.

	Merit	*Distinction*
1 Drawing up plans of action	Student independently draws up plans of action for a series of **discrete tasks**. The plans prioritise the different tasks within the given time period.	Student independently draws up plans of action for **complex activities**. The plans prioritise the different tasks within the given time period.
2 Monitoring courses of action	Student independently identifies points at which monitoring is necessary and recognises where revisions to courses of action are necessary. Appropriate revisions to plans are made **with guidance from teacher/tutor**.	Student independently identifies points at which monitoring is necessary and recognises where revisions to courses of action are necessary. **Appropriate revisions to plans are made independently.**

Theme 2: Information-seeking and information-handling: the way the student identifies and uses information sources.

	Merit	*Distinction*
3 Identifying information needs	Student independently identifies information requirements for a **series of discrete tasks**.	Student independently identifies the information requirements for **complex activities.**
4 Identifying and using sources to obtain information	Student independently accesses and collects relevant information for a **series of discrete tasks**. Student **identifies principle sources independently** and **additional sources are identified by the teacher/tutor.**	Student independently accesses and collects relevant information for **complex activities**. Student uses a **range of sources and justifies their selection.**

Part 1: Grading themes and criteria for the Intermediate GNVQs – continued

Theme 3: Evaluation: the way the student retrospectively reviews; the activities undertaken; the decisions taken in the course of that work; alternative courses of action which s/he might have adopted.

	Merit	*Distinction*
5 Evaluating outcomes and justifying approaches	Student judges outcomes against original criteria for success; justifies the approach used and indicates that **alternatives were identified and considered.**	Student judges outcomes against original criteria for success and justifies the approach used with a detailed consideration of relevant **advantages and disadvantages. Alternatives and improvements are identified.**

Theme 4: Quality of outcomes: the way the student synthesises knowledge, skills and understanding; and demonstrates command of the 'language' of the GNVQ area.

	Merit	*Distinction*
6 Synthesis	Student's work demonstrates an effective synthesis of knowledge, skills and understanding in response to **discrete tasks.**	The student's work demonstrates and effective synthesis of knowledge, skills and understanding in response to **complex activities**.
7 Command of 'language'	Student's work demonstrates **an effective** command of the 'language' of the GNVQ area at Foundation/Intermediate level.	The student's work demonstrates **a fluent** command of the 'language' of the GNVQ area at Foundation/Intermediate level.

Part 2

Action	*Target date*

Briefly explain why you choose to approach the assessment this way

Part 3
What you actually did in order to complete the assessment

Date	*Action*

Certified core skills

	Communication	*Application of number*	*Information technology*
Level 1	1 Take part in discussions with known individuals on routine matters. 2 Prepare written materials in preset formats. 3 Use images to illustrate points made in writing and in discussions with known individuals on routine matters. 4 Read and respond to written material and images in preset formats.	5 Gather and process data using group 1 mathematical techniques. 6 Represent and tackle problems using group 1 mathematical techniques. 7 Interpret and present mathematical data using group 1 mathematical techniques.	8 Input data into specified locations. 9 Edit and organize information within individual applications. 10 Present information in preset formats. 11 Use operating routines which maximize efficiency.
Level 2	1 Take part in discussions with a range of people on routine matters 2 Prepare written material on routine matters. 3 Use images to illustrate points made in writing and in discussions with a range of people on routine matters. 4 Read and respond to written material and images on routine matters.	5 Gather and process data using groups 1 and 2 mathematical techniques. 6 Represent and tackle problems using groups 1 and 2 mathematical techniques. 7 Interpret and present mathematical data using groups 1 and 2 mathematical techniques.	8 Set up, use and input data into storage systems. 9 Edit and organize and integrate information from different sources. 10 Select and use formats for presenting information. 11 Select and use operating routines which maximize efficiency.
Level 3	1 Take part in discussions with a range of people on a range of matters. 2 Prepare written material on a range of matters. 3 Use images to illustrate points made in writing and in discussions with a range of people on a range of matters. 4 Read and respond to written materials and images on a range of matters.	5 Gather and process data using groups 1, 2 and 3 mathematical techniques. 6 Represent and tackle problems using groups 1, 2 and 3 mathematical techniques. 7 Interpret and present mathematical data using groups 1, 2 and 3 mathematical techniques.	8 Set system options and set up, use and input data into storage systems. 9 Edit, organize and integrate complex information from different sources. 10 Select and use formats for presenting complex information from different sources. 11 Select and use applications when they are an effective way of working with information.

Certified core skills (continued)

	Communication	*Application of number*	*Information technology*
Level 4	1 Take part in and evaluate the effectiveness of discussions with a range of people on a range of matters. 2 Prepare and evaluate the effectiveness of own written material on a range of matters. 3 Use and evaluate the effectiveness of own use of images to illustrate points made in writing and in discussions with a range of people on a range of matters. 4 Read and respond to written material and images recognizing the factors which influence own interpretation.	5 Gather and process data using groups 1,2,3 and 4 mathematical techniques. 6 Represent and tackle problems using groups 1, 2, 3 and 4 mathematical techniques. 7 Interpret and present mathematical data using groups 1,2,3 and 4 mathematical techniques.	8 Set up system options, use storage systems and prepare and input data. 9 Set up and use automated routines to edit, organize and integrate complex information from different sources. 10 Set up and use automated routines to format and present complex information from different sources. 11 Evaluate and select applications for use by self.
Level 5	1 Lead and evaluate the effectiveness of discussions with a range of people on a range of matters. 2 Prepare and evaluate the effectiveness of own and others' written material on a range of matters. 3 Use and evaluate the effectiveness of own and others' use of images to illustrate points made in writing and discussions with people on a range of matters. 4 Read and respond to written material and images recognizing the factors which influence own and others' interpretations.	5 Gather and process data using groups 1,2,3,4, and 5 mathematical techniques. 6 Represent and tackle problems using groups 1,2,3,4 and 5 mathematical techniques. 7 Interpret and present mathematical data using groups 1,2,3,4 and 5 mathematical techniques.	8 Set up system options, use storage systems and validate prepare and input data. 9 Investigate and resolve problems in editing, organizing and integrating complex information from different sources. 10 Investigate and resolve problems in formatting and presenting complex information from different sources. 11 Evaluate and select applications for use by self and others.

GLOSSARY

Accommodation services are provided to care for customers when they are visiting an establishment. The term refers to the services required by customers who have booked sleeping accommodation. The services include the cleaning and maintenance of the building, the provision of clean laundry and of supplies such as soap and toilet paper. In most establishments it includes some provision for customers to be able to have food and drink in or near their room.

A **bed board** is a flat board which slides between the mattress and the bed base to make the bed firmer. It is requested by customers who have a back problem.

Centralized vacuuming is based on a central dust-collection area. The building is linked with pipes and there are vacuum points around the building. Hoses are fitted to the vacuum points and the dirt is sucked along the pipes to the central collection area.

A **chalet** is a room or group of rooms in a holiday camp or holiday centre. The chalet door opens directly to the outside.

A **courtesy tray** is placed in bedrooms in hotels and in halls of residence for conference delegates and tourists. It provides all the equipment and commodities required to allow us to make our own hot beverages such as tea, coffee or hot chocolate. This will include a kettle, teapot, cups, saucers, sachets of tea, coffee, chocolate, sugar and milk. We may also be provided with biscuits.

Direct labour is the cost of employing people who make the products (e.g. chefs).

A **discount** is a reduction in the normal price.

Double-locking means that the lock can only be opened by using a grand master key. It cannot be opened with any of the other types of key. It is used when we want to prevent a customer or a member of staff from entering the room.

En suite refers to a bedroom with a private bathroom forming one unit.

A **float valve** is fitted to a wet suction machine between the water tank and the electric motor. As the water level rises the valve floats on the surface. When the water reaches a predetermined level the valve closes a small hole, cutting off the air supply to the motor. This prevents any water reaching the electric motor and the operator getting an electric shock.

The **Front Office** is the section which deals with the administrative aspects of caring for a customer to an establishment. Generally, the Front Office looks after advance bookings to the establishment and the reception of customers when they arrive. For some establishments such as hotels the Front Office also prepares and deals with the payment of the customer's bill. It is the area where customers can go if they have any queries.

Gross margin is the selling price minus the materials cost. It is often expressed as a percentage of the selling price.

Gross profit – see **gross margin**.

A **health club** is like a small gymnasium with machines and apparatus for people to use for exercise. These are usually free of charge if we are staying in the hotel. If we are not staying in the hotel we can choose to pay an annual subscription to join the hotel's leisure club which allows us to use both the pool and the health club.

Indirect labour is the cost of employing people who do other tasks to assist those who make the products (e.g. storekeepers, kitchen porters and supervisors).

The **invoice** is a document made out by the supplier and sent to the purchaser as a written record of the goods and services which have been bought.

The **issue price** is the price which is given to commodities which are taken from stores.

Labour costs are the costs of employing staff, including basic wages, overtime, and other costs such as uniforms and free accommodation.

A **locality** is a geographical area which contains the facilities which people need for their daily lives.

The **mark-up** is the amount which is added to the materials cost to give the selling price.

A **mini-bar** is a small refrigerator placed in a hotel bedroom. It contains miniature bottles of spirit and appropriate mixers (tonic, soda, ginger), quarter-bottles of wine and small bottles of fruit juice. Some mini-bars also contain vacuum packs of cocktail nuts or potato crisps. We help ourselves from the bar and this is later checked by hotel staff. We can then be charged for the items consumed.

Net profit is the profit remaining after all other costs have been deducted.

Overheads are amounts spent on items not classed as materials or labour.

Periodic cleaning is carried out at specific times during the year. It is sometimes known as spring cleaning.

Products are items which are sold by an organization, which may be made by the organization or bought in ready-made for sale.

Profit is the money which an organization makes from selling its goods and services, after deducting the costs of providing those goods and services.

Raw materials are the ingredients which go into a product.

Revenue is money earned by selling goods and services.

Room service is when food and drink is served to us in our hotel room. We select our choice from the room service menu, telephone our order and after a short time the food is served. For breakfast service we are provided with an order form which we complete and hang outside our bedroom door before we go to bed. The menu is collected during the night and the meal is served at the time we have stated on our order.

Routine cleaning is the type of cleaning which we carry out on a regular basis, every day, every night or every week.

A **secondary** or **indirect** service is one which is not the main activity of the organization.

A **service industry** is one which provides services to its customers rather than **products**.

A **socio-economic group** is a classification given to groups of people according to their education, background, qualifications, lifestyle and (partly) income.

A **standard recipe** is a recipe which has been tried and tested to produce exactly the dish required.

Subsidized means that part or all of the costs is provided from somewhere else.

Turn-down is a service offered in a few luxury hotels. It is done in the evening. Bedspreads are folded back and the bedding is turned back to make it easier for the guest to get into bed. Any night clothes may be laid out neatly on the bed. The bedroom and bathroom will be tidied and the curtains closed. Before leaving, the room attendant may turn the bedside light on and leave a small box containing two or three complimentary chocolates on the pillow.

A **utility room** is provided in a hall of residence. It provides facilities for storing milk and other perishables and appropriate equipment for cooking. There may also be limited facilities for students to do their own laundry and ironing. The utility room is often a place where students congregate while they eat and socialize.

Wastage is the amount of material lost during storage, preparation, cooking or serving, due to shrinkage, evaporation, boning, cutting, etc.

The **yield** is the amount of usable product from an item, after it has been prepared, cooked and served.

INDEX